Carpworld Yearbook Contents

INFORMATION

FEATURES

Published by

Angling Publications
(The publishers of Carpworld and Big Fish World magazines)
1 Grosvenor Square
Sheffield S2 4MS
Tel: (0742) 580812, 582728

Printed by

Gibbons Barford

Colour Origination

Adlington & Brough

CARPWORLD YEAR

COMPILED BY

Kevin Clifford

Julian Cundiff

PRODUCED BY

Tim Paisley

Steve Wilde

ADVERTISING

Clive Gibbins

ENQUIRIES TO

Angling Publications
1 Grosvenor Square
Sheffield S2 4MS
Tel: (0742) 580812, 582728

INTRODUCTIONS

Eighteen years ago, when grey hair and shrinking trousers were problems encountered by what nowadays, I am reliably informed, are called 'wrinklies', I was just another carp groupie. Oh yes, and I can prove it too. I used to collect the autographs of famous carp anglers (cries of shame and ribald laughter from the masses but confession is good for the soul!). So, traipsing round the 1973 National Angling Show, I harassed my heroes into putting their monicker into a book which, for me, broke the mould of specialist publications. For the princely sum of 85p you could own the first professionally produced carp magazine, the annual of the British Carp Study Group – 'Carp, Carp, Carp'.

We've come a long way since then. I don't collect autographs anymore – well, at least I don't admit to it in public – and the trousers have started shrinking! But so too has the quality of our reading matter. Make no mistake, it has improved out of all recognition. It would not be stretching the truth to say that one man has been largely responsible for those improvements we now all take for granted. Firstly, since 1981, through his involvement in editing Carp Fisher for the Carp Society and then, from 1988, with his own magazine, Carpworld, Tim Paisley has always striven for quality. That has not always been an easy road to follow. There's been a lot of hard work, some sleepless nights, ups and downs and a whole load of personal sacrifices, but the results are there and it is something Tim should always be proud of achieving.

Why it has taken so long to produce the first annual is something of a mystery to me. Probably, like so many of our personal objectives, it just kept being pushed to one side. But finally, Tim managed to fit it into Angling Publications' schedule and asked Julian and myself to act as the gelling agent. I really hope we have 'gelled' it together; we've tried to give it a bit of everything but, first and foremost, we've tried to give it quality.

We hope you enjoy it and we'll see you next year. And, if you're wondering whose autographs I managed to get in that other Annual, I'll tell you if you promise not to laugh. None other than Peter Mohan and Tom Mintram! Ah, happy days!

Kevin Clifford

Meanwhile...

Christmas 1990, and Tim was enquiring how the Yearbook was getting along ready for its April release. Whoops – other than one or two tentative enquiries with potential contributors, it had lain dormant. Time to move boy.

Now, who's a must for the Yearbook? Chris Ball, Harry Haskell, Ken Townley, Tina and Profumo were all regular contributors to Carpworld so wouldn't it be nice to see how they had fared in 1990? Four 'My Season' pieces, a good start but still a long way to go. In my book, Zenon was an absolute must; talented, mad and a hugely successful carper to boot. I wanted to know what was in his tackle box. Do you? Mike Wilson's involvement in carp fishing goes back a long, long way. A feature from him on tackle would certainly be an eye opener for many. Smooth Mike – well, he didn't let us down did he? Gibbinson is hugely respected and a bait piece from a man with no real commercial ties had to go in. 'Long Life Boilies', the piece, now watch a few heads turn in the bait world. Nev Fickling is certainly not one to beat about the bush, so a piece from him on the effects of the NRA would cut through the red tape.

Rigs – everybody loves to read about them and John Tames' bang up to date article had some super line drawings to make its entry assured. Dumpy bombs, round leads, the lot. All explained and not pie-in-the-sky either.

As you will read, we also managed to add a few more pieces as well. The fact is, it turned out to be what **not** to put in rather than **what** to put in.

Tina put together the review of 1990; we have the thirties and forties list; videos, organisations, publications, the lot. Headbanger, Profumo, will definitely raise one or two tempers as well.

Whatever your interest in carp fishing, be it baitings or facts and figures, sit back, pour yourself a coffee (or a beer) and welcome to the first Carpworld Yearbook.

Julian Cundiff

BOOK STARTS HERE...

HOW TO GET YOUR ARTICLES PUBLISHED

Everyone loves a carp story and good writers are in demand nowadays with lots of scope from magazines, newspapers and book publishers. With so many publications you really do have a reasonable chance of seeing your work in print, but a little thought and presentation beforehand can considerably enhance your chances.

1. Try to have your article typed. If not, write the article very neatly. Probably all the fishing magazine editors will accept handwritten material, but certainly some book publishers and editors of other publications will not even consider handwritten material. The first impression you give to a potential publisher of your material is vital. If certain words are illegible then this means the publisher has to contact you to clarify the problem. Alternatively, the office typist might guess and make a nonsense of a point you were trying to make. Use A4 plain paper, with a good sized margin (at least $1^1/_2$ inches) on the left hand side for the editor to make corrections and notes in. Double space your lines (one line of text then one full space blank) and use a black ribbon in a typewriter or black/blue ink if the material is handwritten. If you are using a word processor, do not justify your text.
2. Keep a photocopy of your article. Enclose a S.A.E. for its return (with any photographs you may include) and preferably add a short letter, explaining briefly what the article is about.
3. Write your name on each sheet and number them clearly. Write your name and address on some sticky labels and attach one on the back of each photograph. Don't write direct on the back of prints.
4. Get someone to check your spelling if you do not feel confident yourself and be consistent throughout with words that can be spelt in different ways.
5. If you are writing a technical piece, make sure of your facts. Try to include diagrams - a picture can, literally, be worth a thousand words! Don't worry if you can't draw very well, the publisher will get them redone. Don't forget to write your name on the diagrams as well.
6. Don't waffle. Make your sentences short and precise. As a general rule make one point at a time. After you've finished an article, leave it for a few days and then go through it again. Read it to a couple of friends and ask what they think. Try not to use the same word repeatedly (we don't mean common words like 'a' or 'the'). Be descriptive.Tell the reader about the surroundings. Try and draw him into the setting. Imagine you have someone with you who is blind and the only way you can communicate is by telling him what you see and feel. Then write down what you would tell him.
7. Try not to deliberately copy another person's writing style. Don't steal another author's work and reproduce (I could have said copy here but I used it in the last sentence) his ideas by changing a few words around.
8. Start by writing short articles (about 1,000 words) and don't try to pad the work out. A well written, interesting, short article will be paid for, whereas a long-winded one won't! Try to think of something that hasn't been written about a lot before. For example, "How I caught my first twenty" or "Last season's memories" don't get a grouchy, word-weary editor sitting on the edge of his seat.
9. Excellent photographic material can make all the difference to an editor's decision. Again, try to include imaginative material, not just the same old trophy pictures. Scenic shots of the lake, so the reader can feel he is there, and photographs of anglers playing/landing fish are often preferable. The majority of anglers use colour print film nowadays and prints can be reproduced in magazines. But editors are often desperate for good quality black and white prints so it may be worth considering a change. Colour transparencies also give far better reproduction than colour prints, so if you are considering journalism seriously it might be worth thinking about changing your film type.

The Editors

COVER PICTURE

The good looking fella on the cover is French star Didier Cottin with a brace of 43+lb mirror and a 33+lb common.

DISCLAIMER

The Yearbook contains a great deal of factual information. The compilers and the publishers have done their best to ensure that this information is accurate at the time of going to print, but circumstances change and mistakes can be made. Please check details of holidays, dealers, publications etc., before committing yourself to any expense or unnecessary travel. As they say in the Yellow Pages adverts, let your fingers do the walking and check details by phone to avoid possible inconvenience. Our apologies if any mistakes have occurred.

INFORMATION

We have included as much detailed information about carp fishing as possible in the Yearbook, but we can't include information we don't know of, or don't have access to. If we have missed you off a list you feel you should have been included in, get in touch with us. We will be updating all the lists and information for next year's Yearbook. Don't phone information in, put it in writing. It makes our job easier.

FORTY POUND +

This latest compilation is by Chris Ball – with our thanks to him for his efforts. Thanks also go to a number of other people for assistance, and to Tim Paisley for the information gleaned from the list in his Crowood book 'Big Carp.'

Repeat Capture	Weight	Captor	Location	Date
A	51-08-0 (M)	Chris Yates	Redmire Pool	June 1980
	46-12-0 (M)	Richard Lloyd	Surrey Pond	March 1990
B	46-02-0 (L)	Pete Richards	Erehwon	August 1989
C	45-12-0 (M)	Ritchie McDonald	Yateley North Lake	October 1984
C	45-08-0 (M)	Tony Moore	Yateley North Lake	July 1990
	45-08-0 (M)	Albert Romp	Savay	June 1990
B	45-02-0 (L)	Ray Stone	Erehwon	December 1986
B	45-00-0 (L)	Mark Fitzpatrick	Erehwon	June 1989
B	45-00-0 (L)	Mark Fitzpatrick	Erehwon	July 1989
B	45-00-0 (L)	Ray Stone	Erehwon	July 1987
B	44-14-0 (L)	Ray Stone	Erehwon	November 1986
B	44-12-0 (L)	Keith Longden	Erehwon	August 1987
C	44-08-0 (M)	Graham Mountain	Yateley North Lake	March 1989
C	44-08-0 (M)	Nick Lee	Yateley North Lake	1989
	44-06-0 (M)	Ray Greenwood	Henlow Grange	June 1984
D	44-04-0 (M)	Steve Allcot	Longfield	December 1989
C	44-04-0 (M)	Dave Baker	Yateley North Lake	1985
B	44-00-0 (L)	Mark Fitzpatrick	Erehwon	June 1987
	44-00-0 (C)	Richard Walker	Redmire Pool	September 1952
I	44-00-0 (M)	Steve Burgess	Horton	June 1990
	43-13-8 (C)	Chris Yates	Redmire Pool	August 1972
B	43-08-0 (L)	Ray Stone	Erehwon	September 1985
E	43-08-0 (L)	Keith O' Conner	Harrow	October 1984
C	43-08-0 (M)	Brian O'Bourn	Yateley North Lake	1989
C	43-04-0 (M)	Steve Brown	Yateley North Lake	October 1989
C	43-04-0 (M)	Adrian Tilbury	Yateley North Lake	July 1984
B	43-04-0 (L)	Gary Morgan	Erehwon	August 1986
C	43-04-0 (M)	Sam Fox	Yateley North Lake	September 1984
C	43-04-0 (M)	Ray Fuller	Yateley North Lake	July 1987
G	43-04-0 (M)	Clive Gibbins	Sandholme Pool	1984
	43-04-0 (M)	AN Other	Kingsmead	July 1990
M	43-01-0 (M)	Peter Bond	Yateley Pads Lake	November 1990
	43-00-0 (M)*	Graham Mountain	Tri-Lakes	1983
L	43-00-0 (M)	Jonathan Leigh	Surrey Club Lake	July 1980
C	42-12-0 (M)	Kerry Barringer	Yateley North Lake	1985
	42-12-0 (L)	Martin Symonds	Waltham Abbey	September 1976
I	42-12-0 (M)	Bernard Blight	Horton	August 1990

Chris Yates. 51.08. June 1990.

Ritchie McDonald. 45.12. October 1984.

Ray Stone. 45.02. December 1986.

Albert Romp. 45.08. June 1990.

Chris Yates. 43.13.8 Aug. 72.

CARP LIST UPDATE

1. Ray Greenwood 44.06. June 84

2. Dick Walker 44.00. Sept. 52.

3. Phil Harper 41.08. Sept. 89

4. Jack Hilton 40.03. July 72

5. Phil Harper 40.04. 1984

Repeat Capture	Weight	Captor	Location	Date
C	42-08-0 (M)	Nick Peat	Yateley North Lake	1985
	42-08-0 (M)	Bob Copeland	Harrow	June 1990
B	42-06-0 (L)	Vic Bailey	Erehwon	June 1985
	42-04-0 (M)	Max Cottis	Savay	June 1990
B	42-04-0 (L)	Mark Fitzpatrick	Erehwon	October 1984
B	42-04-0 (L)	Ray Stone	Erehwon	July 1986
	42-04-0 (M)	Mick Dorton	Harrow	September 1990
	42-02-0 (C)	John Lilley	Mangrove	1988
C	42-00-0 (M)	Mark Lawson	Yateley North Lake	1989
D	42-00-0 (M)	John Allen	Longfield	December 1987
	42-00-0 (M)	Ray Clay	Billing Aquadrome	September 1966
	42-00-0 (M)	Ken Hodder	Yateley Car Park Lake	October 1979
E	42-00-0 (L)	Zen Bojko	Harrow	1984
D	42-00-0 (M)	Terry Dempsey	Longfield	September 1989
D	42-00-0 (M)	Jon Holt	Longfield	August 1987
	41-12-0 (M)	Thomas Gelston	Hainault	November 1985
D	41-12-0 (M)	Dave Whibley	Longfield	1989
K	41-12-0 (M)	Alan Taylor	Mid-Northants	June 1990
C	41-10-0 (M)	Jan Wenczka	Yateley North Lake	August 1981
M	41-09-0 (M)	Ritchie McDonald	Yateley Pads Lake	March 1991
	41-08-0 (M)	Andy Grant	Harrow	October 1990
F	41-08-0 (C)	David Westerman	Snake Pit, Essex	June 1988
N	41-08-0 (L)	Robin Dix	Yateley Car Park Lake	June 1985
J	41-08-0 (M)	Kevin Nash	Silver End Pit	June 1985
	41-08-0 (M)	Alan	Standstead Abbott	December 1989
	41-08-0 (C)	Phil Harper	Snake Pit, Essex	September 1989

6. Terry Dempsey. 42.00. Sept. 1989

7. Kevin Nash 41.08. June 1985

FORTIES LIST UPDATE

Repeat Capture	Weight	Captor	Location	Date
C	41-05-0 (M)	Chris Riddington	Yateley North Lake	October 1980
	41-04-0 (M)	Andy MacTavish	Colne Valley Club Lake	October 1990
L	41-00-0 (M)	Jonathon Leigh	Surrey Club Lake	October 1978
B	41-00-0 (L)	Mark Fitzpatrick	Erehwon	September 1984
	41-00-0 (M)	Peter Wilson	Withy Pool	June 1990
K	41-00-0 (M)		Mid-Northants	June 1990
K	40-12-0 (M)	Dave MacIntyre	Mid-Northants	October 1989
N	40-12-0 (L)	Don Orriss	Yateley Car Park Lake	October 1989
	40-12-0 (M)	Steve Hale	M.o.D. Aldermaston	1987
M	40-10-0 (M)	Jock White	Yateley Pad Lakes	1989
H	40-10-0 (M)	Jon Holt	Longfield	1982
G	40-08-0 (M)	Kevin Clifford	Sandholme Pool	1983
A	40-08-0 (M)	Eddie Price	Redmire Pool	September 1959
H	40-08-0 (M)	Colin Swaden	Longfield	1980
F	40-08-0 (C)	Zen Bojko	Snake Pit, Essex	1988
E	40.-08-0 (L)	Bernie Stamp	Harrow	July 1987
	40-08-0 (M)	Dave Cumpstone	Wraysbury	June 1990
I	40-08-0 (M)	Geoff Ball	Horton	September 1990
N	40.08-0 (L)	Ritchie McDonald	Yateley Car Park Lake	March 1991
	40-04-0 (M)	Richard Johnson	Longfield	1985
	40-04-0 (M)	AN Other **	Pit 1	June 1988
G	40-04-0 (M)	Kevin Clifford	Sandholme Pool	1984
	40-04-0 (M)	Nick West	Wraysbury	1980
J	40-04-0 (M)	Phil Harper	Silver End Pit	1984
K	40-04-0 (M)	Alan Taylor	Mid-Northants	January 1989
K	40-04-0 (M)	Kevin Maddocks	Mid-Northants	January 1990
A	40-03-0 (M)	Jack Hilton	Redmire Pool	July 1972
H	40-03-0 (M)	Colin Swaden	Longfield	1980
E	40-02-0 (L)	Paul Fickling	Harrow	1985
D	40-02-0 (M)	John Allen	Longfield	July 1988
D	40-02-0 (M)	Nod	Longfield	December 1988
D	40-02-0 (M)	Matthew McKwen	Longfield	July 1989
	40-02-0 (M)	Allan Partridge	Harrow	September 1990
	40-00-8 (M)	Ron Groombridge	Boxmoor	June 1966
B	40-00-0 (L)	Ian Longden	Erehwon	September 1984
A	40-00-0 (M)	John MacLeod	Redmire Pool	June 1972
	40-00-0 (M)	Henry Weeks	Peckham	July 1972
D	40-00-0 (M)	Clive Williams	Longfield	August 1988
K	40-00-0 (M)	Steve Gombocz	Mid-Northants	February, 1990

* Weight doubts?

Chris Yates – first angler to catch **two** different carp over 40lb (1980) • Ritchie McDonald – first angler to catch **three** different carp over 40lb. (1991) • Harrow – first UK water to produce **four** different forties.

1. *John McLeod. 40lb. June 72.*
2. *Jon Holt. 40.10. 1982.*
3. *Gary Morgan. 43.04. Aug. 86.*
4. *Max Cottis. 42.00. June 90.*
5. *Mark Fitzpatrick. 42.04. Oct. 84.*

IT IS THE ONE AND ONLY IN THE WORLD

35 TONS OF RECORD SIZE FISH

CARP ★ CATFISH ★ PIKE ★ BLACK-BASS ★ STURGEON ★ ZANDER

IN AN 86 ACRE LAKE

THE IDYLLIC UNIVERSE WHERE ANGLERS WILL EXPERIENCE THEIR STRONGEST SENSATIONS.

- NIGHT FISHING IS AUTORIZED
- EXCEPTIONAL DENSITY OF RECORD SIZE FISH
- LUXURY HOTEL COMPLEX
- OTHER ACTIVITIES ARE AVAILABLE FOR YOUR FAMILY

.. AND MANY OTHER SURPRISES IN STORE FOR YOU.

HERE IS SOME AVERAGE SIZE CARP. THEY HAVE JUST BEEN PUT IN THE LAKE.

OPENING ON 18TH MAY 1991

FOR DOCUMENTS AND INFORMATION AT :

EUROPEAN SPECIMEN ANGLING CENTRE

LE LAC – 22230 LOSCOUET/MEU – **FRANCE**

☎ **96.25.27.66**

FISHABIL

BIG GAME FISHING IN FRESHWATER !!!

HERE IS THE SMALLEST SPECIMEN CATFISH THAT YOU WILL BE ABLE TO CATCH, AMONG A MULTITUD OF SPECIMENS SELECTED IN THE WHOLE WORLD.

INSIDE ....

OVAL BROLLYWRAP SPECIAL

"I've had a few bivvies over the years and set a few trends to boot, as the dozens of copies show. I don't really mind being ripped off. Because at the end of the day it keeps me on my toes. So while I'm out there fishing I'm always looking for ways to improve.
Our range of bivvies and umbrella's are the latest in design and innovation using quality fittings and fabrics, and sold direct to the shops, so we can build more in for you the carp angler as we cut out the middle man.
The rip off merchants, well, they're chasing their arses trying to keep up with us,. And scatching their heads to figure out where they can cut down on quality so they can afford to supply the wholsaler. You could almost feel sorry for them. I lead they bodge up."

Kevin Nash.

....OR OUT

FORCE 10 UNDERSUIT

" I do a bit of winter carp fishing from time to time and like the majority of top anglers favour a one piece undersuit, to sit in the bivvy or move around in.
I think we have all come across the faults of the fluffy undersuit. Cold winds cut through them and there not shower proof. So if it is raining and you"re having action you either have to sit in the bivvy with your waterproof clobber on or you get wet.
The suit I have designed is the result of a year's development with Creek performance fabrics, manufactured from a special insulated quilting that repels water and is wind proof. Have a look at it , if you're out there doing the business you"ll agree the Force 10 undersuit is the business."

Kevin Nash.

Features

* Showerproof Creek Performance Quilting. * Waterproof Two Way Zip. * Too Hand Warmer Pockets. * Two Leg Pockets. * Elasticated Cuffs. * Zipped Elasticated Legs. * Reinforced Shoulders & Kneepads.

Force 10 Undersuit RRP £46.71p
Force 10 Undersuit with Hood RRP £49.99p

AT YOUR LOCAL STOCKIST OR FOR MORE DETAILS CONTACT
KEVIN NASH TACKLE LIMITED
34, BROOK ROAD INDUSTRIAL ESTATE, RAYLEIGH, ESSEX.
TEL: (0268) 770238, 745027. FAX: (0268) 775327.

KEVIN NASH

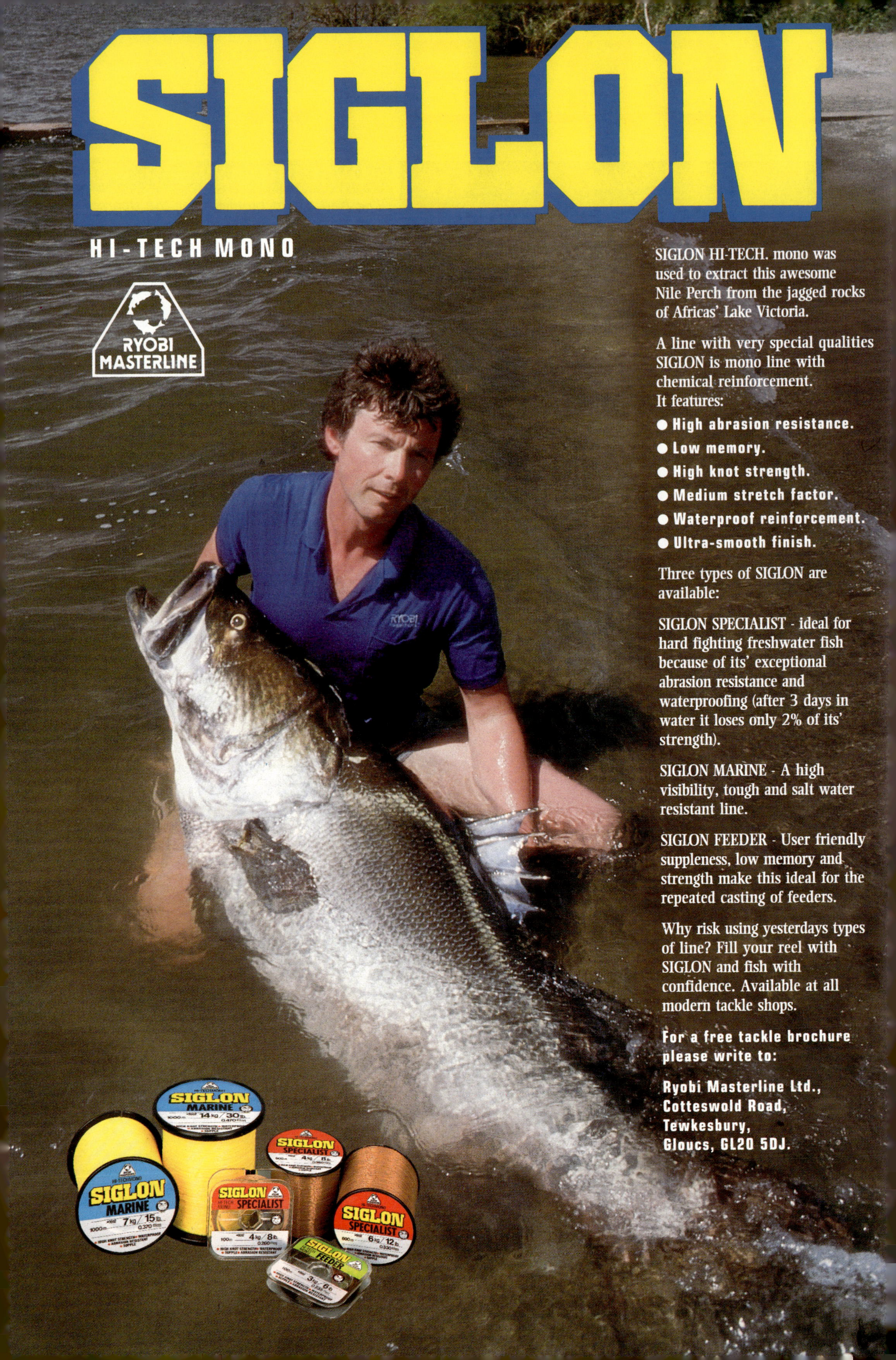
SIGLON
HI-TECH MONO
RYOBI MASTERLINE
SIGLON HI-TECH. mono was used to extract this awesome Nile Perch from the jagged rocks of Africas' Lake Victoria.
A line with very special qualities SIGLON is mono line with chemical reinforcement.
It features:
● High abrasion resistance.
● Low memory.
● High knot strength.
● Medium stretch factor.
● Waterproof reinforcement.
● Ultra-smooth finish.
Three types of SIGLON are available:
SIGLON SPECIALIST - ideal for hard fighting freshwater fish because of its' exceptional abrasion resistance and waterproofing (after 3 days in water it loses only 2% of its' strength).
SIGLON MARINE - A high visibility, tough and salt water resistant line.
SIGLON FEEDER - User friendly suppleness, low memory and strength make this ideal for the repeated casting of feeders.
Why risk using yesterdays types of line? Fill your reel with SIGLON and fish with confidence. Available at all modern tackle shops.
For a free tackle brochure please write to:
Ryobi Masterline Ltd.,
Cotteswold Road,
Tewkesbury,
Gloucs, GL20 5DJ.
SIGLON MARINE
SIGLON SPECIALIST
SIGLON FEEDER

WORTH KNOWING!

TWO PAGES OF INFORMATION THAT MAY BE OF SPECIAL USE TO CARP ANGLERS

WEATHERCALL SERVICE

The Meteorological Office supplies 3-6 days forecasts for areas of Britain. These can be accessed by dialling 0898 500 followed by the regional code below:

Beds., Herts., Essex	407
Berks., Bucks., Oxon	406
Caithness, Orkney, Shetland	426
Central Midlands	411
Cumbria, Lake District	419
Devon, Cornwall	404
Dorset, Hants	403
Dyfed, Powys	414
East Central Scotland	423
East Midlands	412
Edinburgh, Lothian, Borders	422
Glamorgan, Gwent	409
Grampian, East Highlands	424
Greater London	401
Gwynedd, Clwyd	415
Kent, Surrey, Sussex	402
Lincs., Humberside	413
Norfolk, Suffolk, Cambs.	408
North West England	416
North West Scotland	425
North East England	418
Northern Ireland	427
South West Scotland	420
Shropshire, Hereford & Worcs.	410
W & S Yorks., Yorks. Dales	417
West Central Scotland	421
Wiltshire, Glos., Avon, Somerset	405

EUROPEAN EXCHANGE RATES

The actual exchange rate can flutuate slightly, but the following represents the amount of foreign currency that can be expected for £1 sterling.

BELGIUM
60 Franc

FRANCE
10 Franc

WEST GERMANY
2.90 D. Mark

HOLLAND
3.27 Guilder

SPAIN
178 Peseta

WEIGHTS & MEASURES CONVERSION TABLE

LENGTH

1 inch	=	25.4 mm
1 foot	=	30.48 cm
1 yard	=	0.9144 m
1 mile	=	1.609 km
1 millimetre	=	0.039 inches
1 centimetre	=	0.0328 feet
1 metre	=	1.094 yards
1 kilometre	=	0.621 miles

VOLUME

1 pint	=	0.568 litres
1 gallon	=	4.546 litres
1 litre	=	1.76 pints
1 litre	=	0.22 gallons

WEIGHT

1 ounce	=	28.349 gm
1 pound	=	0.4536 kg
1 gram	=	0.035 ounces
1 kilogram	=	2.2 pounds

TEMPERATURE

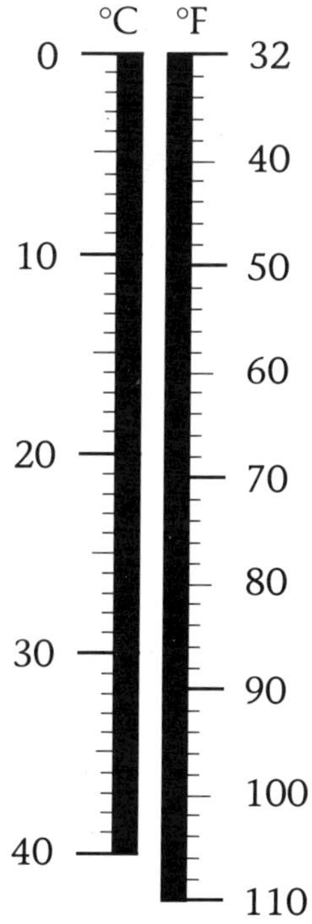

°C
°F
0
10
20
30
40
32
40
50
60
70
80
90
100
110

CONTINUED OVER ➤

SUNRISE AND SUNSET FOR LONDON, 1991

Month	Day	Rise h	Rise m	Set h	Set m
Jan	1	08	06	16	02
	8	08	05	16	10
	15	08	00	16	20
	22	07	53	16	32
	29	07	44	16	44
Feb	5	07	33	16	57
	12	07	21	17	09
	19	07	08	17	22
	26	06	53	17	35
March	5	06	38	17	47
	12	06	23	17	59
	19	06	07	18	11
	26	05	51	18	23
April	2	05	35	19	35
	9	06	19	19	46
	16	06	04	19	58
	23	05	49	20	10
	30	05	36	20	21
May	7	05	23	20	33
	14	05	11	20	44
	21	05	01	20	54
	28	04	53	21	03
June	4	04	47	21	11
	11	04	44	21	18
	18	04	43	21	21
	25	04	44	21	22
July	2	04	48	21	21
	9	04	54	21	17
	16	05	02	21	11
	23	05	11	21	03
	30	05	20	20	53
August	6	05	31	20	41
	13	05	42	20	28
	20	05	53	20	14
	27	06	04	19	59
September	3	06	15	19	44
	10	06	27	19	28
	17	06	38	19	12
	24	06	49	18	56
October	1	07	00	18	40
	8	07	12	18	24
	15	07	24	18	09
	22	07	36	17	54
	29	06	48	16	40
November	5	07	00	16	28
	12	07	13	16	16
	19	07	25	16	07
	26	07	36	15	59
December	3	07	46	15	54
	10	07	55	15	52
	17	08	01	15	52
	24	08	05	15	55
	31	08	06	16	01

Note: These times are in GMT, except between 0100 on 31st March and 0100 on 27th October when the times are in BST (1 hour in advance of GMT).

EUROPEAN TOURIST OFFICES

BELGIUM
Belgium Tourist Office
Premier House
2 Gayton Road
Harrow
Middlesex
HA1 2XU
Tel: 081 861 3300

GERMANY
German Tourist Office
Nightingale House
65 Curzon Street
London
W1Y 7PE
Tel: 071 495 3990

HOLLAND
Netherland Board of Tourism
25-28 Buckingham Gate
London
SW1E 6LD
Tel: 071 630 0451

SPAIN
Spanish Tourist Office
57/58 St James Street
London
SW1A 1LD
Tel: 071 499 0901

FRANCE
French Govt. Tourist Office, 178 Piccadilly, London W1V OAL
Tel: 071 491 7622

BRITISH TOURIST AUTHORITY OVERSEAS OFFICES

FRANCE
63 rue Pierre-Charron
75008 Paris
Tel: 42 89 11 11

GERMANY
TaunusstraeBe 52 60, 6000
Frankfurt 1
Tel: 069 23 80 711

BELGIUM
306 Avenue Louise
1050 Brussels
Tel: 02/511 43 90

HOLLAND
Aurora Gebouw (5th floor)
Stadhouderskade 2,
1054 ES Amsterdam
Tel: 020 85 50 51

SPAIN
BTA, Torre de Madrid
6° of 7, Pza Espana 18
28008 Madrid
Tel: 541 13 96

Compiled by

Kevin Clifford and Julian Cundiff

Please let the editors know if you feel there is any further information we should make available in future Yearbooks.

OBITUARIES

'B.B.'

1991 was marred by the sad loss of several of angling's esteemed figures and, for many of us, they are a reminder of our own mortality and frailty. Denys Watkins-Pitchford was revered by many carp anglers but his books reached a far wider audience. He was a highly respected writer of books about wildlife and the countryside, as well as children's stories, and he wrote many articles for the angling press including a regular column in Shooting Times. There is no doubt, whatsoever, that his writing had an incalculable influence, directly and indirectly, on the development and direction of carp fishing. This fact was recognised by the Carp Society when they made him their President in April 1990. Sadly he was to honour us with this office for so short a time for he passed away, at the age of 85, in September of that year.

A kind and gentle man with a fine sense of humour, yet he suffered greatly throughout his life. His various forms of illness was more than enough for any man to develop a little bitterness, yet this and the loss of his son, Robin, at the age of eight and his wife, Cecily, through pesticide poisoning did not affect his considerable qualities.

His first book, The Sportsman's Bedside Book, published in 1937 was soon followed by many more. They covered many topics but all had the common thread of his love of the countryside. He was not a practical carp angler and would fail abysmally on today's carp scene. But he knew the real secrets of carp fishing, something which many carp anglers nowadays are ignorant of. That is their inestimable loss – read his books and learn.

"The wonder of the world, the beauty and the power, the shapes of things, their colours, lights and shades; these I saw. Look ye also while life lasts."

DICK'S MUM

Dick's mum at the Dick Walker Remembrance Conference in 1988.

In January Dick Walker's mother, Mrs Elsie May Walker, died at the age of 97. She commenced work as a secretary, with Lloyds of Letchworth, and rose to the position of Company Chairman, still running the company until her death. This gives an indication as to her will and determination, qualities which were clearly passed on to her son, Richard. Those who attended Dick's Memorial will remember her abilities for public speaking, which was reinforced to those who also heard her impromptu speech, about her son, at the Carp Society Conference. A truly remarkable woman who will long be remembered fondly as "Dick's Mum."

SONNY WARREN

Another sad loss to the angling world was that of Samuel T. Warren, known universally as Sonny, who died in the Battle Hospital, Reading after a short illness. He was 86.

Sonny had lived alone in Reading since the death of his better known brother, Bill, who died in 1978. Unlike Bill, who once held the chub record with a fish of 7lb. 6oz., Sonny shunned publicity. His many captures of specimen fish, from the Hampshire Avon and Dorset Stour, were seldom reported – even to his friends! If you wanted to know what Sonny had caught you really had to squeeze the information from him. As often as not Sonny's captures never even left the water; he played them in, slipped out the hook and nursed them for a few seconds before they swam away. Landing nets and spring balances were rarely part of Sonny's tackle.

Sonny was a true angler; he went fishing solely because he loved the sport and he will be sorely missed by his many friends and acquaintances.

JOHN SIDLEY

Just a week after his 44th birthday John Sidley died on December 8th, 1990. Well known for his tremendous eel and pike catches, John was becoming more interested in other species and had recently spent a lot of time barbel fishing. He was a tremendously enthusiastic angler who gave up work to spend as much time as possible by the waterside. He wrote many articles for the angling periodicals, several chapters for other angler's books as well as two books of his own. He was also instrumental in bringing a new awareness to the care and welfare of big eels, and in so doing initiated the highly successful 'Put Eels Back' campaign. John was also a founder member of the British Eel Anglers' Club.

All those who knew him said how likeable and innocent John was. Many of his friends and acquaintances from the specialist world gathered to pay tribute at his funeral. As his great friend Des Taylor said, John was a one-off, and he will be sadly missed by all who knew him – and the many who only knew him through his writings.

NORMAN WOODWARD

Norman Woodward died, after a long illness, on the 15th December 1990, he was 65 years old. He was one of the early big fish anglers of the Walker generation and specialised in tench. A fine angler, with an enviable record of most species, he caught lots of big tench, chub, barbel and roach. He also fished for game and sea fish catching several shark over 100lb. He was a regular contributor to the angling periodicals as well as local angling papers and, in the late 1950's, opened, in Leicester, one of the first specialist angling shops in the country. Dick Walker and Fred J. Taylor, being good friends of Norman's, appeared at the opening ceremony and, over the years , a great many famous anglers passed through the shop's doors. The younger generation of big fish anglers also spent many hours in his shop and well-known anglers such as Dave Ball, Brian Culley, Mike Muse and Mike Prorock became good friends. He was always helpful and had a marvellous sense of humour. An excellent craftsman and meticulous in everything he did, he will be greatly missed by all his old customers and friends.

BRIAN GODFREY

Brian Godfrey sadly died at the young age of 45, in December 1990. He was born in Holywell, North Wales but moved to Liverpool as a child. His job, as a civil servant, took him to many parts of the country and this gave him wide experience in fishing for big fish in different situations. An accomplished angler he caught a tremendous number of big fish of all species, including chub, big barbel from the Ribble, Severn and Wensum and carp. He spent a good deal of his spare time helping youngsters and was also involved in putting something back into angling. He wrote a great many excellent articles for the angling press and was, latterly, living in Norwich and fishing with Jim Tyree and Dave Plummer. He leaves a wife and two children and a great many friends around the country.

PAT RUSSELL

Yet another loss to the angling world was that of Pat Russell, who died in March, 1991.

He was a childhood friend of Pete Thomas and through this friendship, took up fishing in 1950. He was soon making trips with Dick Walker and

Pete and, in 1954, outfished them both on a memorable visit to Redmire. Refusing to take advice on where best to fish and how to wait for proper runs, in a few hours he caught three carp up to 27lb.

As a young man he was an enthusiastic hockey player. In later years, he developed a love of trout and salmon fishing and also took up wildfowling.

He attended the Carp Society Conference in honour of Richard Walker in June, 1988 and made many new friends amongst the modern generation of carp anglers. He will be sorely missed by all his friends.

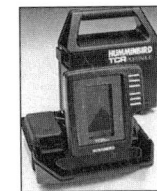

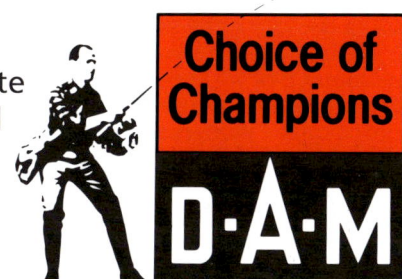

WILD COMMONS -

Geoff Shaw with his magnificent brace of commons weighing 35lb & 39lb.

'Stunning shots of big European fish', the Carp Society letter had said. How right that was! Geoff Shaw was showing slides of his French trips and the room was packed with carp men, held spell bound by shot after shot of huge carp.

I'd been living in France for two years and wondered if we had fished any of the same waters. The next shots answered my question; first, a shot of a lake I'd fished the previous year came up on the screen, then a shot of the very same swim.

We had a long chat after the show and found that we knew a lot of the same waters and were both totally hooked on the pioneering style of carp fishing, searching out new waters for big fish. We decided to organise a trip after big commons for later in the year, when the 'Barrage' would be at its best...

This article is about that trip. The ups and downs, the excitement and the problems of fishing for big carp a long way from home, in a wild, unspoilt water.

It was the beginning of October. My little Fiesta was loaded to bursting with a mass of gear, and the roof rack piled high with inflatable, engine, oars, echo sounder, the lot.

Geoff and I were full of excitement and anticipation as we headed for Dover with ten days in front of us. We drove straight on the ferry (that's unusual), dinner on the boat, three hours' drive and we stopped at a friend's house in Paris for breakfast. Chat about carp fishing with Steve and Dick over breakfast, a couple of cups of coffee and we were on our way again.

Three hours later, cruising nicely along the autoroute when the car jumped out of gear. "Strange", I thought, and put it back in; a few miles later it did it again, with an ominous noise from under the bonnet. We were stuck in third gear. Limping off the autoroute, we were lucky to find a friendly garage, where an inspection on a hydraulic ramp confirmed our worst fears - the gearbox was seized and, at best, would need rebuilding, at worst, an exchange box. Okay, no need to panic, I had RAC Eurocover for such

A view from the bivvy.

WILD WATER

an emergency; they'd have a man who would help us in no time – at least that's what the advert says.

That day's drama was just beginning. Eight hours of phone calls, waiting and frustration later and we were eventually loaded up in a replacement van and on our way. My car was to be shipped back to England by the RAC (it eventually arrived three weeks later), and we would get home in a hire car. The whole saga with the RAC was a nightmare; in fact, as I write, I'm still waiting for a final settlement.

However, back on the road we began to feel better as the lake was only a few hours away. We came off the main roads and climbed into thickly wooded hills as the light faded, and it was pitch black as we reached the 'Barrage' and drove the last two miles of winding road following the water.

We pulled off the road just short of the area we wanted to fish and both stared in disbelief. A camper van, with all its lights on – obviously fishermen – was pulled off the road by the next bend, in the area we wanted to fish; in the stark blackness of night in the mountains, it stood out like Blackpool illuminations. Exhausted after driving all night and day and the drama of the day's events, this was the last straw. It was a group of English anglers who had stumbled on the place by chance(!); after a couple of days they had been caught night fishing and the police had threatened to confiscate all their tackle so they planned to leave the next day. In years of fishing in France, neither Geoff nor I have ever had any trouble and now we were faced with the problem that the police would be on the lookout through the lack of discretion and sheer stupidity of one group of English anglers. Geoff was seething and told them exactly what he thought. At least they would be leaving the next day so we could fish the area we wanted.

We left them with a bee in their ear and parked in a nearby campsite to get some sleep. We had just settled down when an Optonic went off. In a valley where, in the silence at night, you can hear the farmer's bed creaking half a mile away, a Delkim at full volume must have been heard by everybody in the valley (very discreet!). Ten seconds later it was still going. Suddenly, Geoff was off his bedchair, boots on and running down the hill in the dark. It was a good 100 yards but he still got to the rod, struck, and almost landed it before the owner arrived. The owner had "just been having a chat with my friends." Unbelievable.

The morning came quickly and, revived by the night's rest, I could put the trauma of the previous day's events behind me and began to feel the excitement and anticipation as we walked down to the water.

Geoff had described the 'Barrage' and the surrounding countryside in some detail and was obviously taken by the beauty of the place and, as the sun came up, I could see that his enthusiasm was well founded; the scenery was magnificent. As the sun cleared the trees behind us, it cut through the mist that hung on the water and lit up the autumn colours of the steeply wooded slopes opposite. To the left the slope was gentler and a herd of cows stood out sharply in the sunlight against the green of the lush pasture, the colours and outlines

The author with his tremendous common of 39lb +.

John Llewellyn

heightened in the crystal clear air. To the right we could just make out a stone cottage amongst the trees as the 'Barrage' meandered into the distance. The cottage belonged to Michael, a friend of Geoff's since he first fished the 'Barrage' two years before.

We wandered along the bank, Geoff pointing out different areas, chatting about the water and working out the best approach. We couldn't fish the swims we wanted because of the police problem, but Michael had baited that area for us so we decided to make new swims in the bushes further along the bank and fish across to the same area at an angle. Apparently the fish visited this area mainly at night, so we would fish there and hide our gear in the day to avoid being seen in the area at all. I had packed some army camouflage netting 'just in case',which was to prove invaluable.

The morning was spent preparing swims and, once finished, neither would be easily seen from the bank and could only just be made out from a boat. Geoff's experience on the water was that we needed a lot of bait, so we planned to pile in a big bed of maize at the start and keep topping it up. A couple of hours in the boat with the echo sounder and we had a good idea of the area. No big fish had shown on the screen so we hoped that the fish were still moving in to feed at night.

The margins out to the old river bed which ran along the far side, some 90 yards away, were thick silt and full of bloodworm. From my swim, the nearside shelf sloped to 15' two thirds of the way down, sloping quickly to 25' in the original river bed. A marker was set at 20' and placed on the drop off and I baited heavily in a line from the river bed well onto the silty area to intercept fish moving along the 'Barrage'.

Geoff had set a similar trap some 100 yards or so to my right. Both swims were difficult to fish from. Geoff had built a real cubby hole in the bushes, but he had to cast from a clear area 20 yards to his left and the steep bank and deep margins made life difficult, particularly as he had to slide down to the rods on his bum.

My swim was surrounded by bushes and rocks and protected by an undercut bank behind with trees hanging well over the swim. I needed chest waders to cast and I'd also need them if I was to have a good chance of landing a big fish, as a mass of submerged branches to my right looked a real problem.

Rods were set up and cast out. 15lb line straight through, semi-fixed lead, short hooklength with maize or pop-up on a short hair. The day had passed quickly and I could only just make out the marker as I cast out and clipped up the third rod.

Yet another lovely 30+ common for the prolific Geoff Shaw.

Darkness falls quickly in the mountains and it was soon pitch black. Lying back on the bedchair, I relaxed properly for the first time in two days. The lake was flat calm, disturbed only by the splashings of small fish.

Around 10 o'clock, carp began jumping well to the right. The walkie talkie crackled and Geoff was saying that the fish were jumping around the corner. They continued to jump all night, but didn't come any closer. Geoff had one fish, a lovely mirror of 24lb. Rods and gear camouflaged for the day, we walked back up the hill for breakfast.

Michael arrived on his way to work. Geoff caught up on events since his last visit and we chatted about the barrage. The water level had been dropped right down in the spring and the carp had been forced towards the deeper waters near the dam, which may explain why, on previous trips, Geoff had found fish moving in from both directions; but this time we were to find that the fish always came from the right and returned towards the dam during the day.

That morning we met John, the local farmer, and his wife; a really friendly couple, with ruddy cheeks and ready smiles. They offered us the use of a washroom and toilet only 100 yards from where we were fishing, which was a real bonus. This became our base for cooking and bait preparation (the pressure cooker seemed to be on non-stop) and we were able to lock up all our gear and leave the bare essentials at the swim.

More maize was cooked and the swims topped up. The day passed quickly and, at dusk, we were settled back in the swims. That night the fish again crashed way out to our right.

5a.m. Two bleeps on the right hand rod. Off the chair and as I pulled on the chest waders the line pulled out of the clip and screamed out. Picked up and struck to the left to avoid the overhanging branches. The rod pulled round hard and as the fish took line I waded out about 10 yards with the net. The fish stopped running and came in really easily to a few yards out then with an enormous swirl powered off to the right. No way could I have stopped it, but the angle I'd got by wading out seemed to have worked as it surged past the submerged branches and ploughed along the margins further down. As the run stopped I felt pleased that the tactic had worked, but the feeling was short-lived as a nasty grating sensation came up the line as the fish went round an unseen snag further down the margins and the line parted. I stood there shaking, stunned by the power of that fish. I'd missed my chance for that night. Geoff had five fish, a roach of nearly 2lb. and a long double figure common.

We began to get into a routine. Weigh and photograph the fish, camouflage the tackle, breakfast and prepare bait. A couple of mornings we strolled along the bank a few miles to the nearest café or motored around in the boat with the sounder checking out other areas.

Lunch was a real feast. Slices hacked off a huge 'pain de campagne' (a flat crusty loaf over 2 feet in diameter) with French bread and cheese, followed by walnuts and fresh strawberries from John's jam, washed down with a bottle of wine – magic. Michael's wife and kids came to visit us and often brought an extra treat of hot chestnuts. After lunch (usually a 3 hour affair) we would bait up, cast out and settle in, as dusk would be approaching.

On the third night the fish homed in on Geoff's bait and huge fish crashed continually all night. When these fish crashed, it was like no other fish I'd heard; the huge 'BAADOOSH' sounded like a cow falling in: incredible!

8p.m. The walkie talkie crackled and Geoff's excited voice exclaimed "I think I've got a 50lb common, get round here quick."

In the confined space and with the steep bank, Geoff had trouble since the fish was in the net and one of the arms had broken. In the pitch black it's impossible to guess the size of a fish until you lift it out. This one had fought like a demon and Geoff had only seen a big flash as it went in the net. Geoff and Michael have both seen 50+ commons and mirrors in the 'Barrage', so it would easily be a fifty. I lifted the fish out and carried it to the clear area along the bank. It was certainly heavy, but not THAT heavy, and I hoped it might be a forty. Geoff prepared the mat, scales and weigh sling and we watched excitedly as the pointer swung round. It settled on 39lb. Not a fifty, but still a real cracker. Only the second night and already a huge common. I've caught plenty of big fish, but all mirrors and as I scampered back to my swim I hoped it would be my turn next.

5a.m. again and line's pouring out on the middle rod. It was another powerful fish and I let it have its head whilst I waded into position. I'd decided to change tactics to keep fish out of the snags along the bank and waded along the margin to my right to stand at the edge of the submerged bushes, hoping that the fish would fight away from the snags. It worked perfectly. I hadn't realised how difficult it would be to net a fish standing waist deep in water unable to see the net or the fish in the blackness. I had a few anxious moments before it went in. Elated at my success I waded the 20 yards or so to my swim. Lifting the mesh I could make out a long common and I guessed it to be mid-twenties. Fantastic. Geoff had caught another big common soon after the first and lost a fish when the line parted on a snag.

The photo session was a real event that morning. Three glorious commons posed with two grinning anglers. A brace of big thirties, 39lbs & 35lbs and a 27.

The day was spent in the boat and as we motored towards the dam the valley sides became much steeper, towering above us and plunging steeply into the water, which in some places was 60ft. deep in the edge. The line on the sounder plunged and climbed sharply, the bottom reflecting the harshness of the rocky scenery. Approaching the dam wall was an awesome experience knowing that the other side was a sheer drop of over 100ft.

At this point the water was 40 yards wide and 80ft. deep. Suddenly, only ten feet from the dam wall, a mass of fish showed on the screen.

Excited by our discovery, we motored round a few times to check, and sure enough a huge shoal of carp was lying next to the dam wall at a depth of about 40ft. in 80ft. of water. We were a good mile and half from our swims and had only found three likely feeding areas, the rest of the water being almost unfishable due to the nature of the bottom. An area of shallows, a mass of sunken trees in 25ft. of water and a small plateau 20ft. deep surrounded by deep water. The area we were set up in seemed to offer the best feeding ground, (15ft. to 20ft. deep), large beds of silt thick with bloodworm.

We only found fish in two areas, amongst the snags and by the dam. A few had shown up in mid-water elsewhere (travelling fish?) but not in any numbers. We also tried for a mile or so above our swims and only saw a couple of fish. Makes you think,

They weren't all commons! This lovely mirror weighed 30+ too.

doesn't it? Four miles of water and carp only concentrated in only two areas. I tried fishing amongst the snags. The fish were there, but not feeding. Those fish obviously felt happier there during the day and travelled to the rich feeding grounds at night. It was an interesting day and underlined the importance, not of finding *fish*, but their *feeding areas*.

They were back that night and just after midnight a couple of fish crashed near my marker. I lost a fish at 2a.m. The hook point had bent over, probably on the throat teeth.

6a.m. and I was standing in the water again with a very angry fish ripping line off the spool. Suddenly it stopped and I pumped it in easily, just a heavy weight. I thought for a moment I might surprise it and got the net ready, but a yard short the rod pulled down hard and I had trouble holding onto the rod as line was stripped off at an incredible rate. The same thing happened a number of times, but I would feel the fish tiring and the runs became shorter. I had whipped isotopes to the spreader block and tips of the arms to make the netting easier and positioned it ready. The fish was on a short line and I could see the swirls, but not the fish, and netting a swirl isn't easy! Almost there when the water erupted and the rod yanked down hard. With that incredible surge of power I was pulled off my feet and was up to my neck in water, as line was once again ripped off the spool. I dragged myself back to the snags, chest waders full of water. The fish grudgingly came to a stop and as I pumped it back yet again I was determined it was going nowhere but in the net.

Wading back I knew this was a big fish and lifting it onto the mat my heart jumped with excitement. It was a common and looked massive. Carefully adjusting the scales, I lifted the fish in the swing, pencil torch in my mouth. The needle jumped between upper thirties and forty-five. I had to lower the sling to calm down for a moment. Lifting again the needle settled on 39lb. I was out of the universe, never mind over the moon. The fish sacked and secured, I wound in the rods, checked on the fish and went for a hot shower to warm up.

Geoff also had a fish that night, another 20+ common and lost two, again the line parting on snags, a real problem in his swim.

The fish was deep bodied and looked absolutely magnificent; its golden scales shining in the sunlight. With solid muscular shoulders and huge tails, these were truly glorious fish.

Sunday lunch was a memorable affair, as Michael's wife treated us to a paella, her speciality. Stuffed with every type of seafood conceivable, it was delicious and after washing it down with a bottle of wine and finishing off with a glass of home-made fire water, life had never seemed so good.

The pattern continued for the rest of the trip. The fish appearing after dark over Geoff's bait, moving up to me later in the night, then disappearing with the dawn. Geoff's runs came mostly in the early evening and mine between 2a.m. and 6a.m.

We caught 13 fish between us, with 3 thirties each, topped by the big commons and had a great time into the bargain. The trip had been a real success, and to me, fishing for big, wild fish in beautiful and wild surroundings, that's what carp fishing is all about.

Sadly, the 'Barrage' is to be emptied in 1991 and we left with a final 'au revoir', knowing that this magnificent water would probably never be quite the same again.

We've been looking at other waters that hold really big fish and planning the next trip. I wonder if we'll get a 'fifty' in 1991?

NRA - ALL CHANGE?

By the time this is published we will be fast approaching the end of the second year of operation of The National Rivers Authority. Carpworld subscribers, who also read Coarse Angler, will know that my parting comment on leaving the N.R.A. was not at all complimentary! I had no need to exaggerate in that series, though I will admit some of what I said was aimed at hitting back at the few individuals who tried to make my life miserable. I will therefore not be continuing in this vein, having got these grievances off my chest. What I will look at is how the new N.R.A. will influence carp fishing.

In spite the formation of the N.R.A., the Byelaws we operate under still remain those of the old Water Authorities. These are as varied as the anglers who have to live with them. Now I cannot speak for all anglers but, because I do fish around quite a bit, I am going to suggest what most anglers consider to be acceptable methods of fishing. Most anglers who fish for carp, and certainly also pike, zander and eels, like to fish with three rods. There are some who like four, five or even six rods. I myself use four rods for some of my pike and zander fishing, but not for carp. In general, I find three rods are acceptable for most of my fishing and would happily conform to this.

As far as the N.R.A.'s are concerned, the rules are different in several regions. For example, if you use three rods in Anglian, or Severn Trent, you could be prosecuted and face some embarrassment, in addition to running the risk of a small fine. Fish three rods in the North West, Yorkshire or Southern and you have no problems. A lot of carp anglers ignore the two rod rule in those areas which enforce it. This is sad because they should not have to break byelaws to fish for carp. While it is true that carp can be caught on two rods, it is the principle that matters, i.e. something is illegal in Nottingham, yet legal in Sheffield!

2, 3 or 4 rods? In some areas extra rods are legal. In others they aren't.

Daiwa
Daiwa

A 20lb Trent mirror. Pollution control by the NRA protects these fish.

Nev Fickling

This is why many people break the rules. Moves are afoot to rationalise the Byelaws and N.A.S.A. and P.A.C. have already voiced their fears to the central office of the N.R.A. concerning a 'rounding down' of the regional Byelaws to make them all the same. This would entail everyone fishing with no more than two rods.

The problem with the present system of representation is that the specialist angler is still left out in the cold. This is, in many ways, his own fault. Let me explain how the system works. There is a system of angling consultatives around the country. Each operate as a line of communication to, and from, the N.R.A. The members of the consultatives are generally officials from angling clubs in the area and, as such, represent the average angler. Sadly, their views can tend to be narrow and not all appreciate the different needs of the specialist angler. The biggest stumbling block tends to be number of rods in use. Because the consultatives relate to normal fishing, where one rod is quite sufficient to catch large numbers of shoal fish, they tend to think that the use of more than two rods is unsporting. They do not realise that fishing for a very few large fish is helped by the use of the extra rod. It enables varied baits and one extra area, in a swim, to be covered. There lies our problem. Though the consultatives are a democracy, a democracy does not work well for minorities such as ourselves. On a straight vote the specialist angler always loses. I have been a member of The Great Ouse Fisheries Consultative for a number of years. The travelling to meetings is hard work and the time could be spent fishing. However, it is vital that someone hangs in there to represent the specialist interests. In other areas our representation is non-existent, while in key areas we could do with more specialists to get involved. The problem is a serious one because we, as specialists, would rather go fishing than attend meetings! So while the system is as it is we must be careful. N.A.S.A. has the best system of liason with consultative organisations, but this could be improved. Indeed, it must be improved, otherwise we could find new, more restrictive byelaws coming down to limit our activities even further.

There are quite a few other problems lurking here and there. Luckily, most N.R.A. regions have turned a blind eye to carp sacks which are, in many areas, an illegal method of retaining fish. This "I see no ships" attitude has come about simply because there are sensible people working for the NRA, and they appreciate that carp sacks are beneficial or, at least, better than keep nets for retaining carp! However, the legislation should be changed quickly otherwise we could all come unstuck! Another area where the N.R.A.'s are involved is fish diseases. Much is said about diagnosis of fish diseases, and the limiting of the spread of diseases such as S.V.C. (Spring Viraemia of Carp). However, only a handful of the N.R.A. regions are capable of testing fish and, in the case of S.V.C., it has not been shown that the disease is not already widespread. Too few carp populations have been checked. The protection that the N.R.A. can offer to us, in terms of checking the health of fish due for restocking, is limited. However, when stocking is being considered great care should be taken, especially if the water holds existing stocks. New stock fish may stress the old fish, bring out disease symptoms which may, or may not, be due to S.V.C. It does pay to take the greatest effort to get new fish health checked, but do not rely on every N.R.A. region to be able to do this. The only one that seems to be able to do this in detail is Anglian, so be warned. Most carp fisherman fish stillwaters and these are seldom affected by factors over which the NRA has control. River carp obviously face the risk of death from pollution, so it is essential that the N.R.A. is there to monitor water quality. However, reductions in the water table, due to borehole abstraction, can threaten both lakes and rivers and here I do not have great confidence in the N.R.A. Hopefully, they will get their act together and prevent over-exploitation of the groundwater by the privatised Water Companies. So far they have not done very well, particularly under their former guise of the Fisheries Departments of the Water Authorities. In the past carp anglers have benefitted from the activities of the old River and Water Authorities. Many carp waters were stocked by these bodies and today there are several fish farms producing carp, along with other species. I doubt if carp anglers will benefit much in the near future, simply because goodwill, free stockings, along with free fisheries advice, has ceased in many areas. This is not a problem for those such as myself, who run their own fisheries. I buy my fish and stock them into my waters and do not expect any favours. The average angler, fishing the rivers, might derive some benefit from the N.R.A.'s, particularly if a river is polluted and fish stocks need to be replaced. Indeed, Anglian Water have stocked a few rivers and drains in the Fens with carp, and there are now some limited carp fishing possibilities in certain areas. Generally however, the fish stocked are roach and bream, the staple quarry of the average angler.

The picture I have painted is a fairly realistic one: the N.R.A.'s offer us, as carp anglers, very little but plenty of 'aggro' if we break the rules. Nevertheless, sitting on the sidelines and moaning will not change things. We must get involved, become more political and I dread to say this, we must show what good anglers and conservationists we are. N.A.S.A. did a good job with the work they did a couple of years ago, but that momentum could be carried on, not by organisations, but by us as individuals. Only in this way will we be heard by the N.R.A.'s. I am not one for throwing a load of mindless rhetoric at readers, so forgive me if some of this article sounds like that. However, I believe I am doing my bit, how about a few others joining in?

TEAM
DAIWA

Most carp anglers now fish still-waters – few of which attract any involvement by the NRA.

"Write a piece about your year from January to December 1990", they said. "You haven't actually CAUGHT that second thirty yet have you? No... Oh, good. Well, keep it light if you can and keep trying!" Nice people at Angling Publications. Always rooting for their guys.

"Do you ever get the feeling that some things just aren't meant to be? I mean... I've been carp fishing on and off for over twenty years now and I've only caught one thirty. I'm not complaining (not many Benny!) but what's a guy got to do to keep his 'street cred' intact these days, when every little bum-fluffed schoolboy is staggering away from Darenth with half a dozen under his belt each season. Come on someone, give us a break.

So then I sat down and thought about it a bit more carefully. You see, Carole and I have just come off the back of our best ever season for big fish. Now I don't care what your criteria is as far as 'big' is concerned; mine is anything over 20lb. At the same time I have seen five 30lb. plus fish landed while fishing either next too, or not far from, the angler concerned, and have come to the conclusion that it's all a matter of pure luck! At least, that's my theory and I'm sticking to it.

I did try putting a sign on my hookbaits saying "Only Thirties Need Apply" but that didn't work. Then I was still scratching my head over Plan B when Franck rang from France to say that he'd just taken his second thirty from a water we'd fished together earlier on in the year. Then we'd both had nice twenties out, but we thought that they were tops for the water... but now clever clogs has to go and prove that wrong.

Then I had to sit and suffer at Savay (a not uncommon occurrence for me) while Max (millions of bloody carp) Cottis stuffed his thirty and three twenties up my left nostril, and Nige (Chum Mixer) Bryant did the same to my right. Piggy in the middle caught nine bleeding tench, which has got to be some sort of record. What's a guy got to do?

I remember a few years back feeling a rather condescending sympathy for Derek Stritton. At the time people were saying that he was one of the best carp anglers never to

Ken Townley

A YEAR IN THE LIFE...

Savay sunset: From Sunken Island looking up towards Alcatraz.

Ken with a twenty plus common.

have caught a thirty. I'd caught mine by then, so I could afford to be patronising (or should that read "a smug little bastard?"). But then I never, for one moment, thought it would take so long before I caught another. I understand Derek has caught more than enough 30lb. plus fish now, and I'm still floundering along in just about everybody's wake... or am I. Is it just a perceived conception, of my inborn inferiority complex, that the world and his wife catches bigger fish than I do? I don't know.

My search continues. I've realised Savay isn't going to play the game for me. It is the only water I have ever fished that intimidates me. I've fished some hard, small waters, and some easy, big waters... and then I've fished Savay. My three years on the syndicate have produced four 20lb. fish and four doubles (plus P.B. tench and bream), and the only reason I caught them was because they felt sorry for me. The very gate itself challenges me whenever I drive through it, as if to say "what the hell have you driven all this way for again? You know you ain't gonna catch!" Hate that Gate!

So this will probably be it for me on 'Savs'. My last fish out was a magnificent creature that looked at least thirty in the net and dwindled to just under 24lb. on the bank. I was pleased of course, any Savay fish is a blessing from on high. But why was it THAT fish that had to take my floater when it had maybe two or three companions, of at least 30lb. plus, swimming around with it by the sunken island.

I knew I wasn't going to catch a thirty at Birch... or rather, I thought I knew. Tim doesn't reckon there's a thirty in there, but I'm not so sure. One of the fish I watched under one of the snag bushes looked to be all of thirty, but then again I'm useless at assessing weights, either in the water or on the bank. One thing I do know, there are one hell of a lot of twenties in there. Mind you, if there WAS a thirty in there I certainly wouldn't catch it!

The summer of 1990 provided some good memories, but the Honeymoon Week at Birch has to be the highlight. Tim's since described that first Sunday afternoon as "ridiculous" and maybe he's right. To be frank, my lasting impression of that lazy afternoon was that it wasn't all that "wet". Tim tells it different and has the photos to prove it. My trouble is that I tend to get serious and sleepy when I've had too much and certainly my powers of recall aren't what they were. All I can tell you is that it was a wild and woolly day that did nothing to enhance my reputation as a drinker. I'm not macho about my capacity, but when you're in with the Paisley's and the Sly's of this world, you must know when to take the pass-out option! That didn't apply to Micky. I don't know how much of Fred J's home-made, red wine he managed to put away but anyone who can mistake a 19lb. 8oz., common for a bream must have suffered some severe muddling of the brain cells! There were ten twenties out that week and Carole and I had three of them. It was surely no coincidence that we didn't start catching until Fred and Mickey had departed and our headaches had moderated.

Talking about headaches... that same Savay trip, when I was catching tench and everybody else was catching carp, drove another nail into the coffin of my big drinker reputation. I had a heavy cold that night in the North Bay. Andy Kellock heard me coughing and spluttering across in Maylin's Pads and told everybody I was throwing up all night. Not true... honest!

I came very close with a 29lb. 6oz. in September. There were three of us there, in the early hours when it was landed, and all of us put it well over thirty as it looked huge in the torchlight. I even ran back to the car to get the 40lb. scales. I suppose those of you who have caught stacks of thirties NEVER make those silly mistakes. Early next morning we did the photos and confirmed the weight. Even then I couldn't accept the evidence of the scales, it was so big across the shoulders. We'd no sooner put that one back than I had another run and this time the fish went 27lb. 12oz. Steve was winding me up when he said it would go thirty, but for a moment I almost believed him. What is it about this magical number that makes addicts of us all? Is it that the age of innocence has past and, in this great, 'go get-it' era, excellence can only be judged by ever increasing standards? Thirty years ago a double would have made the headlines in the weeklies. Now they turn down Yorkshire 28's because there are too many Home Counties thirties to fit in.

I sometimes wonder if the angling editors realise how often they use photographs of the same fish week in week out. I know there are some spectacular fish in the Home Counties but not all 'whackers' live in the Colne Valley. Keep one hand on the perspective lever lads... please!

I knew I wouldn't catch a thirty in Rashleigh either, but it's such a lovely water that we always like to have a couple of weeks in high summer stalking the fish in the edge and off the top. A few years ago the water was not one to be taken at all seriously. These days it is getting to be a bit special, from a parochial viewpoint at least. When Carole caught the lovely, 21lb. 8oz. mirror that appeared in the Mail, I thought it was a record for the water. I apologise to Tony Chipman who has since put me right. Busted Tail was the record at 22lb. 8oz., but then Carole's fish came out again a pound up so it all got a bit confusing. This has got to be one of the best club waters in the South West, thanks to a huge extent to the stupendous amount of work (hard graft) done by the Committee to improve water quality and productivity. More power to yer elbows Tony, Steve, Nigel, Colin etc., etc. Oh, yes... and to Graham who came and watched!

I did think there was a chance of a thirty across the Channel. So much so that I went across three times in 1990. I came close again with mirrors of 28lb., 27lb. 12oz. and 27lb. 8oz., and a common of 27lb. 8oz., but once again it was that spawny, French git Franck who copped for the big 'un with a 32.04. Same bait, same rig, same swim, he gets the whacker. I'm getting ready for the first foreign trip of 1991 at the moment. Another French friend of mine has just told me about a 46 pounder and three 35lb. plus mirrors from a northern lake, so I suppose I'll have to go on there and get another hiding from all and sundry, but at my age I can take it. I keep telling myself I'm past caring and sometimes I almost believe it.

I've been in heaven and hell this year. I came back from a Savay week in July to be greeted by the news of the Salamander fish theft. At the time, over-reaction was rife in the county and there were carp anglers going around with murder on their minds. I fished the water for a while after the dirty deed and caught nothing over 14lb., which seemed only to add weight to the genuineness of the story. Then, towards the tail end of the year, came the best news I've heard for ages. Big Daddy hadn't gone missing after all. He turned up on the back page of the Times at 28lb. something. (Clever disguise that Mark... why not draw people a map!). The fact that he's still there doesn't mean that the Salamander fish nicking didn't happen. It did, most assuredly and many of the well known twenties did go missing. Luckily, dear old Daddy wasn't one of them. Of course, the picture has stirred the masses again and the bounty hunters are hot on his trail once more. I had three phone calls within 24 hours of the photo appearing! As a result I can't get near the water for love nor money just now. And one million tufties aren't helping, either. Still, it's really nice to know my old friend is still there. Somehow I doubt if I'll go after him again, it would be a bit like sticking a hook into your best friend.

Lasting memories of 1990? Well, after the deafening buzzer silence of 1989, it has been lovely to find out that the Delkim's wheels haven't been superglued-up. That really is a lovely noise, isn't it? I suppose the most pleasing fish was the British 29.06, but some of the French carp were very special indeed. Carole upped her P.B. three times in the year and, the way I see it, she'll get the next Townley thirty. The lass is on a roll and good luck to her.

I've found a couple of brand new waters too. I've got high hopes of both of them. One hasn't been fished for something like twenty years. You wouldn't think there were waters like that still waiting to be discovered, but there are. And it's nice not to be just another one of the crowd, going the rounds of the circuit waters on the big carp, magic merry-go-round. It's nice to be able to fish for unknown fish again. I had Salamander to myself, more or less, for much longer than I ever believed I would and, no doubt

Nigel Bryant – Savay 32.

in time, these others will get discovered. But I'm not giving away any soppy clues this time, other than to say they are in the U.K.

I've just read through what I've written so far. It isn't very light and it doesn't really tell you anything about 1990 either. But because this year has been such a good one for us both it would have been only too easy to list the successes. I have in fact done this for the next Nutrabaits catalogue, which looks at our year in glorious, successful detail and you can read all about it in there. Instead I thought I'd dwell, in my customary gloomy fashion, on my continuing failure to bank another whacker.

To many of you our results will be nothing special. To others they may be a source of wonder. It all depends on where you live and what your carp fishing terms of reference are. It just goes to show what a tricky tightrope it is that we all walk, trying to put our season into perspective with others who may, at first, seem much more successful that you. For what it's worth, the statistics will show that we had 34 twenties over the year which makes it our best ever; but then, when did statistics ever matter? They ain't everything are they? I don't know if my attitude towards big fish is changing, but the non-appearance of a second thirty doesn't seem so important these days. Or perhaps it's this constant yearning that keeps me going.

Another thirty I didn't catch. Franck returning a 32.04.

Perhaps it's a good thing I haven't caught it, maybe I'd just have lost interest once the magic barrier had been broken for a second time. Somehow I doubt it but only time will tell. Perhaps Sgt. Pepper will sing it for me this year. "I read the news today, oh boy, about a lucky man who made the grade."

EFFECTS OF BOILIES ON CARP

We see a great deal of unconfirmed comment and wild conjecture about the effects of boilies on carp and the possible damage they may do to a water and its inhabitants. Bruno Broughton is very highly qualified to comment on this controversial area. He is a Fisheries Management Consultant, holding the qualifications of a B.Sc (Hons) degree and a Ph.D. in zoology. He is active within the Institute of Fisheries Management and has been awarded full membership. He has been employed within the water industry for ten years as Fisheries Biologist and Fisheries Officer, has been a successful and enthusiastic angler for over 25 years, has edited angling magazines and is a regular contributor to the angling press.

One of the recurring questions in the enormous amount of correspondence I receive each year, is one about the possible effects of large numbers of boilies on the health and/or survival of carp and non-carp species. This is an area which is subject to a great deal of ill-informed conjecture, so here are some of the facts.

Obviously, fish must eat to survive. If they consume more than their bodies need to simply 'tick over', this extra nutrition is available for growth, the production of eggs and milt, increased movement etc. Because fish are so-called 'cold blooded' animals, their body temperatures are more or less the same as the water surrounding them. Furthermore, their internal body processes – their metabolism – are governed by the temperature of their environment. Thus, if water temperatures increase, their metabolism increases and they require more food.

Carp metabolism is geared to water temperatures higher than those of this country. Everything else being equal, they will grow fastest at water temperatures of 25-27° C, and maximum growth will continue for as long as the water temperature is at this sort of level. (This is the main reason why carp in southern France, Spain, parts of the USA and Africa grow so much larger than in this country – it's hotter, for longer, than in Britain).

Carp have a catholic diet which might include most forms of aquatic invertebrate animals, some plants and, occasionally, other material (e.g. fish fry, tadpoles). The the best of my knowledge it has not been proven that they will actively select certain natural food items and ignore others, although this may occur. Usually though, they eat what is most readily available.

That said, their appetites certainly seem to be stimulated by certain tastes/smells. Even in the 1940's, American scientists discovered that one of the most successful flavours with which to lace poisoned maize (used to eradicate carp!) was synthetic maple.

That fish can be weaned onto non-natural food is well known. This may occur for non-angling reasons (e.g. the famous roach shoals at Cappoquin in Ireland which fed on blood and offal discharged into the river by an abattoir). When large quantities of anglers' baits and free offerings are introduced, these items may be very important in the diet of fish. The best example is that of the River Severn barbel which, according to several scientific studies carried out in the 1970's, thrived on a diet comprising 50-60% anglers' baits, mostly maggots.

There is a growing body of evidence that carp in Britain have benefited from the mass introduction of both particle (i.e. seed and nut) baits and boilies. Indeed, several of the boilie manufacturing companies also run carp fisheries where they deliberately feed the fish on misshapen boilies or 'end-cuts' of boilie paste from the boilie making machines. I have yet to hear of these fish suffering in any way. Indeed, the reverse is true – they seem to thrive on this diet. Despite some of the nonsense put about by a few anglers,

Dr. Bruno Broughton

carp do not **need** a high (80-90%) protein diet, which in any event they would be incapable of finding by eating natural food items.

The inescapable conclusion from these observations, and from numerous studies overseas on the diet of carp (notably in Israel, where they are grown for food), is that the type of boiled baits used in Britain can have but a beneficial effect on carp growth and general health. Given that no one actually force feeds carp, a fish will stop feeding when it's full, or has satisfied its hunger. This fact is used not only by anglers, but also by carp farmers, who often employ self-feeding 'demand' hoppers full of carp pellets to feed their fish. The carp release pellets by nudging a float-operated level, which opens the flap at the base of the hopper.

When anglers' baits are introduced but not eaten immediately by fish, they may remain intact for some time until they decompose slowly, or are eaten by fish, water birds or invertebrate animals. I know of several studies into why some angling 'pegs' are better than others. Although not conclusive proof, it was shown in at least one case that there was a richer than average invertebrate population on the lake bed in the most popular and productive swims. The implication

was that anglers' baits did not just attract fish; they may have attracted, or caused the development of, a larger than average population of invertebrate animals ('creepy-crawlies' if you like) on the lake bed. Indeed, it could be argued that fish might, initially, be encouraged to enter these areas for this wealth of natural food they contain, rather than the bait present on the bottom.

Although the 'skinning' of boiled baits or the use of bait-hardening ingredients renders them less susceptible to consumption by small fish and invertebrates, eventually they do break down sufficiently to enable these animals to eat them. I have heard of – but never witnessed – netting operations on small ponds which resulted in boilies being recovered when the net was drawn to the shore. This has led to suggestions that the bed was covered in rotting boilies which 'soured' the lake – whatever that means. It would, in my opinion, take an unreasonably large number of baits to produce this alleged polluting effect and, in any event, they would all eventually disappear as they were eaten or rotted. On very small waters, it is just conceivable that this might produce a temporary by undesirable change in the water quality from which fish could not escape; on large waters, fish would undoubtedly simply avoid any 'pockets' of pollution – their instinct to survive and their ability to avoid danger is far greater than their desire to feed.

To summarise, I have yet to come across a situation where carp are known to have died because of the use of **any** form of anglers' baits, including boilies, although I do accept that it appears to occur with mass baiting of uncooked particles. Rather, from the point of view of fish health and general well-being, the use of boilies has almost certainly been beneficial.This seems to apply to non-carp species too, which will eventually rip uneaten boilies to pieces, even if they can't get 'em down in one go.

There must be a point at which a water could be polluted temporarily with these baits, but I suspect this would require the input of at least several hundreds of pounds of bait per acre in a very short space of time.

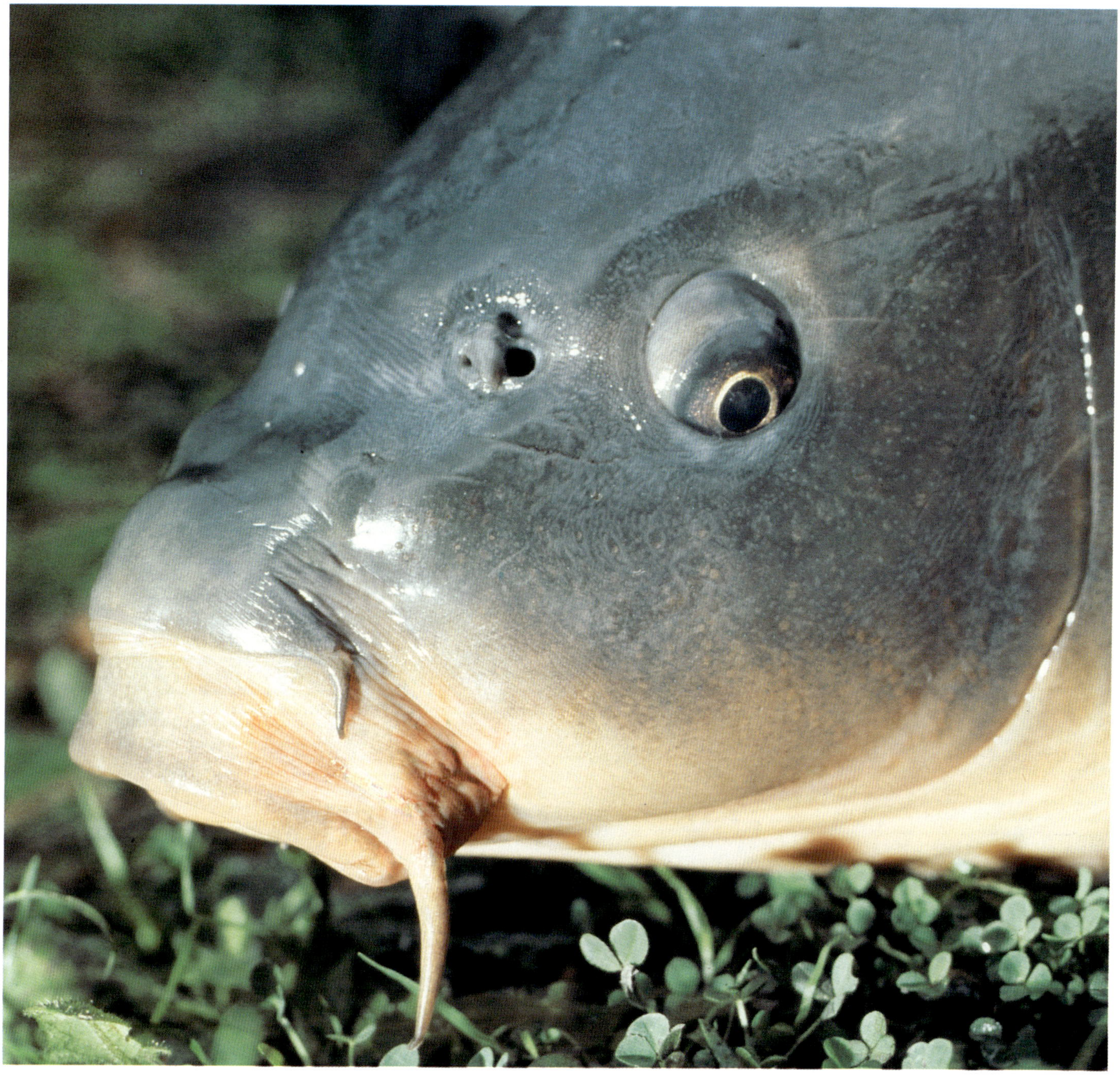

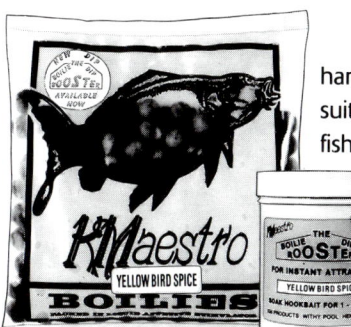

SENSITRON

A major advancement in electronic bite alarms is offered in the new Daiwa Sensitron Bite Alarm. The major feature never before available in this type of product is our Variable Sensitivity Control. This hi-tec computer designed product is certain to take the specimen world by storm. Designed and developed in conjunction with Kevin Nash, one of the UK's top carp anglers, the Sensitron carries his full endorsement.

Kevin Nash – *"After field testing and seeing the benefits the Sensitron offers over all other bite alarms I would not use anything else."*

Sensitron could mean the difference between fish on the bank and a blank.

Daiwa
S
T
OFF V
SENSITRON
SENSITRON

- ☆ **UNIQUE VARIABLE SENSITIVY CONTROL**
- ☆ **FINITE FORWARD OR DROP-BACK INDICATION**
- ☆ **VARIABLE TONE**
- ☆ **EXTRA LONG BATTERY LIFE**
- ☆ **EASY ACCESS SLIDING BATTERY COVER**
- ☆ **WIND-BEATER EARS**
- ☆ **HIGH VISIBILITY LED's – 20 SEC. LATCHING**
- ☆ **RIGID FIXING POINT – BRASS THREAD**
- ☆ **SOUNDER BOX JACK SOCKET**
- ☆ **PROTECTIVE POUCH SUPPLIED**

THINK CARP... THINK Daiwa

COMMITTED TO TOTAL QUALITY

BITE THE BULLET

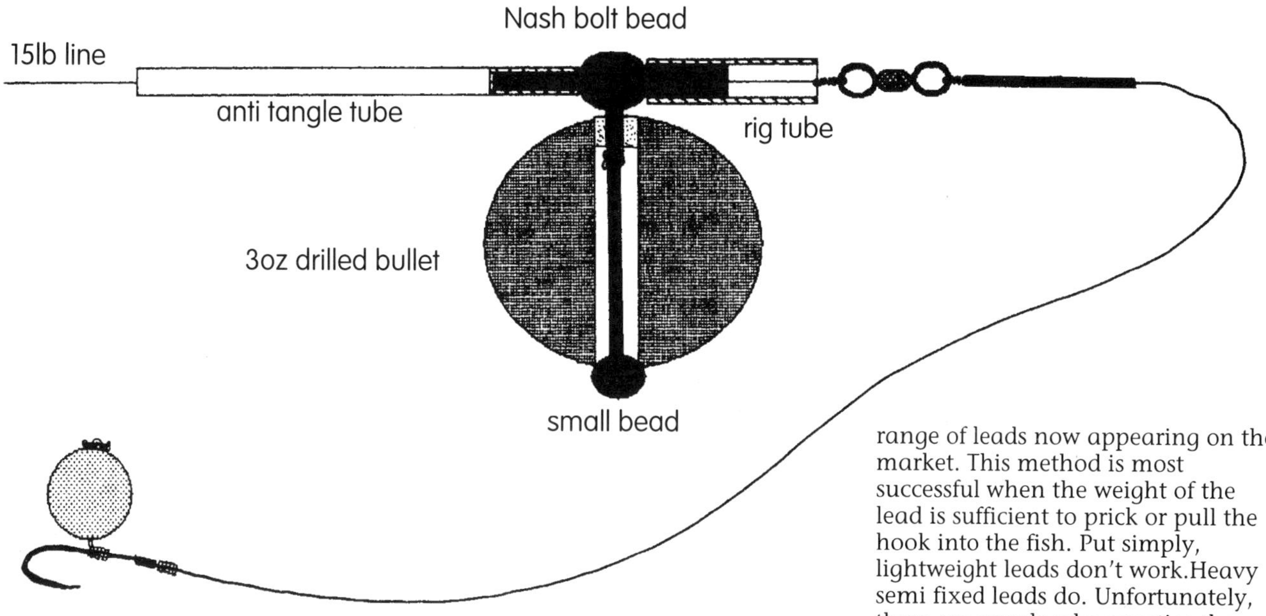
Nash bolt bead
15lb line
anti tangle tube
rig tube
3oz drilled bullet
small bead

I was reminded recently of a conversation I had with Albert Brewer, which took place on the banks of Cuttle Mill during the mid 70's. Well, to be honest, it was not really a conversation in the strict sense of the word. I was more a spectator, a captive audience, an opportunity for Albert to get a few things off his chest.

His bone of contention centred on two lads who were fishing swims on the lawn side of the pool. The very one sided conversation went something like this.

"Two ounce leads! Two ounce leads!!!!! I don't believe it, what on earth are they trying to do? If they wanted to fish this side of the pool, why set up on the opposite bank and cast across?"

Even the dog was growling by this time. On reflection, perhaps he was talking to the dog.

I can't imagine what he would say about the size of some of the leads that are propelled towards the horizon in the new age of distance bashing.

Modern technology, coupled with space age materials, have produced carp rods capable of handling leads in the three to four ounce class a reality. Already models are on the drawing board which are, in theory, capable of handling weights in excess of this figure.

An interesting spin off from the search for 'the ultimate casting tool', is the re emergence of that old favourite the 'bolt rig'. A method ideally suited to the new heavyweight range of leads now appearing on the market. This method is most successful when the weight of the lead is sufficient to prick or pull the hook into the fish. Put simply, lightweight leads don't work.Heavy semi fixed leads do. Unfortunately, there are people who practice the philosophy that heavy fixed leads work best of all. To this small minority I would say "Please think again".

It is accepted that an educated fish will eventually wise up to a 'method'. In this, the bolt rig was not an exception. Ironically, a contributing factor to the gradual fall off in it effectiveness can be attributed to the shape/design) of the lead. The modern 'carp bomb' is a product of man's quest for distance. Its aerodynamic profile is just what is required for the job in hand, i.e. distance. On the lake bottom, as part of a bolt/resistance rig, it's quite a different story.

To understand why this problem has arisen, I would like to quote from Andy Little's recent article in 'Anglers' Mail'.

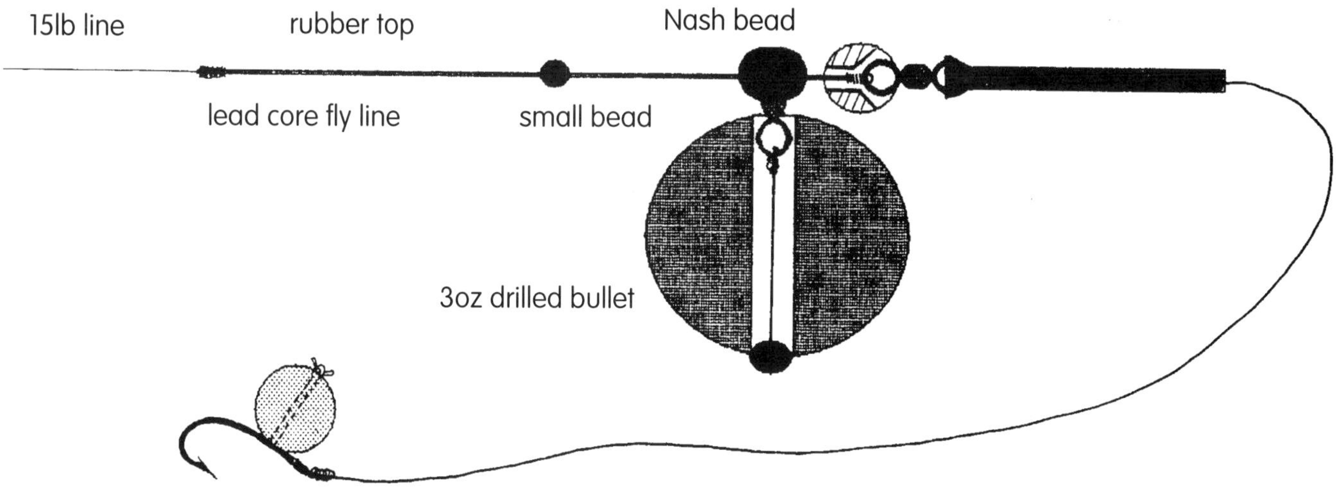
15lb line
rubber top
Nash bead
lead core fly line
small bead
3oz drilled bullet

John Tame

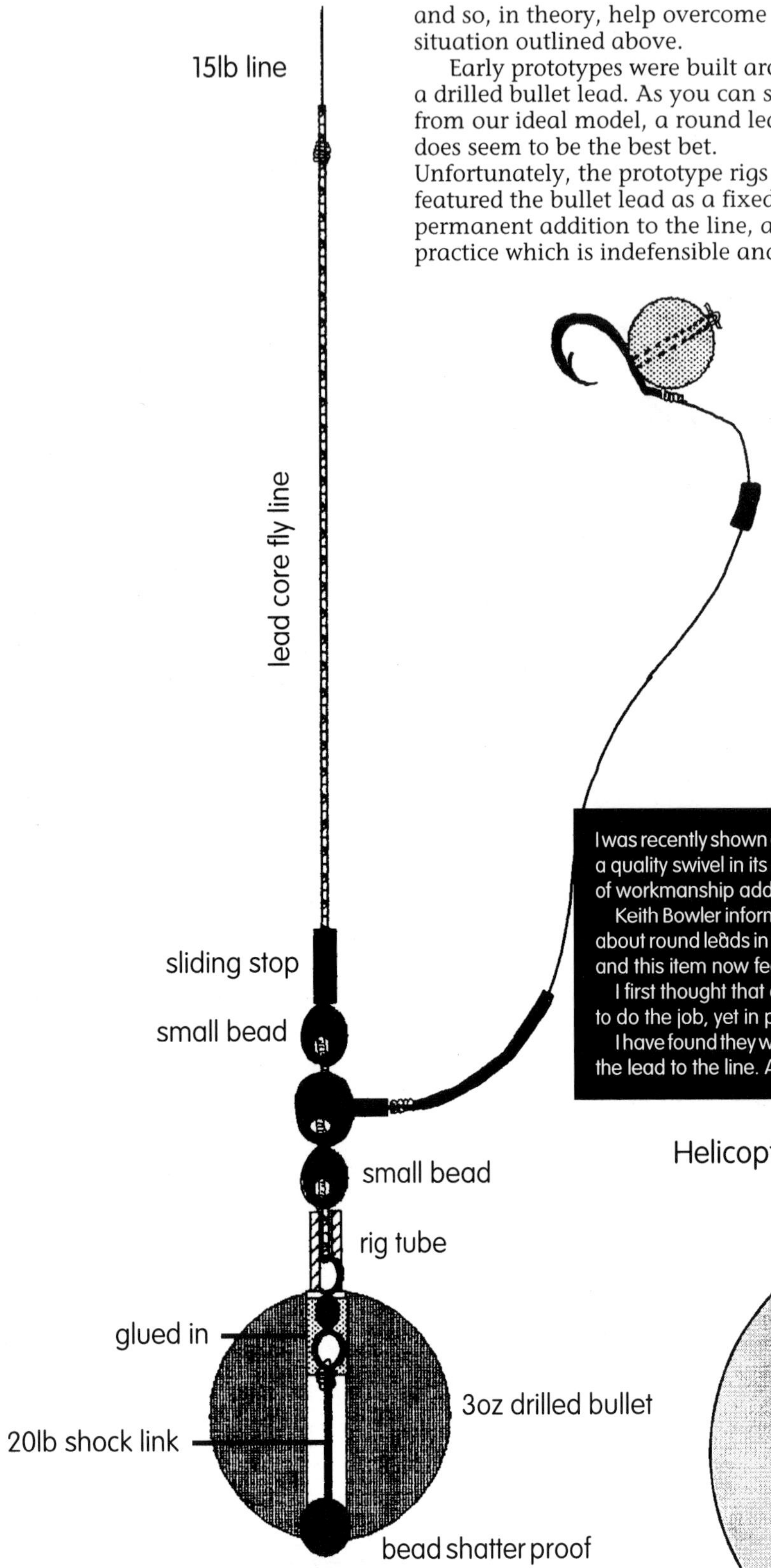
15lb line
lead core fly line
sliding stop
small bead
small bead
rig tube
glued in
20lb shock link
3oz drilled bullet
bead shatter proof

'For some time there has been a theory that on long tailed leads there is a possibility that a pricked carp can gain enough movement by lifting the tail of the lead quite easily off the bottom to help get rid of the lightly pricked hook'.

An interesting theory, which I know is supported by other innovative anglers.

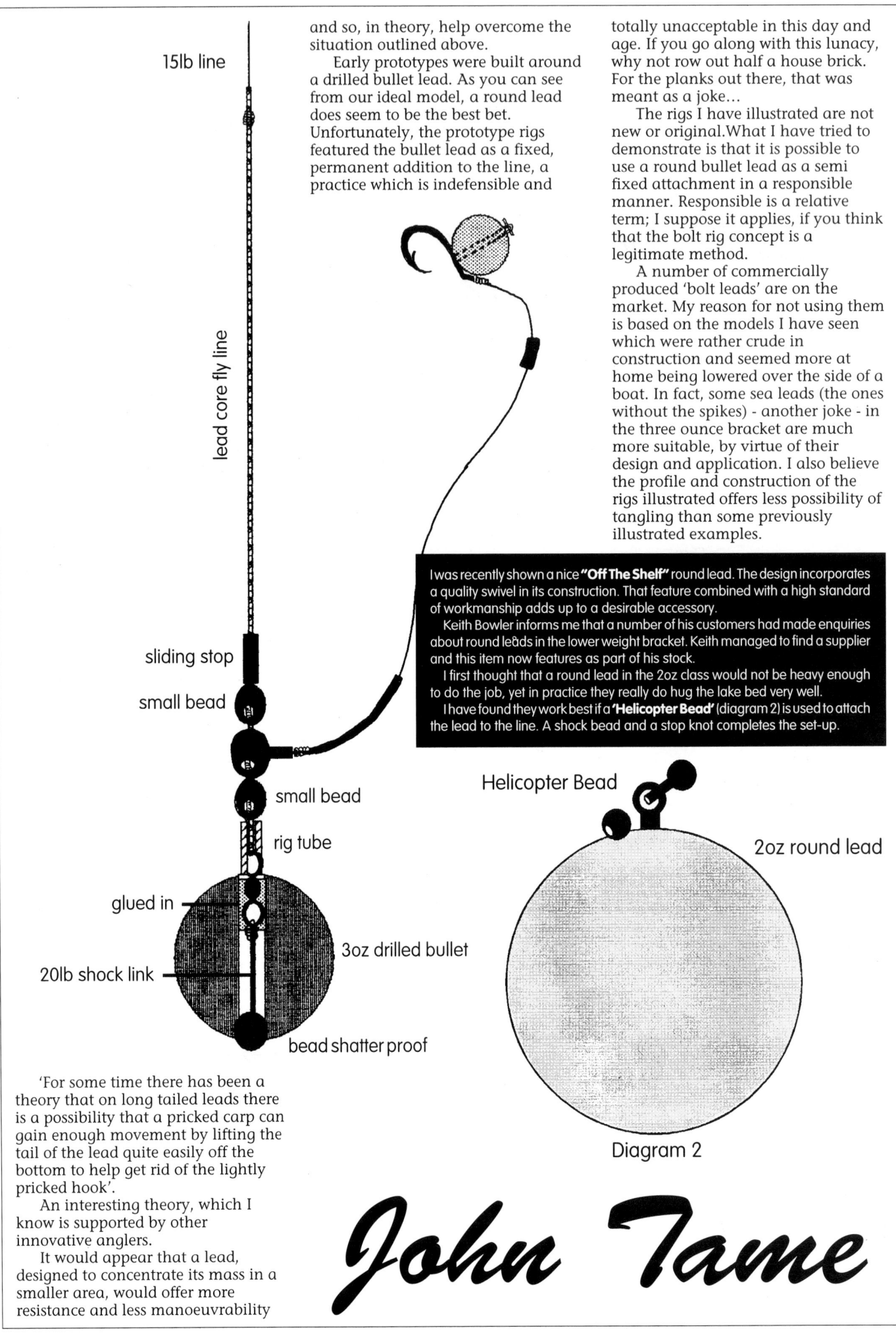

It would appear that a lead, designed to concentrate its mass in a smaller area, would offer more resistance and less manoeuvrability and so, in theory, help overcome the situation outlined above.

Early prototypes were built around a drilled bullet lead. As you can see from our ideal model, a round lead does seem to be the best bet. Unfortunately, the prototype rigs featured the bullet lead as a fixed, permanent addition to the line, a practice which is indefensible and totally unacceptable in this day and age. If you go along with this lunacy, why not row out half a house brick. For the planks out there, that was meant as a joke...

The rigs I have illustrated are not new or original.What I have tried to demonstrate is that it is possible to use a round bullet lead as a semi fixed attachment in a responsible manner. Responsible is a relative term; I suppose it applies, if you think that the bolt rig concept is a legitimate method.

A number of commercially produced 'bolt leads' are on the market. My reason for not using them is based on the models I have seen which were rather crude in construction and seemed more at home being lowered over the side of a boat. In fact, some sea leads (the ones without the spikes) - another joke - in the three ounce bracket are much more suitable, by virtue of their design and application. I also believe the profile and construction of the rigs illustrated offers less possibility of tangling than some previously illustrated examples.

I was recently shown a nice **"Off The Shelf"** round lead. The design incorporates a quality swivel in its construction. That feature combined with a high standard of workmanship adds up to a desirable accessory.

Keith Bowler informs me that a number of his customers had made enquiries about round leads in the lower weight bracket. Keith managed to find a supplier and this item now features as part of his stock.

I first thought that a round lead in the 2oz class would not be heavy enough to do the job, yet in practice they really do hug the lake bed very well.

I have found they work best if a **'Helicopter Bead'** (diagram 2) is used to attach the lead to the line. A shock bead and a stop knot completes the set-up.

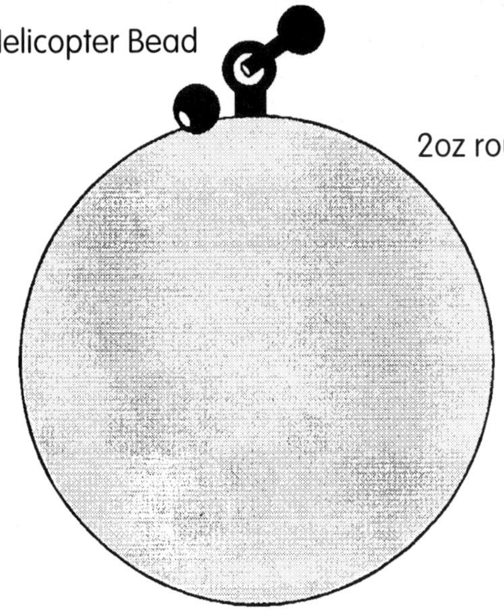
Helicopter Bead
2oz round lead

Diagram 2

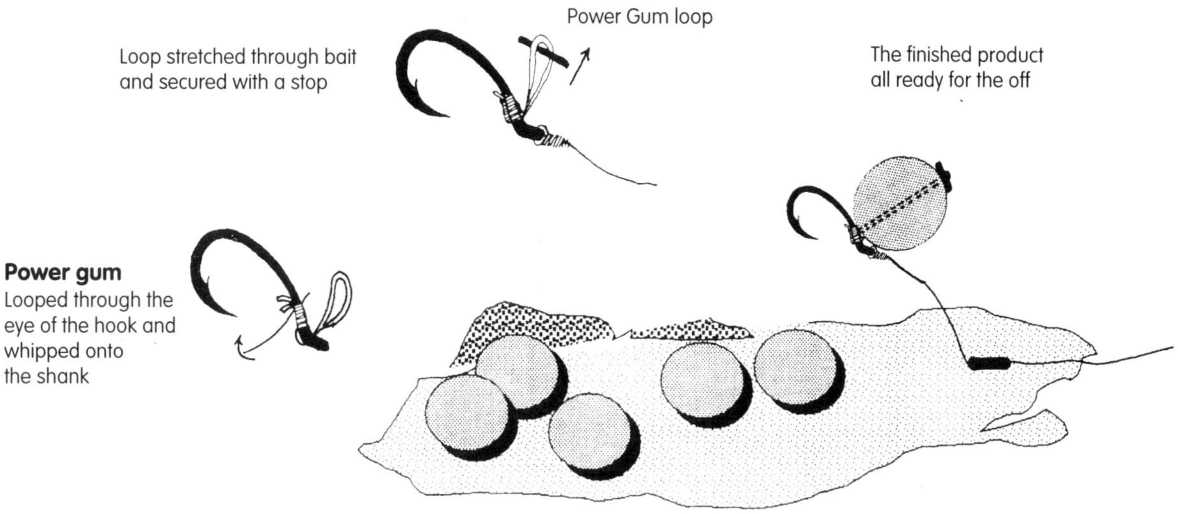
Power Gum loop
Loop stretched through bait
and secured with a stop
The finished product
all ready for the off
Power gum
Looped through the
eye of the hook and
whipped onto
the shank

CONSTRUCTION NOTES

The use of heavy leaders are recommended with leads of this size and weight. Whatever material you decide to use, it is important that all stops, beads, etc., are of sufficient size to pass over any knot that is used to attach the leader to the main line.

Lead core flyline can be attached to the mainline using a needle knot which hardly increases the overall diameter of the line at all. I have not used flyline in traditional leader lengths so I can't comment on this application. I have incorporated this line in some of the rigs in the article for its strength and anti-tangle qualities. I understand that a question mark has been raised concerning the durability of the lead core during extended use; perhaps somebody has current information on this point.

The use of a barbless hook may be worth consideration if snags are a real threat. Even without the lead it is possible for the fish to get caught up on the leader. After using barbless hooks for a number of years, any fish that I have had to get the boat out to,had slipped the hook and was well away before I arrived on the scene.

The method I use to attach the bait to the hook seems to give good presentation and it speeds up bait replacement when needed. A small loop of Power Gum is attached to the back of the shank or, in the case of rods, hooks the eye by means of a whipping. It is then a simple matter to pull the loop through the bait and secure with a small stop. You then have a bait tight to the hook without the possibility of the bait obscuring the hook point.

GRAPEVINE – TINA'S

It's February 1991 and I'm sitting in the study looking out over a winter wasteland. Snowflakes cascade down outside my windows and the thaw is obviously a long way off. Somehow this seems indicative of the season 1990-91, which for many anglers has been a season of extremes. Long hours with no indications and then brief periods of activity. For some it's been a good season, while for many more it got harder and harder. Sure, rigs, baits and information on carp have improved tenfold but the carp's awareness seems to be up even more. A lot seems to be down to the extremes we've had in the weather. The mildest winter in 1989, warmest spring in 1990, hottest summer in 1990, wettest autumn the same year and now the coldest winter. Long, settled periods, coupled with drastic changes, have spelt out blanks for some and an increase in "tackle for sale" in Anglers Mail. However, Tina seems to grow and grow and, for all of you who enjoyed Tina in 1990, we will be back in 1991; and here's the review of 1990-91.

KENT

Without a doubt 1989-90 was the year of the fishmeal, with Premier Baits mixes finding themselves in great quantities at most Kent waters. At **DARENTH**, the water had been well hammered all summer and autumn on fishmeals and it was no surprise when winter 1989 to spring 1990 brought a decrease in chances. Whether it was due to fish wising up to fishmeal, or just a decrease in feeding fish (more likely), the first few months of 1990 saw more than a few blanks for the boys. The two 'biggies' fell to Tony Moore and Micky Kavanagh, both at 38lb. Incredible fish, and not too far away from that magical 40lb mark. Thirties also for the well known, baiter extraordinaire Ian Booker (31-00, 34-00- Tip Lake fish), Steve Newman (32-08, 'Big Bollocks' at 35-12; part of a 7 fish catch), 14 year old Richard Bacchus (32-08). Twenties for Frank 'The Blank' (though not on this occasion), Steve and Paul Payne, and one or two others. Last knocking, in late February/early March, showed an increase in action as some of the lads moved off the fishmeal onto the protein or birdseed. Using Chris Haswell's new Buttcracker (now Carpbuster) mix, Gary Harrow and 'Nobby' had an incredible weekend with 11 carp to 28lb. Horrendous conditions and a new bait seemed to put the fish on the move. Jackson's seemed to be the swim to get in and Jason Brown wasted no time taking 'Chubbys Mate' at 36-00 from it on the fishmeals. As the season drew to a close people tended to fish all four lakes on the complex, (Tip, Big, Long and Tree Lake) and some super carp were caught including a 24-00 common to Ian Smith.

During the close season Darenth came under new Leisure Sport rules, regarding the running of the fishery, in an attempt to rid itself of some of the more obnoxious malpractices that some session anglers were getting up to. Coupled with an increase in fees, and an improvement in bailiffing, it was hoped to get things off to a good start in the 1990-91 season. The fish started the year slightly down in weight from 1989's highs but one or two anglers had good catches, whilst others really began to struggle. Many of the lads who did well in 1989 moved off to new venues (Horton, Yateley etc.) so pressure did decrease somewhat. Early season soon drifted into mid-season and it wasn't until autumn that the big fish really got on the move. Steve Kingsley had a 28-03 and 3 doubles in one session. Big fish for Frank Matthews at 30-02 and 22-10, Dougie Jones came up with a 33-08 ('Lumpy' on Buttcracker), and Colin Lovett at 28-00. Thirties to Glen Robinson at 36-00, Daniel Cox at 30-14, Clive Scholes at 34-00, Tony Olivo at 36-00, Barry Middleton at 38-08, Ronnie Barnes at 30-01 and Mark Dean at 33-08. Two of the best catches went to Peter Matthews who had a 7 day session which produced 11 carp to 33-06, and Nicky Birch 7 fish to 26-10. No forties from the venue in 1990 but we shall wait to see what 1991 produces.

The **SUTTON-AT-HONE** fishery had a quiet end to the season but Martin French, aged 15, took a huge carp of 33-10 and others weighing 26-06 (common) and 19-04 (mirror). As the season drew to a close Gary Thatcher, who's even younger at 13, took two beauties at 24-08 (mirror) and 30-08 (common). Not much from the adult lads on the water, although Bill Green managed to take a 26-13 mirror. Early season produced little of note due to angler pressure, soaring temperatures and low water levels, though pride of place would have to go, in the 1990 season, to 'Suttons' fully-scaled mirror. It is up to 27-03 and its last lucky captor was David Mann.

Many of the lads who left Longfield on its demise have made

The Buttcracker boys (now Carpbuster) with part of their fabulous January catch.

REVIEW OF SOME 1990'S CATCHES

their way over to another well known Kent fishery, **JOHNSON'S PITS**, a complex of three lakes comprising the Road Lake, Island Lake and Railway Lake. Probably more famous at one stage for its tench than its carp (tench to 12lb and a high average over 6lb.), it has always seen a good turnover of carpers such as Andy Little, Rod Hutchinson, Dickie Caldwell, Terry Gage etc. Now it's the turn of the 80's and 90's lads to give it a bash! Winter '89/90 produced little of note and, as the water has a close season, the fish didn't begin to trickle out until June 1990. Rob Maylin and crew stuck mainly to the ultra-hard Railway Lake (subject of Peter Jones chapter on the big leather in Fox Pool) and began to grind away at it. No huge catches but Rob had the big leather slightly down in weight, Steve Allcot had a 33-06 and 'Travolta' and crew kept sneaking 'em out. A very hard water and it won't get any easier in 1991.

BROOKLANDS (see Curly Hatchman's feature in Carp Fisher 4) had an indifferent season. Some carp well up in weight, though it's got to be one of the most pressurised waters in Kent. Brian Murphy had the biggest, at 32-12, and quite a few 20's have been out as well. **COTTON FARM** is another well known venue in Kent which see lots of early season pressure that fades out from autumn onwards. However, anglers such as Malcolm Underwood and Dave Cooper stuck it out all season and were rewarded accordingly. Dave had the big one out at 29+ and Malcolm had over 100 carp, including 2 over the magical 30lb. His 100th fish was a 20lb common, which is a hell of a way to do it!

Another water in Kent which had a relatively slow year was **HORTON KIRBY**. Faversham's **SCHOOL POOL** biggie, 'She', has been out on more than one occasion but, up to press, Lee Jackson has still to have her! Boy, oh boy, is there going to be some celebration when he does! 15 year old Andrew Nigers did catch the famous lady and John Wade had Lee's big common at 33-02 (down slightly).

TackleBox

Lee Jackson with the big common from School Pool. Came out for John Wade in 1990.

GREATER LONDON

Probably the biggest news, in early 1990, was the announcement that Leisure Sport would be closing **LONGFIELD** (Fox Pool, Staines) down and moving the carp to the Horton fishery, near Slough. So quick was their announcement that many anglers, who were familiar with the water, didn't realise until it was too late. However, the fishery, which is a legend in itself and subject of a publication called the Longfield News, did finish on a high, if somewhat controversial, note. Steve Allcott, despite being banned from the fishery, continued to poach it and took a huge brace weighing 44-04 and 37-12. The 44-04 was the known 40 at, its then, largest weight and the 37-12 the equally well known, and formidable looking, 'Parrot'. An incredible brace, I'm sure you will agree, but one that had poor, old Steve writing to the press to explain his actions.

Another water subject to a 1990 closure order was the **RODNEY MEADOW** fishery, popular with many of the country's top carp anglers. It was due to close in March, 1990 but threats, or belief of threats, to move the carp to other waters caused the lake owners to move the stock earlier than expected. Prior to its closure, the consistent Tony Cheadle had a 23-05 (he's the lad who had the 31lb plus fully-scaled beauty earlier in the year) and a 28-04 on last knocking. Robert Hill had a 23-12 and Colin Brandon a 25-10. Approximately 250 carp were moved during the transfer. The biggest (fish over 20lb.) went to Harefield and the doubles to Farlows. 'Nelson', Rodney's famous fish, fell to Robert Kirby and now swims happily in Harefield eating boilie after boilie as per usual. And then it was all over for RODNEY – sad, very sad.

HAREFIELD, even before the injection of Rodney's fish, had been a big fish venue for quite some time and the fish only went to add to its potential. However, the period of winter 1989 and early 1990 was still a grueller and not many faces decided to brave the elements. Mud and open water can be daunting at the best of times, in winter even more so. Come early season, it turned out to be a real grind with anglers hoping to catch these recently moved carp whilst their defences were down. After all, newly moved fish can often be quite catchable (Tilery/Horton) until they get accustomed to their new surroundings. However, it wasn't the bumper year many expected and you really had to get it just right, or get lucky, to put a fish on the bank. The June/July period was a real grueller but, come autumn, fish started to show and get caught. Stuart Gillham (of Llandegfedd fame) had some bumper sessions on a new Richworth bait, taking 8 over 20lb., 5 doubles and a thirty weighing 34-04. Twelve of these fish came in one session as well! The gorgeous, fully scaled carp came out to Kevin Guillford at 33-06 (Catchum baits) and to David Courtney at 33-04 (Premier). David also added fish of 25-04 (common) and 14-08 (mirror). Kevin's good friend, Chris Ladds (as featured in Catchum's advert), upped the fishery record to 36-08 with 'Nelson', the one-eyed, boilie eating machine. Not content with that Chris took a 33-05 mirror and a massive common weighing 28-08; (again Catchum – read about it in the advert boys). 'Nelson' likes to put himself about a bit and also came out at 34-00 to Eddie Lancaster (early season) and to Tim Hodges at 36-08. Tim's fish were caught on the popular K.M. Maestro range of 'ready mades', whilst Eddie's was a Premier victim. Three 30's for 'Big' Rob Hill, the Harefield bailiff, at 30-06, 33-04 and 34-04 – again Premier and long chucks did the trick. Thirties for Tony Long at 32-08 (Catchum) and Kev 'the Frog' at 36-08 (plus a 29-08 as well). Big 20's for Martin Clarke at 27-00 and John Watson weighing 26-12, 29-05. John, as many of you remember, is the man who likes his pic's taken without his shirt on. Good God, imagine Maylin or Stuart Barry doing that. Rob has got into the Harefield syndicate but is finding it as hard as everybody says it is! Just ask Kevin Nash.

Only 300 yards away, across the road next to the Horse and Barge, is probably the county's most talked about venue, SAVAY. You don't even have to be a carp angler to have heard of it, as 1990 was no different to other years in that it found itself all over the angling papers. Our Albert made the news in 1990 but let's go back to the previous season. Unprecedented weed had written off the Cottage Bay, Shallows and North Bay and, it seemed that, unless your name was Broxup, Selleck or Harry, you might as well go home as start fishing. Our Jules did hook one but lost it when he became tangled in his own hair (or ego!). Most syndicate members gave it a miss until January/February 1990 when the weed might have dropped, moving the fish out down to the Colne or Canal banks. Unfortunately, the fish never really got past the bailiffs and only odd syndicate members caught. Roger Smith had a low 20 from the North Bay and Bob Copeland had his first ever Savay carp at 16lb plus. Last knocking produced the biggest when Martin Locke had 'Jeff' at 34-00, Paul Brooks had a 31-08 and Dave Woods a 33-10 and 28-00. It was the baillifs' year though, and 1990 saw Pete Broxup break all Savay records with 59 carp, including four over 30lb. One late season catch included 12 carp to 33-04. Nice guy, Keith Selleck, kept his end up with a good number of carp, including 2 late season super sessions of 8 carp to 29-12 and 5 carp to 29-06. John 'the Bollox' Harry also having an equally good session with 5 fish to 29-08. No close season fishing at Savay of course, so June 1990 was the first chance of a real biggy. The first big one was caught by Max (bite yer tongue Hally) Cottis who took Savay's first ever forty, at 42-00. A huge bellied mirror that was obese yet not even Max's personal best (which was, of course, the subject of the acid jibe by the ageing D.H.). That wasn't the end of Max's year as he stuck at the venue and caught fish of 30-08 (linear), 28-08, 22-00, 30-15, 27-01, 25-04 and 20-03. A tremendous result and Max also unfortunately lost a few biggies as well. Savay's other forty fell to the irrepressible Albert Romp. Albert's first fish including carp of 45-04, 39-02, 3 over 20 and 3 lost. He then went on to catch carp of 38-12 and 35-04 to make him Savay's 'unero numero' big fish man. All caught on Richworths and all down to heavy baiting and accurate casting. Albert's forty is the carp that appeared in Rob Maylin's book, Tiger Bay, at 32-12. Other, early season big fish fell to Steve Reeve at 32-12, 31-08 and 29-00. 'Curly' Hatchman had a 33-04, Terry O'Brien a 32-00 and Keith O'Connor a 34-08. Lots of early season twenties for many of the syndicate members off the top (where else?) to around 20lb. Mid-season it slowed down a bit, but autumn onwards saw a run of big fish to numbers of anglers. Carp angling's big boy Bruce Ashby had a stunning catch of 9 carp to 37-04 in a couple of days, all on a heavy baiting session on M.A.C. baits. Keith Selleck had a bit of a struggle but upped his personal best to 35-08, whilst Peter Broxup had carp of 30-00, 29-04, 27-08, 24-00 and 22-08. Not much 1990 joy for John Harry – however later on...! Mr. Bedchair himself Cliff Fox got on the scoreboard with fish of 34-06 and 25-08, whilst John Holmes (that's a mouthful) took carp of 30-04, 25-13, 18-03 and 15-08. 'Curly' upped his personal best to 33-06 and Keith 'the Tooth' O'Connor's been giving 'em the Savay seed mix to take fish of 34-08, 29-00, 24-08 plus some low 20's. Also taken on Locke's mix were fish of 27-08 and 24-00 for Terry O'Brien and Bernie Stamp with carp of 36-08, 31-08, 30-04 plus 6 others. Once again heavy baiting did the trick, so well done Bernie! A 32-12 for Clive Rigsby, 2 big twenties for Carpworld contributor Ken Townley, weighing 29-06 and 27-12, and Steve Reeves adding to his early season success with fish of 32-12, 31-08, 20-06, 15-08 and 12-00. As temperatures dropped it got really hard and, come November time, it was almost impossible. John 'the bollox' Harry made the papers with a huge catch of carp to 35 plus before, once again, it dried up. Very few chances from December onwards and, yet again, no sign of Sally! I wonder what this year will hold?

We did mention Longfield a little earlier and, as many of you know, the fish went to the Leisure Sport water **HORTON**, near Slough. Every carp that was in Longfield made its way across to the venue and, eventually, 14 doubles, 13 twenties, 6 thirties and a forty found themselves resited in this former trout fishery. The 40 left Longfield at 42-00 and by sheer coincidence was the last fish to be rescued from the venue. For many of these fish it's their third move (Yeoveney, Longfield, Horton) and a certain wag was overheard to comment that if they live long enough to see another trip we'll be able to describe them as musical fish! The Leisure Sport Pool at Horton is a completely different type of venue to Longfield, and many old faces didn't fancy the change. No stalking, day tickets only and mown grass banks don't appeal to the die-hards and it was left to various new boys to see what they could do. Early success came for many, despite soaring temperatures and heatwave conditions coupled with prolific weed growth. Steve Burgess had the forty at 44-00 and he also added carp of 16-13, 17-04, 17-06, 18-14 and 20-06 (all on Richworth baits). Geoff Ball took her at 40-08 on his first visit to the fishery and John Hampton (he should get together with John Holmes) had a 37-08 (Parrot) and Big Scale at 33-06. There was no need to fish at long range as many early season fish fell to baits at under 50 yards. Steve McNeil put his bailiffing abilities to good measure with the 'Lady' at 29-02 and Joe Holdsworth had 'Shoulders' weighing in at 35-01. 'Lady' fell again later to Steven Galliver at 33-12. The Angler's Mail ran an excellent Action Replay at the venue and stars, Andy Charles and Steve Newman, produced carp to 38-

08 (8 in all) for the readers. A most remarkable fish was John Buckley's new grass carp record, at 16-01, which could have been even bigger but he weighed it late the next day. The fish soon began to wise up and from September onwards was a real struggle. Rumours of a 'famous five' winter assault on the water never materialised and 1990-91 drew to a quiet close on the fishery. For 1991 the venue has been turned into a £200 per year restricted season permit water and we may now see some of the old faces creeping back if certain rules are amended.

The other famous big fish water, **SPRINGWELL**, got off to a flier in early 1989 when Alan Smith broke all records, and surprised even himself. He managed a cold water 39-15 (how's that for honesty!) but January through to March 1990 saw very few fish caught due to diving ducks and seagulls. June 1990 was a warm month to put it lightly and bumper catches fell to all anglers at the fishery who managed to get on the carp. Bob Copeland had a huge 42-00, which made 8 over 40lb recorded all over the country in the first two weeks. Alan Partridge, again a very talented angler, had a 40-02, but even Alan Smith found it a bit of a struggle as autumn crept into winter. Some bumper catches came out in October but then it went dead once again. Diving ducks and seagulls completely took over and it became literally impossible to get a 'freebie' out, never mind a bait. Some anglers gave it best, the carp went torpid and 1990 bowed out at Harrow on a very dour note. However, the venue did produce 11 carp over 40 in 1990 so many anglers were not too disappointed.

WRAYSBURY, as many of you will know, is not a water you go down to 'set up and wind 'em in' on. In winter, it's even worse. There was nothing to report early in 1990 but the close season months found fish still taking the 'old chummies' like there's no tomorrow. However, once June came, most of them did a disappearing act, though Chris Ball's '36' made the grade at 40lb plus to Dave Compstone. Ken Hodder also had a marvellous 29-00 mirror on bird seed; Jason Chater took a double on floater and a publicity shy angler took a 35 plus, which was over 36 inches long. That's a Burton type fish (Leney Strain). As the season progressed fish which had previously been in shoals split up and only a few fish fell to the boys. Chances during the winter 1990? – well, what do you think?

FARLOWS LAKE, which enjoys close links with Harefield due to John Stent, had a good summer in 1989 and many expected early 1990 to be no different. However, despite the injection of fish into Farlows from Rodney Meadow, it wasn't until late in the close season that carp were caught in any number. Farlows is classified as an 'any method' trout fishery so carping in the close season is allowed. As a testing ground for new baits and rigs it's ideal and the close season months of 1990 saw many of the top lads giving it some 'welly'. Driving down the M25 you could see a veritable army of bivvies each weekend in April and May – wonder if they actually caught any trout? As a consequence, despite its high stocking levels, it's no pushover, so beware. Chris Hull had a nice 25-04 mirror on Richworth's and feed inducing oil, with corn as a hookbait (is this true?). Peter Jones, of Fox Pool fame, got his act together with fish (6) up to 21-04 (common), all on Locke's mix with Premier's oil. Steve Knowles had a personal best leather of 24-04 and Peter Truckles a 21-12 common and 4 more doubles. Plenty of bream and a 19lb plus mirror for Chris Cornwell, again on the Nodd oil. Once into the season it began to take off and Albert Romp had a super 26-08 mirror on Richworth's. Albert followed a new approach of not moving the baits for hours and it seemed to work for the big fish. England's most expensive goalkeeper, Dave Seaman, got his name on the scoresheet (sic) with commons of 19-12 and 17-08. However, the two boys who have really been doing the business are Chas Newman and Paul Mepham, Farlows regulars. Paul's fish included a 31-12 mirror (The 'Pet') and a 28-00 mirror. Chas took a brace of mirrors weighing 33lb and 27lb. All on fishmeal and the lads added another 11 big doubles to boot. When you get it right you get it right, eh! One or two good commons also came out at 23-00 (Neil Scholey plus 2 more), Darren McCann (18-00) plus others. Big fish also for Alan Spurlock (21-12 'Mad Max') and Mark Pospiech with a 28-00 mirror. Again autumn didn't bring a deluge of carp and, not surprisingly, the water didn't see much pressure this winter, so results have trailed off accordingly. However, Gary Venus did manage a 25-12.

SURREY

The carp man's Mecca and home of more big carp than anywhere else I can think of. However, it's also home to a lot of carp anglers and even those that don't live there seem to want to fish there! Pressure – not much, mate. Top venue must, of course, be the **YATELEY** complex of lakes situated around the River Blackwater. Heather de Leather, Ritchie's 40, Big Scale Mark 2, The Parrot, Piglet – they all live there but unfortunately so do loads of 'keenies'. Big surprise, early 1990, was Jock White's (Yateley Ya-hoo crew) 40-10 from the little fished (then) Lily Lake (No. 7 on your guide book, Squire). An absolute monster of a fish and just reward for all the hard work and fishmeals Jock's been putting into the water. This was a Match Lake fish (1980 at 23lb.) so it's really done the business hasn't it! Of course, once this monster came out everybody wanted a go at it. All the boys were down including the three big M's – Maddocks, Maylin and MacDonald.

Kevin took a super 25 plus, but angler after angler on one water doesn't suit Kevin so off he pulled. Ritchie Mac came good finally knocking out three beauties of 25-00, 29-00 and 36-08. Well done my son! Maylin, fact is he didn't do anything

Richworth

Albert Romp – Farlows 19lb+ common on Richworth baits.

(that'll teach him) and he even had a go at Ritchie telling him his rigs "were the best ever anti-pickup rigs" he'd ever seen. Ritchie went on to remind him who'd had the fish – exit (tail between legs) Rob. Ritchie did the business with Richworth bird food, whilst most other boys were heavily baiting with fishmeal and gallons of oil (must have had premonitions about the Gulf War).

The other lakes also came under a lot of early pressure but Phil Thompson had the Match Lake's first 30. A very underrated angler Phil, who has had a LOT of big carp from a variety of venues. Plenty on the Match lake and some good 20's out as a result. Martin Dalby took a 28-03 and David Beagley a 25-12, both on Premier. Across the road, at the Car Park Lake, Andy Martin put it together and took fish of 36-12, 33-10 and 24-00. This on a lake which only contains a dozen or so carp anyway. Andy had taken 'Heather' earlier in the year at 39lb plus so he had done himself proud as the 1989-90 season ended. The Car Park Lake also produced late season carp of 30lb plus (an unknown thirty – yes, it does happen), 29-00 to Phil Calloway and 28-00 to Jeff Pink. Most of the fish have been out at least once.

No close season carping allowed on this venue so it was sit on your hands until June 1990 arrived. Not surprisingly, early season it was madhouse on the water. Favourite swims went early with lines and baits everywhere. Huge quantities of bait were introduced by the majority of anglers and, understandably, a lot of them saw blank after blank. Jock White moved onto the North Lake, Ritchie gave it a miss, Maylin didn't fancy it but everybody else and their uncle did! Odd carp trickled out between June and October but generally it didn't fish well under pressure. Best fish fell to 'Big' Tony Moore at 45-08 from the North Lake. He also added a 38-10 for good measure and all on that deadly combination of Fish Meal (Premier), Nodd Oil and Peach Melba. Jock White found his way in again with a 36-12 and he's an honorary member now at Yateley. I'm not surprised that with the amount of bait he puts in most of the fish are up a couple of pounds. Nick Peat, who had already taken 'Basil 40' (Fawlty!), added a 36-12, Tom Cooper a 28-00 and Kevin West the leather at 32-04. Of course, as autumn moved into winter many of the lads began giving it the 'full-works' on the Lily Lake with the forty in mind. Pete 'the painter' produced the goods. Now it's up to 43lb plus and Pete added a good 20 as well. Not content with that, as the 1990 season drew to a close, he had a brace of good 30's. Tremendous result in anyone's books!

CUTT MILL seems to get harder each year and, despite a high turnover of good anglers, fails to produce the goods which it did in the early 1980's (watch the Richworth videos to see what I mean). Andy Little, Chris Ball and Mike Starkey used to really rave about it as a winter water, but early 1990 produced only 3 carp despite constant weekly pressure. No close season carping but June saw most carp on the top giving anglers the finger. Quite a few fell to basic floater tactics but, within a week or so, became ultra-wary of anything unusual. Mass carpets of 'chummies' failed to work as well. Best catch was taken mid-season by young Adam Cole who had a 27-01, 16-06, 14-14 and 12-06 on fruit boilies. Odd fish did come before the thaw but the season ended on a sad note when the lake's biggest inhabitant perished, believed to be due to old age. It's been many anglers' personal best and was, at one time, quite a catchable carp.

HAMPSHIRE

Another beautiful part of the world with many carp waters, a number of which are syndicated or restricted to give some peace and quiet. No such restrictions at the famous **BROADLANDS** lake where, providing you've locked up and got your Richworth's, you are always in with a chance. 1989 was a good season and the fishery continued to fish well early in 1990 as mild weather kept the carp and carp anglers on the move. Nick Denlow took a 17-14 and plenty of doubles for those winter 'keenies'. Like Farlows, you can fish Broadlands in the close season and plenty did with good results. Twenties for Mark Jones (20-09), Neil Warrington (21-03) and Jeff King at 21-07, all on the Richworth's, of course. Once into June it really took off and a deluge of the old 'ready rolled' had 'em queuing up (so it seemed). Steve Carter has taken around 120 carp (doubles) to 25-02, all on basic baits and rigs, but well applied. One session produced 17

*Some captures from the prolific Broadlands Lake in Hampshire. **1** – Lee Seymour, 22lb. **2** – Kristian Hill, 20.04. **3** – 16 year old John Welton with Mandy at 19.06. **4** – Steve Whittington with the Pig at 20.06.*

1

2

3
Richworth

4

carp, including two over 20lb (23-00 and 25-00). Mark Murrell had 'Yuppie' at 23-06 from Pets Corner. Mark has also had 30 plus 'Penny' from the venue. Chris Halliday had a new, fully scaled mirror at 17-08, Steve Whittington 7 doubles in 24 hours and Pat Wilson, from Kent, his first twenty at 20-06. Andy O'Brien also had his first twenty at 20-05 and similarly, for Lee Seymour, the 'Pig' at 22-00. Again, most fell to Richworth's Strawberry Yoghurt/Tropicano. Big fish also for Matt Ayres at 23-13, Adam Ayres 20-02 and 20-03, Tony Merrett with mirrors of 23-00 and 19-03 plus an 18-00 common, Luke Kenning's a 17-05 and Kevin Chalk an 18-08. No respite, as winter approached, and the slaughter continued until the last knocking. This venue is well worth a try at any time of year and don't forget the Richworths! For your first double, or twenty, you couldn't chose a better venue. Talking of productive waters, **WILLOW PARK** near Aldershot continued to live up to all the expectations of anglers who fish it. The year 1990 didn't start off very well at the venue, due to an absence of carp anglers and bait, so the carp had definitely got into a state of torpidity. One, or two, chances a day at most and mainly small fish. 'The Selby Flier' had a few trips for a small number of fish, including a lovely, fully-scaled carp, but generally it was very slow. However, come April it really began to take off and carp were on the move all over the lake. Both bays produced well and luncheon meat scored for anyone who used it. The Lake's biggest fish, 'The Pig', came out probably half a dozen times up to, and around, 27lb., and then levelled out later in the year. Wind surfers ruined a lot of Sundays on the venue but most lads caught. November to January saw quite a few anglers really putting in a lot of bait. John Raison lifted the boilie ban and it was 'reach for your wheelbarrows time'. Ninety-seven doubles in two months for Jules and good catches for Harry Haskell, Andy Little, Chris Ball et al. Chris had an amazing summer at the venue, taking some huge catches off the surface on Kryston and 'Chummies'. January's cold winter winds put the fish down and even the 'boilie boys' really struggled. Tim Paisley had a personal best, January common and the Winter Video turned into a real corker. Odd, better carp came in February but it froze over in that horrendous February freeze up. Boilies allowed until March and then it was back to the meat.

PIT 4, also known by many of its anglers as Fir Tree Lake, produced some early winter twenties for Harry Haskell and Andy Little. However, these carp are the cutest of the cutest and very few of the syndicate members caught at all. No close season carping and come June it wasn't giving them up any easier. Nevertheless, some carp did fall to anglers who were prepared to stalk fish. Sitting behind rods produced very few chances indeed and Andy took a superb catch of 29-00, 27-04 and 21-00. Unfortunately, the water did not live up to expectations during the winter of 1990/91 due to a massive fish kill. It is estimated that over 80% of the stock died (most being twenties) and its loss of Leney carp, which no-one can replace, is an absolute tragedy. A few fish have survived but, much like the Frensham water, it's a loss on a national scale.

PIT 5, next to the aforementioned water, on the Hollybush complex also had a chequered year. A good winter, a good summer and then a large fish kill at the Plank Island. Mostly doubles, but fish which are dear to many a Hampshire carper.

Graham Rowles' other water, **OLD BURY HILL**, had a slow start to the year despite some anglers giving it serious attention. Chris Day succeeded where many have failed, taking cool water carp of 21-12, 19-10, 15-00, 11-06 and 9-03. The main problems are the tench and the bloody geese! If you crack either of them you should get some good results.

SUMMERLEASE LAKES, Ringwood. 1990 proved to be a good season with John Hampton (of Horton fame) taking the year's best fish of 28-10. Lots of good doubles to anglers on the top and one, or two, twenties to the locals. Produced well in autumn and fish weights seem to be on the up for June 1991.

NORTHAMPTONSHIRE

1990 was the last year that Duncan Kay's **MID-NORTHANTS FISHERY** was going to have. The reasons are well documented in Kevin Maddocks' Carp Fever video; suffice to say it was yet another loss to carp fishing, even though the carp were moved to another water. Anyone who has seen the video, or read Carp Fever, will realise how good a winter water it was and late 1989, early 1990, proved no exception. Pride of place must go to Kevin who had the Bi-Tech Viper fish at 40-08 (his first U.K. 40). Kevin's been on Duncan's water for 16 seasons and 13 years ago had the same fish at 19lb. Quite literally he has seen it grow and grow. Alan Parberry (boilie-maker extraordinaire) had the other biggie at 34-04 and, between Alan and Kevin, they accounted for most of the carp caught that winter. All caught on 'ready-mades' with good angling technique applied to their use. Out came the 40 again to Steve Gombocz at 40-00 and Robin Dix (of Heather fame) had an amazing foul weather catch of 36-08, 28-00 and 22-08. The 22 plus fish was his personal best common despite taking fish to over 40lb over the years. Back to the 1990's season and the first biggie fell to Neil Warner at 38-14 on a K.M. Oceanic boilie. His personal best, and that fish was only slightly down from its winter weight. Out she came at 40-04 when Dave Willets had her in the early part of the season, and then Alan "Gino" Taylor went a pound better at 41-12. His personal best U.K. carp, however, he has bigger foreign fish to his credit. Boilie maker Alan Parbery didn't miss out and proceeded to take both the big fish at 39-14 and 38-06. He also added a 37-02, 31-08, 20-02 and 18-08 for good measure. Old J.J. himself, John

Harry Haskell writes about the death of the Pit 4 fish in Carpworld 14... and John Pooler has a feature about the closure of Duncan's water in the same issue.

Pooler, of Carpworld fame didn't miss the boat either and took some big 20's at 28-08 and 28-04 on Locke's Seed Mix. Last capture (?) of the forty was when Northants. regular John O'Driscoll took it at 39-08, also adding fish of 33-08, 27-04, 25-00, 23-00, 21-12 and 20-12 in two weeks! Unfortunately, it's now all gone and the fish have been transported to a new complex of lakes that Duncan has at Ringstead. All the biggies were transferred, plus 30 new big doubles, to a new 10 acre lake. A 7 acre lake is being used to set up a new syndicate.

CORNWALL

Probably one of the most written about waters in the country, **COLLEGE**, does actually fish well all year round. Any of you who have read Ken Townley's articles in Coarse Angler/Carpworld will realise that he and Carole had some magnificent catches on the water. However, that was in its early days and now much thought is necessary if you want to catch consistently. Winter 1989 and early 1990 produced odd fish, but decent catches didn't start to appear till April. Ian Smith had 5 fish to 25lb in mid-April, all to Hutchinson ingredients. The boys from Kent came up to give it go and Steve Hayes (Billy Bunter) had a 22 linear, Dan Cox a 20-00 common and eight other back-up fish. Pete Howard caught nine carp to low-twenties with most being big doubles. Ken got in on the action with a fully-scaled 18lb beauty featured in many a publication. Lots of close season activity on the Lake, one or two 'stroke-pullers' and plenty of anglers made it hard for most lads. Summer tended to be a real grueller with the heatwave conditions making it difficult all round. Tony Tallot managed to get it right though and landed six twenties to 24-12, including the big common. Winter has been a real pain on the venue and the big freeze-up in February played havoc with any thoughts of serious carping.

First '30' from Angler's Paradise fell to the irrepressible owner, Zyg Gregorek.

DEVON

ANGLER'S PARADISE, owned by our Zygy, had a fairly quiet start in 1990 but really took off from about March onwards. The fish are growing well and the year turned out to be the bumper year everybody expected it to be. Dave Watkins started the ball rolling with a 24-08 linear on his first trip to the fishery. Mick Whitfield also had a twenty-plus linear at 21-10 and Steve Gills caught a 20-06 on the Premier gear. Sputnik came out to Peter Metcalfe at 22-08, Kevin Woodacoth landed a 25-04 off the top and Paul McKewon similarly a 16-04 mirror. Fifteen year old Simon Tomlinson has had a personal best each time he visited the fishery and his best fish (so far!) stands at 15-12. Even younger, at 14, Carl Mincher took a 13-12 mirror and the two Messenger brothers (Darren and Neil) caught nine carp to just under 16lb from the main lake. Vincent Jenkins brought a 14 pounder to the net, hooked on a tiger nut, whilst Paul Kingston went 12lb better with a fabulous 26-10 on a peach boilie. Best close season catch went to Chris Coarse who had 14 carp in a session (best 16lb.). With all the pressure on the fishery, and fish being repeatedly caught, many expected it to slow down from June onwards. However, it didn't – it got better! Chris Coarse went back to the fishery and caught a lovely 26-08 mirror and, not content with that, added a further 25-04. Best fish for quite some time fell to Ben Cook who took Jumbo at 29-08 (up from 25lb.). Brothers Wilson visited the fishery and landed carp of 23-04 (Ulysses for Andrew) and 28-08 (Neptune for Rob). Twenties also for Nick Moseley at 21-00 (common and his first 20) and 25-12 for Alan Cheeseman. As the nights drew in the number of carp caught did decrease, but it finally turned up its first 30 to none other than Zygy himself. Zyg reckons this one is only one of five possible 30's in the complex. I wonder what 1991 will hold?

BEDFORDSHIRE

It seems that Kevin Maddocks' hard work has now come to fruition as 1990 turned out to be a spectacular year for **WITHY POOL**, including it's first ever 40 being caught. As with many places the year started fairly quietly but really took off when Kevin, himself, took a 35lb mirror on one of his Oceanic Boilies. This was made even more special in that at the time he was making a video for his Carp Fever Series. No close season carping, of course, but June saw a glut of big fish for the boys. Dave Thorpe had four twenties in a day from the Pool, which is rated hard by anyone's standards. These were only 4 of the 40 plus twenties he had in 1990! Big fish No. 1 fell to Withy Pool regular Peter Wilson, weighing in at 41-00. An absolute monster of a carp (one of 8 forties caught in June) and looks like it could well end up a mid-forty. K.M. Maestro boilies did the trick. Robert Cook also had the same fish at 39lb., again it fell to the Maestro range – Mellow Lobster flavour. Another regular, Phil Cousins, continued to up his personal best managing a fish of 30lb followed by another of 35-08. Both on 'ready-mades' as well for you so-called purists out there. Odd fish have been caught all year round from the venue but a cold end to 1990, and the freeze-up in early 1991 have restricted the carp feeding.

HEREFORDSHIRE

REDMIRE POOL (which isn't in Wales as I've been informed) is, of course, now under Carp Society control giving anybody with £100 spare the chance to fish it. Winter 1989 and early 1990 ended on a wet and dreary note when the big storm caused a lot of damage to trees. The coloured water also made fishing all but impossible. Odd carp were hooked but red-mire it was indeed. Once the gales dropped one or two anglers managed to get their trips in and were rewarded accordingly. Gordon Owen had the big common at 27-04 from the Stumps peg; this was poetic justice as Gordon was one of the people who had lost out on the Clive Diedrich Rent-A-Week Scheme. Jim Wilson had the same fish a little later at 28-07, this time from the Willow Pitch. Early season saw carp all over the surface and tiny baits, on balanced tackle, seemed to be the only way to get a pick-up. However, after the carp had finished spawning it was business as usual. Len Arbery, who is a regular Redmire Pool visitor, took 7 to 25-07, Tony (Len's son) had 5 to 24-00 (Raspberry) and a friend, Peter, 4 fish to 19lb. Another famous Tony, Tony Higgins the owner of Cuttle Mill, visited the Pool and took five carp to 25-02. Alan Gover had Raspberry again at 26-04 (well up on it's previous weights) and Jim Wilson, Trevor Chinney and Phil Marvel found themselves on the Angler's Mail front cover with carp to 25-15 (a common). All told the lads had 30 carp that week, most being good doubles as well. Odd fish have been caught during the winter, but a freeze-up in late January caused problems.

YORKSHIRE AREA

TILERY LAKE, Newport had a poor end to 1989 when even a mild winter couldn't keep the carp feeding into 1990. Most consistent, early on, was Doncaster Mark, Andy and Mel taking good carp to mid/upper twenties. All carp well up in weight and feeding strongly. Carp also for Mally, Long Haired Ian and Brian Skoyles. No sign of Ian 2 plus Robin Reliant. June was soon upon us and twenties for Eric Hodson (Uncle Backstop), Long Haired Eric (up to 25-12 with 3 twenties in an hour!), Mick Dinnigan, Stuart Hirst, Jim Matthews, and John Morrell. July and August were gruellers for many with dust, mossies and heatwave conditions driving some anglers potty. Twenties for Jules (4 to low 20's), Eric Hodson, Mally etc. Clive Gibbins had the biggy (Sumo) at 29-15 (hard luck Clive!), Andy got very consistent with lots of upper twenties and carp most weeks. Predictably, as October drew into November chances were at a minimum but Andy continued to winkle 'em out making him and Long Haired Eric the most consistent anglers on the water in 1990.

Moving out of Humberside, and actually into North Yorkshire, two lakes have really had bumper seasons in 1990. **THREE LAKES**, Selby, produced 'bugger all' of note during winter 1989 and it was well worth avoiding. Fish did start to move about in February 1990 and Kevin Watson went to town on them. He'd never had a twenty, prior to 1990, but in 4 short sessions had carp of 22-07, 21-03, 20-03, 20-10 and 15-11. Phil Beck managed to leave the women alone long enough to take a 21-12 plus 20-10 and Dean took a 21-12 as well. September soon crept up and twenties to Jules (plus doubles) with 25lb plus carp to Noel Teale and John Bassham. Mark Kaye had the biggy at 27-13 and also a 23-04 on Premier's gear.

Another 'Selby Flier' venue, **DRAX**, had a bumper year in 1990 despite a dire winter in 1989. One, or two, carp out in February but March and April saw swims 30 to 36 producing good carp to upper doubles. A few carp died, due to parasites in the gills, but it wasn't the deadly S.V.C. that many believed had got onto the water. May/June saw twenties coming out to 23-00 (Mark Stephens), and fish on the whole were up by 2-3 pounds to an average 14-16 pound weight. Over half a dozen twenties out by late June and suddenly the big boys started to feed. Spot came out at high 27's for Geoff Bradshaw and then Uncle Eric moved onto the water. In 5 sessions he took carp of 27-13 and 28-04 (same fish Spot) and also other twenties and a few big doubles.

Noel Teale with a Selby Three Lakes 25lb+ cracker.

WENTWORTH, home of Donkey Dave, Big Bill and Handy Andy has always been rated as an all year round venue and 1989-1991 proved this in a big way. A well-known, excellent winter carp fishery it produced well in late 1989 and early 1990. Cold weather carp for Keiran Snodgrass at 26-02 and to Andrew Smith at 22-07. 15 year old Steve Holmes managed one at 25-00, again a cracking common. No close season carping here, but plenty of carp coming out all season to regulars and visitors alike. It's not an overly large venue and you do have to fit in with the no night fishing rule and give due accord to the bream/roach boys on the fishery. Dave Collage had a 21-00 mirror, 23-00 common, Wayne Shaw a 20-00 common, Andy Smith carp to 20lb plus (commons and mirrors). The biggy came out to golden oldie Ernie Scott at 27-07 (early season) and looked like it could do a lot more. A combination of 50% Enervile/50% fishfood and Cotswold's Salmon and Shrimp produced well for a few of the lads. Dave Glossop had a 21-00 and 20-07, Rob Heald a 23-00, Dave Guy 21-09, Dave Pratt 25-00, Dave Moore 21-00, Nigel Wrigglesworth 20-02 and 20-08, Steve Powell 22-12 and Andy, from Nutrabait, kept scoring on a regular basis. The cold weather didn't seem to affect the fish and anglers who moved onto the Hi-Nu-Val seemed to do well. Another 20 for Rob Heald, Guy David had the big common at 29-08 (2 pounds up and looking like it might make 30). Guy also added two mirrors at 21lb plus on the Nutrabaits gear. Andy Pratt took fish of 23-06, 19-02, 17-10, 17-08, 17-00 (all commons) and Mark Shepherd a 22-06. Ray Marshall managed the biggy again at 28-14 with back-up fish of 15-00, 17-06 and 19-05, all on Hi-Nu-Val and essential oils. Nick Morley created some kind of record with 3 different 20's from 3 different swims on 3 consecutive days, (on 3 different rods on 3 different baits – no, I'm only kidding). All low 20's but what a run! Donkey Dave kept his hand in and, with tuition from Bill, advice from Andy and Ray and baits from Jules, caught some nice carp. Bill Cottam, now a married man, had a good run of twenties, including an unknown leather. Winter 1990 has seen a few on the bank but a cold January/February has seen a big freeze up.

Nutrabaits' employee Andy Pratt with a lovely 23lb+ Wentworth common.

MIDLANDS

Everybody's favourite Midland's fishery, **CUTTLE MILL**, continued its bumper year (2,000 doubles) and 1990 surpassed even that legendary amount. Consistent pressure all year round but cold weather carp for Adam Latham, at 27-10 and 21-05, in early 1990. If you do fish the water don't expect to have it to yourself, show some degree of patience, take a rod pod and get ready to learn all about liners. David Archer got it right with a 24-08 mirror and Norman Moon managed 11 carp to 26-02 in 2 days. That super session included 2 over twenty and 8 good doubles. Hundreds, and I mean hundreds, of carp all season fell to a variety of baits and rigs. Too many to mention and it did include some good twenties as well. The fish in the Mill used to top 30lb plus (ask Terry Eustace) but have dropped and levelled out somewhat. Would Autumn 1990 bring their weights up at all? The answer, as many of you know who read the papers, was yes. Cyril Hare had the venue's thirty at 30-04 on S.B.S. Quest Mix. An incredible fish, and one which fought for 75 minutes before Cyril got it to the net. Trevor Brindley kept the average up with a 27-10, on the Premier gear, and then, of course, there was the Carpworld/ Angling Publications 'Fish-in', to raise money for the Dexter James Appeal. In the 2 days the fishery was occupied, 55 doubles were caught including 6 twenties, up to 24-08. Biggy fell to the multi-talented Bernard Loftus, who we believe has yet to discover women or barbers! Norman Moon returned to the fishery and had another bumper session, with 13 carp to 28-00 all on the Nutrabait's gear. 13 year old Mark Cot got it right with carp of 11-10, 13-03,14-03, 14-05, 17-14 and 24-14, all on home-made bait. Walthamstow's top boy, John Pope, visited the Mill for some late season carping and had a huge catch totalling over 300lb . This included 4 over twenty to 28-04. Best mid/late season catch went to Martin Barratt who'd never had a twenty in 5 years of carping, but then took 13 fish including 3 over twenty to 25-12. Nice one Martin! Even as the cold months fell upon us the action didn't drop off too much and most of the lads received some action. Best catch was undoubtedly to Norman Moon, who once again decided to turn over the water. Best fish went 31-01 (yes, 31lb 1oz!) which is the venue's best fish since Tony Higgins took over in 1985. Norman also added 5 more carp to 27-02 for good measure. Come 1991 you know where to go lads, don't you?

PATSHULL PARK probably appears under more guises than even Tilery or Savay used to do, but I think all Carpworld readers know what a good venue it can be for those who get it right. Late 1989/early 1990 saw one, or two boys, doing just that with Alan Smith taking a 22-08, Ross Bradley (age 11) landing an 8-04, John Butler amassing 9 carp to 20-12 with plenty of other good doubles and low 20's coming out. The usual end of season spree continued with Paul Fox taking the big mirror at 30-08, a 24-08 common and 19-08 common. Rob Hales, the Midlands own, self-made superstar had carp to 26-01. Have a look at S.B.S.'s bait book to see just how successful Rob is with the big commons! No carping on the venue until later in 1990 but plenty of boys got it together then. Baz Griffiths had a nice brace at 24-02 and 24-08 (Shoulders again) and then proceeded to take a big November catch of 2 good doubles, 2 twenties and a thirty. Rob Hales had his 30-00 common, spot on, and Alan Hales, who is no way related to Rob, took 16 carp to 23-00. Jim Grimmett had carp to 20-08 and John Freeman a 30-08. Onto the twenties list for John Harding, at 21-11 and 20-10, and many, many more. End of season success for Rob Hales, with good commons and mirrors, but cold, easterly winds killed the venue in January/February.

Moving further up into Shropshire and the north west, information isn't easy to come by regarding some of the waters. The lads play their cards close to their chests in that part of the world! Main report for the back end of the winter was that Brian Garner had a terric Mangrove result over the last week or so of the season. Odd fish had come out to John Lilley, but fishing the flooded mere wasn't easy, until Brian took seven fish in as many days, five of them being twenties. No winter captures reported from Erewhon, and Birch Grove proved much tougher than the lads expected, very little coming out apart from a one-morning three twenties catch to Gary from Liverpool. Odd fish from Hawkstone, but Redesmere proved difficult to all but Paul Nixon, who delighted Brian Garner by pulling a couple of whacking commons – 33.12 and 27.04 – out in successive trips.

Into the new season and information more freely available for a while. The Mangrove fished its socks off for a month or so, with biggies to Dave Phillips, John Ankers and Joe Bertram – who all had Scaley at 32.08. Eka Green, Bob Tapken and John Lilley all had unknown big twenties. After two years of struggling Joe and Eka really got their act together and rivalled the consistent John Lilley in terms of the number of good fish caught. On into the season and the action slowed, although Tony Baskeyfield banked a lovely 29lb+ mirror, John Lilley had the magnificent common known as Trio at 35lb and Joe Bertram had Scaley again at 34.12. Little to report here after the end of August, although Tim Paisley managed a brace of twenties to 25.14, and Tony Baskeyfield's persistence paid off with a couple of fish in successive weekends – both low twenties. Only fish reported after the end of October fell to John Lilley.

Erewhon didn't fish as well as the previous summer but continued to produce a string of big fish for the persistent. The Longfield brothers got their act together best and were rewarded with consistent results, including a one night five twenties catch and Perky at 36lb+. Contrary to popular rumours Pinky did not come out during the 90/91 season. Stoney didn't score as heavily as previous seasons, managing odd fish to 20+. Farmer Dave Morgan did well with a string of fish to mid twenties: Fitz, Steve, John Blumfield, Vic Bailey and company scoring well, if inconsistently – but no big 'un. What an incredible water, though.

Hawkstone weights consistently up, with big twenties being the rule rather than the exception. Reports patchy but young Ben Seal started his season with two twenty sixes – one of each. Dad missed out on the biggies – and did so again when the family fished Birch, both sons being among the twenties again, Richard going biggest at 23.08. Weights well up on Birch, with Liverpool Gary upping the lake record to 26.08. Mary's fish came out to Eric Hodgetts at 25.03, the water's first reported 20lb+ common fell to Tim's rods (22.02), and by the end of October (when Alan Young's rods had upped the lake record to 27.08) the water had yielded almost fifty twenties to the anglers fishing it. Mary Paisley had five of these, and our Steve Wilde managed to find the time from work to claim his first twenty.

Reports from further north patchy. Grey Mist not as prolific as in previous years – and the same can be said for Redesmere, although the water did make a nice present of The Male to David Sawyer at 33lb. Brian Garner struggled to come to terms with Redesmere, but finally did so in a big way with a five fish catch including a 28.00 and a 31.00 mirror late in the season. Bernard Loftus got up the locals' noses by achieving unheard of results from Treetops Lake – and other northern waters.

Well, this could go on, and on, but we are going to have to stop it somewhere. Hope you've all enjoyed Tina's review of the major waters news in 1990 – see you in Carpworld soon.

Tina

HNV's AND PROTEIN DIGESTING ENZYMES

The author is a B.Sc and a research chemist at the University of Nottingham. In this article he gives us the benefit of his knowledge of his subject as it relates to the use of enzymes in carp baits.

In recent years many special anglers, myself included, have experimented with protein splitting enzymes in their HNV bait. Also, many bait suppliers are now offering enzymes, bait mixes containing enzymes, and now even predigested baits. From reading the angling press it would seem that these baits are very successful.

As a research chemist at the University of Nottingham, the use and the mechanism of action of these enzymes has been of great interest to me, as well as their potential application to my own fishing. What follows are my thoughts on the use of these enzymes and on some of the claims made about them. The conclusions I have come to are as a result of a lot of study of both angling and technical literature over several years.

Protein digesting enzymes act by splitting peptide bonds between the component amino acids of the protein, this process is known as hydrolysis. There are two general types of these enzymes:

1. Endopeptidases – Attack only inner peptide bonds, and are specific to certain bonds. For instance, Trypsin attacks adjacent to Arginine and Lysine. The major product of endopeptidase hydrolysis are peptide chains.
2. Exopeptidases – Attack terminal peptide bonds at the end of peptide chains, producing free amino acids.

The consensus of opinion in the angling world is that by predigesting the protein in a bait you are increasing the Net Protein Utilisation (N.P.U.) by the fish, and all other things being equal are creating a more nutritional bait. By doing this you would be increasing the chances of your bait being accepted in preference to other baits or natural food – I think the theory of nutritional recognition is now generally accepted. I have also seen it written by some anglers that enzyme action increases the Biological Value (B.V.) of the protein, but this cannot be the case as I understand the meaning of B.V. The B.V. of a given protein is a measure of the degree of fit of its amino acid profile to the essential amino acid requirements of a given organism. It is a fixed value. Hence a protein containing all the carp's essential amino acids in all the correct proportions has a B.V. of 1.0 for carp, whereas casein, for instance, has a B.V. of approx. 0.4 for carp. Predigestion does nothing to alter the 'overall' amino acid profile, and so does not alter the B.V. The only way to increase the B.V. of your bait is to use a mixture of proteins to reduce the effects of limiting amino acids.

Now the above all sounds very plausible, a predigested bait must be more nutritious, and I must admit when I first read about it I was quite convinced. That is until I came across several papers in the literature which suggested that the opposite was true. Aoe et al (1) found young carp unable to grow on diets in which the protein component (casein, gelatin) had been replaced with a mixture of amino acids similar in overall composition. A trypsin digested diet was also equally ineffective. It would seem that carp are unable to utilise free amino acids or predigested protein. This is exactly the opposite of what we hoped to achieve.

In order to understand these results we need to take a somewhat simplified look at protein synthesis and amino acid metabolism in general (Fig 1).

Consider the passage of the protein component of the carp's diet, through the gut. The higher order structure of the protein is destroyed by a whole series of enzymes, known as endopeptidases, to give peptides. Some absorption of peptides does occur, but most are further hydrolysed by enzymes, known as exopeptidases, to give free amino acids. This is rather like unravelling a ball of string and then chopping it into small lengths. The free amino acids are absorbed through the gut wall into the body pool of amino acids, where they suffer one of two fates:

1. An enzyme (tRNA synthetase) joins the various types of free amino acids together in a precise order to form new proteins, which the carp requires to grow.

Mark Symmonds

Fig 1. AMINO ACID METABOLISM

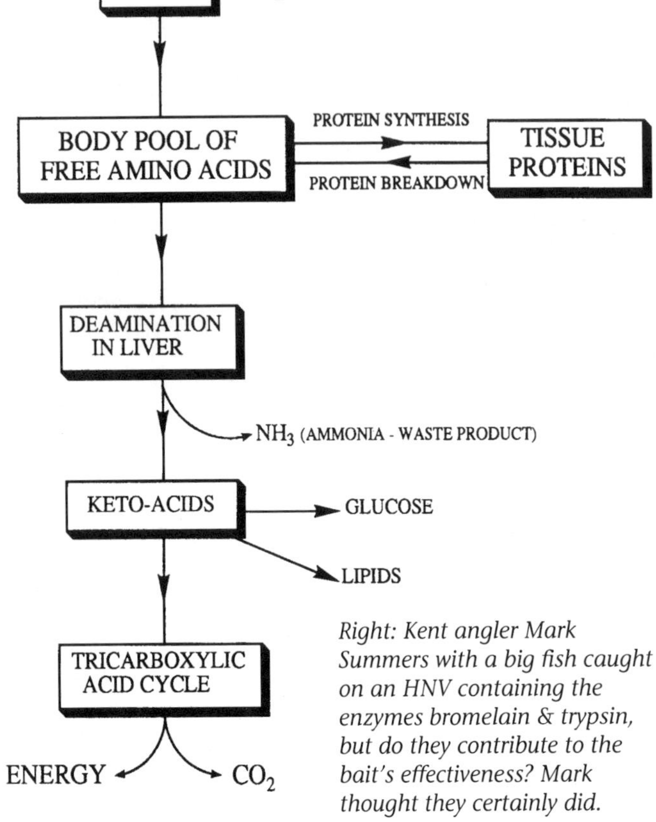
DIET
BODY POOL OF FREE AMINO ACIDS
PROTEIN SYNTHESIS
PROTEIN BREAKDOWN
TISSUE PROTEINS
DEAMINATION IN LIVER
NH_3 (AMMONIA - WASTE PRODUCT)
KETO-ACIDS
GLUCOSE
LIPIDS
TRICARBOXYLIC ACID CYCLE
ENERGY
CO_2

Right: Kent angler Mark Summers with a big fish caught on an HNV containing the enzymes bromelain & trypsin, but do they contribute to the bait's effectiveness? Mark thought they certainly did.

2. There exists no mechanism for the storage of amino acids in the fish's body. If an amino acid is not used for protein synthesis within a short period, it will be deaminated and 'burnt' to give energy. There is quite a rapid turnover.

The key to the whole problem is that different amino acids are absorbed through the gut wall at different rates, dependent on their chemical structure. The normal process of protein digestion has evolved so that amino acids which are absorbed slowly, are released from the dietary protein first, and the fast amino acids are released last. The overall result is that all the amino acids arrive in the body pool at the same time – a necessary condition for efficient protein synthesis.

However, with the free amino or hydrolysed diet, all the amino acids begin absorption at the same time, and hence arrive in the body pool at different times. When a rapidly absorbed amino acid arrives in the body pool, the other slower aminos will have been deaminated. In both cases no protein synthesis is possible – no growth.

This 'rate of absorption' theory is backed up by the work of Murai et al (2), who coated amino acid supplements with casein and found comparable but not better growth rates to a casein/gelatin control diet. They concluded that the coating minimised the variation in amino acid absorption rate, resulting in relatively simultaneous availability of all amino acids to tissues for optimal protein synthesis.

But, these baits are catching lots of big carp for a lot of people, so we must be doing something right. I believe that enzymes added to the bait mix are a relatively inefficient way of hydrolysing the protein due to the difficulty in achieving the right conditions. Only a small proportion of the protein is hydrolysed, and as most modern bait mixes have protein contents far in excess of the optimum literature values of 38-55%, plenty of undigested protein will remain for normal digestion to occur. Whether this will be the same for pre-digested mixes now available is another thing. So an enzyme bait can still be HNV, but it will not be 'Higher HNV'.

Where these baits do score, is in their inherent attractor value. It is well known that free amino acids are olfactory and gustatory feeding stimulants for carp. An added bonus is that the free amino combination released by that enzyme from the bait, is directly related to that bait – what you smell is what you get. This will be the case for the commonly used, naturally derived enzymes – Bromelain, Ficin and Papain, which although they are endopeptidases, are so general in their action that they release many free amino acids. More specific Trypsin type endopeptidases will tend to produce mostly a peptide product, which may be attractive in itself but will, in my opinion, be less effective. I don't know if there is an exopeptidase available at the moment, it would be interesting to compare results.

I think that there is a lot of mileage in using enzyme baits without any artificial label, just let the amino 'signature' be the label. There is also some evidence that the searching/feeding response of fish to amino combinations is not a genetically inherited response, but a conditioned response from eating its natural diet, such as occurs with artificial flavour labels. It should, therefore, be possible to educate carp to associate your particular amino combination with nutritious food, be-prebaiting in the normal way. Different enzymes act on different sites in the protein, releasing a different amino combination, so changing the enzyme, changes the label for the same base mix. The major advantage is that your label will be exclusive to your bait – less common denominators.

I should add that, apart from the referred to work of Aoe et al and Murai et al, most of the above is educated guesswork and conjecture. It seems that some of the claims made for enzyme baits, apart from the fact that they work, are mistaken.

I hope this is of interest to anglers, like me, who find bait as interesting a topic as the fishing itself.

REFERENCES:

1. Aoe et al. Bull. Jap. Soc. Sci. Fish, 1970. 36, 407-413.
2. Murai et al. Bull. Jap. Soc. Sci. Fish, 1981. 47, 523-528.

Harry Haskell

ONE YEAR'S CARPING

Contrary to what I might have once envisaged, as the years roll by demands on my time have increased. This results in seemingly less and less time to spend actually carping and is something I keep meaning to rectify. The fact remains that, generally speaking, consistent success in terms of results requires a relative element of time. This is a summary of how my time spent carping turned out, between January 1990 and January 1991. I apologise in advance because it's all about me, sorry!

January 3rd – fished the pit from 7.30am to 6pm with Andy Little, and both of us blanked when we shouldn't have. Two days later I drove over to Darenth and spent some five hours looking for a carp under the bushes in the Tip lake, and found nothing! Then I fished from late afternoon till after dusk in the 'Rats', without a bleep.

My son was now desperately ill again, and all fishing stopped until Andy persuaded me to have a day on February 5th at an easy water. What a tonic! Andy had twenty five to my fifteen! (I'm not complaining). Just pure fun fishing, with the best four fish being low doubles.

This inspired me to visit the pit again on the 17th for a day session. The weather was perfect, mild and overcast, but I had to wait till 5pm when the bobbin twitched and out came a lovely mid-twenty linear. A further three, one day sessions at the pit were made, which resulted in nothing. And I see from my diary notes that I should have caught. Somehow or other, despite giving myself a good talking to, my heart wasn't in it. I fished badly, without much thought, paid the price, and so the season ended.

All close season plans were scrapped, and I only ventured forth on one occasion with a fly rod in hand. The pit fishery had been let go over the past few years, and what with the previous two winters storm damage, needed urgently attending to. So, during the next three months, a thousand miles and as many hours were clocked up on work parties. This proved to be very strenuous but rewarding work and, by June, everyone was well pleased with their efforts.

During May two major problems arose on this water. The first was a power struggle to gain control of the fishery, (this was later to have disastrous results). The second was that a borrowed punt, with much sentimental value, was left unlocked and subsequently stolen –(this matter has yet to be resolved). Whilst I have no wish to go into any further detail, all this caused an awful lot of unnecessary upset, to the point of resignation on my part and others.

The 'glorious sixteenth'? – this is when I always 'biv-up' for three or four days, as opposed to a normal one or, at the most, two 'nighter'. Past experience has proved that opening week can be somewhat unreliable, but I still have a go anyway. Swims are drawn for on the 'pit start' and, as with last year, you can guess who drew the short straw! My plan and tactics were well thought out and executed, and you would have loved my bait, a cheeky little number, even if I say so myself. The trouble was that during my stay all the carp were down the other end of the lake spawning, or going through the motions. So much for mice and men!

During this time only three carp were spotted visiting my end of the lake, and they didn't stay more than ten minutes. However, at 2am on the second morning a belting run materialised, and a 17lb. mirror lay in the net. This turned out to be 'Old Scaley' the 'mug' of the pit, a tatty but much loved fish for all that.

My next session back on the pit was June29/30th and still the weather remained cool and wet, with very little moving. After a blank day and night, the sun finally smiled down on us during the following late afternoon, and everything looked roses. A fish was spotted, and my static rods were promptly swapped for the nine foot stalker and 'pin'. By 8pm, after some two hours of effort, this particular mirror took a bait; a whacker at last and just a 'herring short' of a thirty. My first big one of the new season; I was, as they say, well pleased.

As you will remember, July saw the start of the heat wave and I will not bore you further with day by day accounts. This hot weather provided me with some of the best stalking at the pit I've had for years, and lasted up until early October. There were several one day multiple catches of twenties – the best, number wise, were five carp including three big twenties, twice, in successive days!

Despite what you might think, these fish are very shrewd and required a lot of work and thought. They would run a mile if a single mixer appeared, and the definition of this type of stalking refers to bottom baits, in shallow water, at close range. Close range means, where possible, no more than the hook link length out from the bank – six to twelve inches!, with the lead as tight

in as could be. Two things scared the pants off them. One was line and the other was too many baits about! The tolerance limit seemed to be three 14mm jobs at the time of actual fishing. Mostly, it was singles or plus one on a stringer (to pin-point the freebie).

This was really exciting stuff, but it would be wrong to think they just upended and off it went. If only it could have be captured on video, you just would not believe the caution exercised by them in picking up and putting down a bait. Each bait would be inspected time and time again, taking hours sometimes. All this on my very best presentation too, although it's true I did have several 'quickies'.

This caution was, no doubt, being shown on static baits fished at distance, all taking place unseen. It went, some way, in explaining why normal style carping here was so slow. This 'hot weather behaviour' was later discussed with Andy Little, who had also been tearing his hair out at their 'spookyness'. His experiences and solutions were similar to my own, at least in some aspects. Further details of this period will, hopefully, appear in a future issue of Carpworld.

One thing was clear, fine tuning of presentation and of thought upped my catch rate, I would guess, by a factor of two. The home-made bait seemed of less importance than pin pointing 'the spot'. And as everything was just lowered in off the rod top, in spite of being belly down in the grass, great accuracy could be achieved.

Several other waters were visited during the summer and autumn, including three 30 hour sessions on Darenth. Apart from the carp, Darenth offered me the chance to gain some experience in 'communal carping', which to date I've always avoided like the plague. So far I can't say I've enjoyed it, which is in no way a reflection on those Darenth lads. It's probably more to do with having to fish whatever swim is left, and the time available, in relation to time required. And the fact that, to date, I haven't had much success there!

Despite what you might think, the returns per rod hour, even by the best of the regulars, is pretty grim. What was once a prolific, easy doubles water is now far from so. Indeed, in the broadest sense of the word, Darenth is fairly hard, unless you have lots of time to spare and lots of bait, or so it seems.

Anyway, the end results of my other excursions resulted in a sprinkling of doubles. The one other highlight of summer 90 was a trip to Redmire, the details of which may appear in a future Carp Fisher. A wonderful experience, and whilst not handling long sessions well, it was very enjoyable, and I did catch. Was it necessary? Well, I'd be telling porkies if I said it wasn't.

Redmire seems so easy, all those lovely 'silt feeders' everywhere you look, and I have a long list of excuses for not catching what I should have! Preconceived plans, no matter how successful they may have been in the past, often let you down at the point of fishing. The two big chances I had,

I blew, and only saved myself from failure by the skin of my pants. But at least I caught, and held a few of those beautiful Leney Redmire commons. Please Lord, give me another chance!

So the summer ended, and already I had experienced several 'happenings'. Here's one at the aforementioned pit, which was beyond my experience. September 15th – it was almost time to go and all the gear was packed except one rod, plus rest, and net. On the way out there was just time to drop into one tiny area for an hour before dusk. So, leaving most of the gear back on the pathway, I threaded myself through the undergrowth with rod, net and small chair in hand, squeezing into a very tight spot beneath some bushes. A few baits had previously been placed here, tight to the bank, and was, as yet, untried. An hour passed, dusk set in, and there was just enough light left to check my watch – almost 7.15pm, it's no good I'll have to go. As the chair legs were being folded up, purring like a cat, off went the Bait Runner! There was something heavy on the other end, intent on distancing itself away from me. After some twenty minutes or so, I realised this was something special and soon my arms and back began to ache. On at least two occasions it had actually gone some fifty yards behind me with the line running through a willow tree. Each time it all pinged out as it set off down the lake. It ploughed itself through every bush and reed bed possible yet still everything held together. I thanked the stars for being tooled up with the heavy stuff (11lb. Sylcast).

Now this was not only getting silly, but I was really hurting! In fact it got so bad, I was beginning to wish the damn thing would fall off, which is a terrible admission. The facts were it was pitch black, no one for miles, and I had now got severe cramp – what the hell was this thing? Every time it came anywhere near the net, off it went again. It had to be foul hooked but it didn't feel like it at all. It began to dawn on me I was winning, albeit slowly. After heaven knows how long, I also realised it was necessary to feed the 12' foot rod (what a twit!) behind me, due to the over-hanging trees, to get it anywhere near the net.
By holding the rod above the middle joint this feat had been tried several times already. The moon was now peeping out a bit and, at long last, just in a wee patch of light shimmering on the surface, an enormous head came up six inches from the net! The line went straight to her lips! For a second it was stale mate, in desperation I gave a last heave. Then, amidst a huge boil of water, she went down again. Horrors, I couldn't give any line! It all pinged up into the tree above, as the hook hold gave, and I cried out in agony and relief. After crawling back to my bag, still in pain, to get a torch, I found the line had gone around and under the spool and, God's truth, the time was 8.31pm! Now please don't ask, because I just don't know!

A couple more 30 hour sessions, in October, at the pit gave me several more 'biggies' including two 20lb. plus commons. On October 20th I was duly informed by an assistant bailiff, that during the previous week there had been a stocking of carp put into an adjacent water, by a well known FISH SUPPLIER? And that two of these fish, around three pounds each, had been slipped into our water. This, though I didn't know it then, was to be the start of my worst nightmare!

On November 3rd I had my first blank there, except for the opening period. My diary tells me that not a thing moved during those 30 hours; ironically my notes say "dead as a door nail.' Back for a day trip only, on the 16th, I found small groups of carp on the top. By mid morning, having fruitlessly tried to stalk them and get one to take a bait, it dawned on me something was most decidedly strange about their behaviour. They appeared unusually lethargic and, at first, I put it down to low dissolved oxygen, what with all the leaves and low water. What I didn't know then was they were dying! My notes say "I'm not happy about this" and, indeed, I asked a local member to check them out during the week if he got the chance to call in.

On December 1st the nightmare came true, and I found five dead carp and others very distressed. On December 2nd dead carp were also found in the nearby pit, which had received all but two of the stocking. To date we have lost eighteen carp, mostly twenties to nearly thirty pounds, and the other pit some forty fish in total. We can expect more of the same, come the spring, because the suspected virus introduced by the stocking is temperature dependent. I suppose we will be lucky to have 10% survive, which will mean just a handful of fish.

This outrageous killing has occurred in the past in exactly the same circumstances, and has happened because of others' greed and ignorance. At the point of writing this, the matter is under investigation. I've heard recently that a pit in the Colne valley was stocked some weeks after ours, by the same supplier (ask around), and the pattern is repeating itself yet again! With regard to this 'fish dealer', you can be assured that when all the evidence is collected their name will appear in foot high, fluorescent letters, as a warning to others. Hopefully, the Carp Society will, in due time, publish a list of approved fish dealers, when this business has been sorted out. Remember, if you are thinking about additional carp, especially if your existing stock is old Leneys, you need specialist advice. The N.R.A. Health Certificate, as it is at the moment, is useless.

I'm sorry to end this piece on such a sour note, but it is a truthful account of my season from January 1990 to January 1991. I'll treasure, forever, those long, hot summer days and I'll remember the sadness which followed them. I'm a year older now, and a lot wiser, and there's a lesson here for everyone. May I wish good luck, and good health, to both you and your carp in 1991.

WHERE TO GO TO CATCH...

I suppose we get three main enquiries at the office in the course of a week. "When's the next Carpworld out?", "I'm looking for a bait that...", and, finally, "Where can I go to catch my first...?" Sure, there are books on this subject, some even dealing specifically with waters but many of you, and we take this as a compliment, want it direct from the "horse's mouth".

Despite the apparent glut of big fish, week in and week out, appearing in the 'weeklies' they are not caught willy-nilly. Certainly, many of the people we speak to are still looking to consistently catch 'doubles' with the odd 'twenty' or two. Waters holding carp are on the increase but so are anglers interested in catching them so, unless you can find a little water tucked away from the public domain, you are always going to have company!

Here then is a brief guide to catching your first...

4 GREY MIST MERE, Warrington – Large number of doubles to low 20's. 10 acres. Warrington Anglers' club water.

5 LLANDRINDOD WELLS – Very famous, pretty water well stocked with single and double figure carp. Lovely to fish. Cafe on bank. Tickets on cafe.

14 HORSESHOE LAKE – One of the best doubles waters in the country. Day and season ticket fishery at time of writing, but may have changed. Just outside Lechlade in Gloucestershire.

49 REDMIRE POOL, Llangarron, Herefordshire – The Carp Society now control the fishing on this historic, 3 acre pool. Very attractive and atmospheric fishery, although the large carp are not present in the numbers they once were. Still tremendous potential for its magnificent 20lb. commons. Fairly difficult. Arrangements through 081-551-8250.

7 ARROW LAKE, Redditch, Birmingham – This is tackle manufacturers Shakespeare's own water and contains a large head of double figure carp. A super water for beginners. Day tickets available.

13 DOCKLOWS POOLS, West End Farm, Docklow, Leominster – These Pools comprise four 2 acre lakes stuffed full of small carp, running into low doubles. A great water for beginners. Bookings per day, in advance, by telephone (056-882-256).

39 GAYTON POOL, Northampton – Carp to good doubles. 3 acre pool. Gayton A.S. water.

40 COMMON LAKES at Milton Common – Lots of doubles in this 7 acre water. Day tickets on site.

19 SHILLAMILL LAKES, Lanreath, Looe, Cornwall – These are three small lakes on this complex, all holding good numbers of doubles. The close season does not apply and booking can be made by telephone with John Facey, on 0503-20271.

48 COLLEGE RESERVOIR, off the B3291, near Falmouth, Cornwall – A 38 acre reservoir holding large stocks of carp with a good proportion over 20lb. Fish well educated and easiest between March and September. Day and season permits available from machine in car park. Further details obtainable locally or from South West Water, telephone 0392-219666.

2 MIDDLETON WATER PARK, Darlington – Low doubles to 14lb. Tickets from paper shop opposite fishery.

1 HOLEHIRD TARN, Windermere – Some doubles. Ticket on bank (restricted numbers).

15 COMBWICH POND, Combwich, Bridgewater – Difficult water with a good head of doubles and twenties. Bridgewater A.A. control the fishing.

10 CUTTLE MILL, east off the A4091, Wishaw, near Sutton Coldfield, West Midlands – A highly productive fishery which was created in the early 1970's by Albert Brewer. An excellent and well organised, commercial fishery, situated in attractive surroundings. It is very popular and limits are placed on the number permitted to fish, so prior-booking is recommended. Over 2,000 doubles were reported caught in 1990. Contact the owner, Tony Higgins, on 0827-872253.

9 GIBSONS LAKE, Kingsbury County Park, Bodymoor Heath, near Tamworth, Warwicks. – This 3 acre gravel pit holds over 100 doubles, some going over 20lb. Season tickets available from the County Council Offices, Shire Hall, Warwick.

11 MOLANDS MERE, Packington, Ashby-de-la-Zouch – Lots of doubles. Day/season tickets at venue.

8 TELFORD A.A. have a number of waters, some of them being good carp fisheries.

17 ANGLER'S PARADISE, Halwill Junction, Beaworthy, Devon – A number of popular, purpose built carp waters which hold carp of all sizes to meet different carp angler's aspirations. Most baits work well and close season angling is allowed. The amiable owner, Zyg Gregorek, will be pleased to advise about day and extended bookings. Night fishing is allowed. Telephone Zyg on 0409-22559.

18 LOWER TAMAR LAKE, Bideford, Devon – This large reservoir holds a very good head of doubles and is not heavily fished. The close season does not apply and day tickets are available on the bank. Very pleasant fishing.

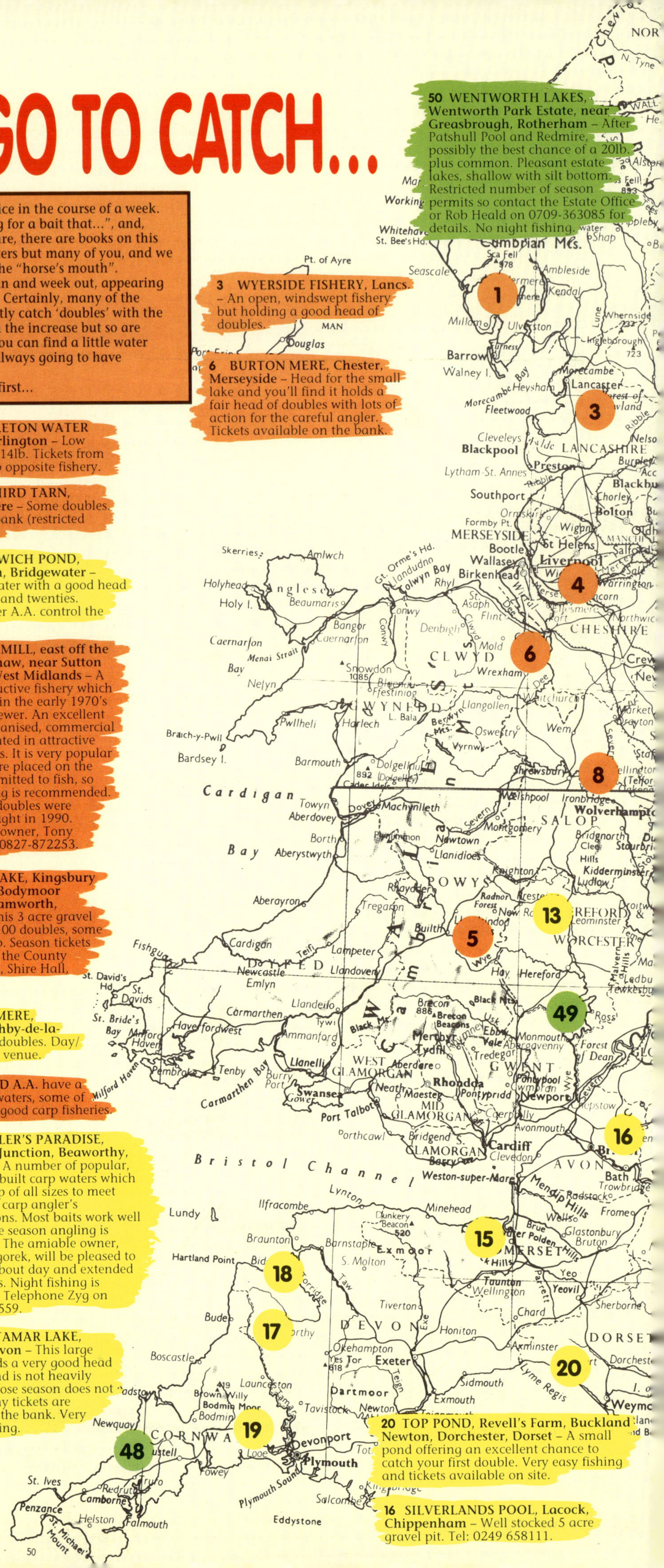

Cumbrian Mts.
Scafell
Ambleside
Kendal
Pt. of Ayre
Seascale
Millom
Ulverston
MAN
Douglas
Barrow
Walney I.
Morecambe
Lancaster
Heysham
Fleetwood
Cleveleys
Blackpool
LANCASHIRE
Preston
Lytham St. Annes
Southport
Blackburn
Chorley
Bolton
Formby Pt.
MERSEYSIDE
Bootle
Wallasey
St. Helens
Birkenhead
Liverpool
Wigan
Warrington
CHESHIRE
Skerries
Amlwch
Holyhead
Holy I.
Anglesey
Beaumaris
Bangor
Caernarfon
Conwy
Rhyl
Colwyn Bay
St. Asaph
Flint
Denbigh
Mold
CLWYD
Wrexham
Menai Strait
Snowdon
Ffestiniog
Nefyn
Pwllheli
Harlech
L. Bala
Llangollen
Oswestry
Vyrnwy
Wem
Braich-y-Pwll
Bardsey I.
Barmouth
Dolgellau
Shrewsbury
Cardigan Bay
Towyn
Aberdovey
Machynlleth
Welshpool
Ironbridge
Wolverhampton
SALOP
Borth
Newtown
Montgomery
Bridgnorth
Aberystwyth
Llanidloes
Kidderminster
Knighton
Ludlow
POWYS
Rhayader
Aberayron
Tregaron
Radnor Forest
New Radnor
Builth
Leominster
HEREFORD &
WORCESTER
Cardigan
Lampeter
Fishguard
Llandovery
Hay
Hereford
Newcastle Emlyn
St. David's Hd.
St. Davids
St. Bride's Bay
Carmarthen
Llandeilo
Brecon
Black Mts.
Brecon Beacons
Ammanford
Merthyr Tydfil
Ebbw Vale
Abergavenny
Monmouth
Ross
Haverfordwest
Milford Haven
Pembroke
Tenby
Carmarthen Bay
Llanelli
Burry Port
Swansea
Gower
Neath
Aberdare
Rhondda
Tredegar
GWENT
Pontypool
Pontypridd
Newport
Cwmbran
WEST GLAMORGAN
MID GLAMORGAN
Port Talbot
Maesteg
Porthcawl
Bridgend
Caerphilly
Avonmouth
Cardiff
Barry
Clevedon
Chepstow
Bristol Channel
Weston-super-Mare
AVON
Bath
Trowbridge
Mendip Hills
Radstock
Frome
Lynton
Minehead
Ilfracombe
Lundy
Dunkery Beacon
Exmoor
Braunton
Barnstaple
Wells
Glastonbury
Bruton
Hartland Point
Bideford
S. Molton
SOMERSET
Taunton
Wellington
Yeovil
Sherborne
Bude
Tiverton
Chard
DEVON
Honiton
Axminster
DORSET
Okehampton
Yes Tor
Exeter
Boscastle
Launceston
Bodmin Moor
Bodmin
Dartmoor
Sidmouth
Exmouth
Lyme Regis
Weymouth
Newquay
CORNWALL
Tavistock
Newton Abbot
Devonport
Plymouth
Looe
Fowey
St. Ives
Redruth
Truro
Camborne
Penzance
Helston
Falmouth
St. Michael's Mount
Plymouth Sound
Salcombe
Eddystone
1
3
4
6
8
5
13
49
16
15
18
17
19
48
20

50 WENTWORTH LAKES, Wentworth Park Estate, near Greasbrough, Rotherham – After Patshull Pool and Redmire, possibly the best chance of a 20lb. plus common. Pleasant estate lakes, shallow with silt bottom. Restricted number of season permits so contact the Estate Office or Rob Heald on 0709-363085 for details. No night fishing.

3 WYERSIDE FISHERY, Lancs. – An open, windswept fishery but holding a good head of doubles.

6 BURTON MERE, Chester, Merseyside – Head for the small lake and you'll find it holds a fair head of doubles with lots of action for the careful angler. Tickets available on the bank.

20 TOP POND, Revell's Farm, Buckland Newton, Dorchester, Dorset – A small pond offering an excellent chance to catch your first double. Very easy fishing and tickets available on site.

16 SILVERLANDS POOL, Lacock, Chippenham – Well stocked 5 acre gravel pit. Tel: 0249 658111.

YOUR FIRST DOUBLE

(OR POSSIBLY TWENTY)

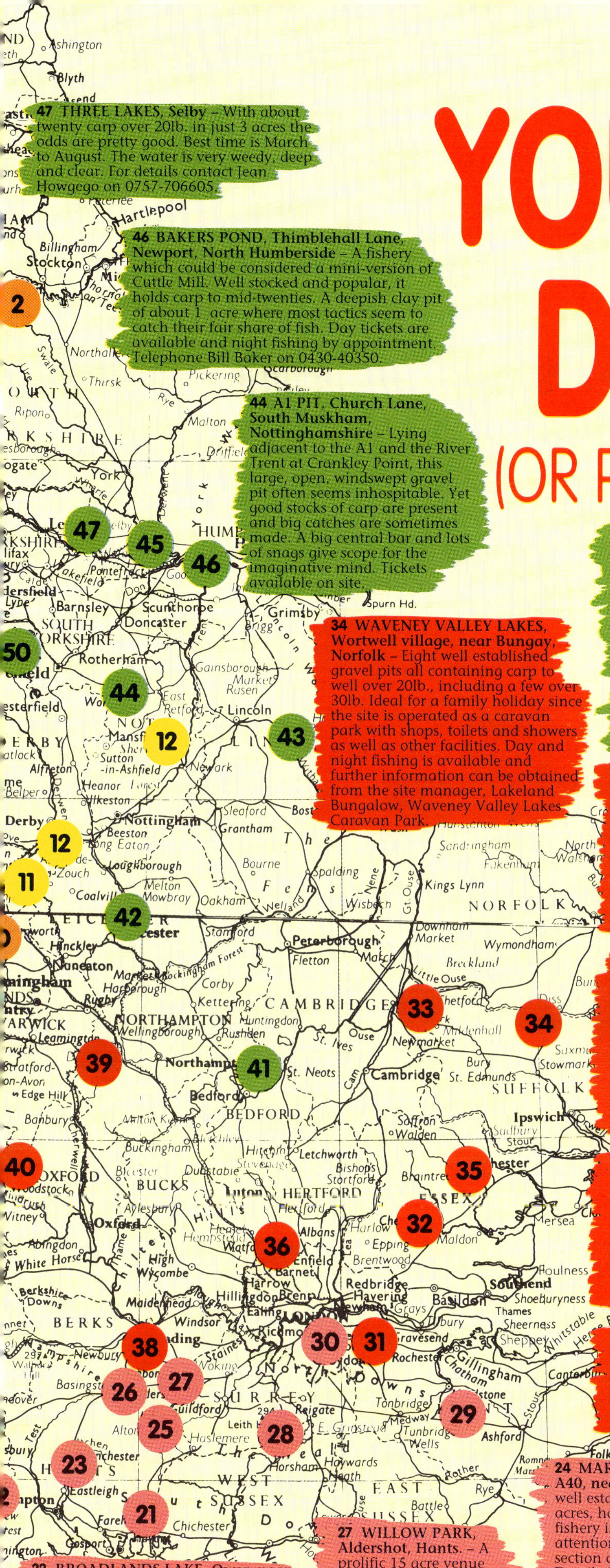

Ashington
Blyth
Hartlepool
Billingham
Stockton
Northallerton
Thirsk
Ripon
Pickering
Scarborough
Malton
Driffield
York
Goole
Pontefract
Barnsley
Scunthorpe
Doncaster
Grimsby
Spurn Hd.
Rotherham
Gainsborough
Market Rasen
Lincoln
East Retford
Mansfield
Sutton -in-Ashfield
Alfreton
Heanor
Belper
Derby
Ilkeston
Nottingham
Beeston
Long Eaton
Sleaford
Grantham
Boston
Loughborough
Coalville
Melton Mowbray
Oakham
Bourne
Spalding
Wisbech
Kings Lynn
Sandringham
Fakenham
NORFOLK
Stamford
Peterborough
Downham Market
Wymondham
Hinckley
Nuneaton
Market Harborough
Corby
Kettering
Rugby
Fletton
March
Brockland
Little Ouse
Thetford
Diss
NORTHAMPTON
Wellingborough
Huntingdon
CAMBRIDGE
Leamington
Mildenhall
Northampton
Rushden
St. Ives
Ouse
Newmarket
Stratford-on-Avon
Edge Hill
St. Neots
Cambridge
Bury St. Edmunds
Stowmarket
SUFFOLK
Banbury
Bedford
BEDFORD
Ipswich
Sudbury
Stour
Saffron Walden
Buckingham
Letchworth
Hitchin
Bishop's Stortford
OXFORD
Bicester
BUCKS
Dunstable
Luton
HERTFORD
Braintree
Woodstock
Aylesbury
Hertford
ESSEX
Witney
Oxford
Harlow
Mersea
Abingdon
White Horse
Hempstead
Albans
Epping
Maldon
High Wycombe
Watford
Enfield
Brentwood
Barnet
Harrow
Redbridge
Havering
Southend
Foulness
Shoeburyness
Berkshire Downs
Maidenhead
Hillingdon
Ealing
Brent
Basildon
Thames
BERKS
Windsor
Grays
Sheerness
Whitstable
Newbury
Reading
Richmond
Gravesend
Rochester
Sheppey
Herne Bay
Basingstoke
Staines
Woking
Gillingham
Chatham
Canterbury
Andover
Guildford
SURREY
Reigate
Maidstone
Tonbridge
Medway
Tunbridge Wells
Alton
Leith Hill
Haslemere
East Grinstead
Ashford
Dover
Folkestone
Winchester
Horsham
Haywards Heath
Romney Marsh
Eastleigh
WEST SUSSEX
EAST SUSSEX
Rother
Rye
Fareham
Chichester
Gosport

47 THREE LAKES, Selby – With about twenty carp over 20lb. in just 3 acres the odds are pretty good. Best time is March to August. The water is very weedy, deep and clear. For details contact Jean Howgego on 0757-706605.

46 BAKERS POND, Thimblehall Lane, Newport, North Humberside – A fishery which could be considered a mini-version of Cuttle Mill. Well stocked and popular, it holds carp to mid-twenties. A deepish clay pit of about 1 acre where most tactics seem to catch their fair share of fish. Day tickets are available and night fishing by appointment. Telephone Bill Baker on 0430-40350.

44 A1 PIT, Church Lane, South Muskham, Nottinghamshire – Lying adjacent to the A1 and the River Trent at Crankley Point, this large, open, windswept gravel pit often seems inhospitable. Yet good stocks of carp are present and big catches are sometimes made. A big central bar and lots of snags give scope for the imaginative mind. Tickets available on site.

34 WAVENEY VALLEY LAKES, Wortwell village, near Bungay, Norfolk – Eight well established gravel pits all containing carp to well over 20lb., including a few over 30lb. Ideal for a family holiday since the site is operated as a caravan park with shops, toilets and showers as well as other facilities. Day and night fishing is available and further information can be obtained from the site manager, Lakeland Bungalow, Waveney Valley Lakes Caravan Park.

45 DRAX POND, (Brock Holes Lake), Drax, North Humberside – Well stocked, shallow clay pit of about 17 acres holding good average sized fish. Contact Gordon Simms on 0757-618641 about the availability of season permits. Night fishing is allowed.

42 MILL FARM, Gilmorton – Nice stock easy carping. Some doubles. Night fishing. Tel: 0455 52392.

36 STANBOROUGH LAKE, Welwyn Garden City, Herts. – This medium sized gravel pit is known locally as the "Cracker Factory." Huge shoals of carp, of all sizes, inhabit this very popular fishery which is also used by other water sports. Only one rod is allowed up until November 1st. Day and season tickets are available of the bank.

37 LINEAR FISHERIES, Little Linford Lane, Milton Keynes – This venue is a large complex of lakes suitable for all types of carp angler, from the novice to the expert. Readily accessible from all parts of the country with excellent stocks of carp. Contact Len Gurd on 0908-607577 about details of day and season permits as well as nightfishing.

35 LAYER PITS, 6 miles south of Colchester, Essex – This well documented carp fishery holds a tremendous stock of carp, which can be tempted by a wide variety of methods. Day and season tickets are available from local tackle shops. Fishing controlled by Colchester Angling Preservation Society.

38 BRITTEN'S POND, Jacobs Well, Guildford, Surrey – Well publicised water, full of doubles (around 200 in under 5 acres of water!). Day tickets obtainable from local tackle shops in Guildford.

12 RIVER TRENT, Nottinghamshire – With the River Thames, the Trent must be the best stocked carp river in the country. Certain areas hold considerable numbers of doubles, with occasional fish going into high twenties. Plenty of effort required in location but this can be repaid handsomely. Enquire local tackle shops regarding day tickets or season permits; alternatively telephone Rob Heald on 0709-363085.

41 CHAWSTON PIT, A1,St. Neots, Cambs. – This 10 acre gravel pit holds a good head of doubles between 10lb. and 15lb. The water is controlled by Chawston Angling Club who issue permits through local tackle shops.

43 WEST ASHLY LAKES, Horncastle – High stock of doubles. Tel: 0507 600473.

31 HORTON KIRBY, Dartford – Some easy to moderate carp fishing available. Dartford Club water.

32 CHIGBOROUGH LAKE, Heybridge Basin, Malden, Essex – This water holds a large head of doubles up to about 18lb.Season and day tickets are available on site. Details by telephone on 0621-852113.

26 LODGE POND, Farnham, Surrey – A pretty lake, set in lovely surroundings, it contains a good head of doubles. Can be fished with a Farnham A.S. year book which are available from local tackle shops. Details from the Secretary, 70 Prince Charles Crescent, Farnborough, Hants.

29 BYSINGWOOD, Faversham, Kent – This well-known carp water, about 10 acres in size, holds a tremendous head of carp running well into double figures.Some membership restrictions, but try writing to the Faversham Angling Club, 5 Kennedy Close, Faversham, Kent.

24 MARLBOROUGH POOL, next to the A40, near Whitney, Oxfordshire. – This well established gravel pit, of about 10 acres, holds a large head of carp. The fishery is very popular and receives a lot of attention. Mentioned in the Winter fishing section of Kevin Maddock's Carp Fever. Details from the Secretary, Oxford & Dist. A.A. , P. Weston, 18 Linden Road, Bicester, Oxfordshire.

22 BROADLANDS LAKE, Ower, near Romsey, Hampshire – This hugely popular and very productive 25 acre gravel pit, running alongside the M27 motorway, is full of double-figure fish with a fair sprinkling of larger fish. Richworth boilies are very successful here and for details about the fishing ring Mark Simmonds on 0703-733167. Day tickets and night fishing are allowed.

27 WILLOW PARK, Aldershot, Hants. – A prolific 15 acre venue which is stuffed full of carp of all sizes. They mostly average 9 to 14lb. and are reasonably easy to catch all the year round. Day tickets and night fishing are available from John Raison by telephoning 0252-543470.

23 FISHERS POND, Winchester, Hampshire – A ten acre estate lake holding a fair head of doubles. Tickets are available from the house on the site. Ask for Mr. Paton.

30 BROOKLANDS LAKE, Dartford, Kent. – A huge head of carp reside in this prolific 28 acre gravel pit. The majority are between 10lb. and 20 lb. with a few larger fish. Day tickets are available on the bank although no night fishing is allowed. This water comes under a lot of angling pressure and bankside space is at a premium.

21 NUNNERY LAKE, Wyke, Chichester – Well stocked. Day ticket on site.

25 CUTT MILL, Puttenham – Farnham A.S. water, with good head of doubles and twenties. Very pressured.

28 A number of carp lakes of varying difficulty at **PIPPINGFORD CORNER**. All are season ticket waters. Permits obtainable from A. Norris, Pippingford Estate.

33 NUNNERY LAKES, Thetford – Excellent carp waters on a syndicate basis. Enquiries to Jason Davis.

HEADBANGER AWARDS 1990

Paul Selman in hiding. Someone's just whispered those magic words. "It's your round."

Talker of the Year

Selman went to the trouble of sending us a copy of his phone bill in an attempt to win this highly coveted award, but he's only a run of the mill mega-talker in the Bamford/Griffiths/Haswell league. Chris Ball and Des Taylor are talking megastars, but even they cannot match the exploits of one Steve Edwards of Kent in his prime. In the middle of one of Steve's phone conversations his listener was startled to find himself talking to Steve's wife, who had to pick up the phone to apologise for the fact that Steve had fallen asleep in mid-conversation! Must have been listening to Bamford...

Book of the Year

Fairly quiet on the book front after the flurry of new carp titles last year, but for the most part what did come out was well worth waiting for. "Carp in Focus" is probably a few years ahead of its time, and the production doesn't quite match the concept, but it's a classic, nonetheless. "Big Carp" is terrific, mainly because most of it isn't by the author. Yatesy's "Deepening Pool" is lovely but suffers slightly from unfair comparison with "Casting at the Sun", which can't really be improved upon. Chris Turnbull's "Big Fish from Famous Waters" is different, lovely and great. Those carp paintings are something special. "Famous Anglers" is an astonishing book and does John Bailey great credit for the amount of research and effort that went into its production. The book's two demerits are that it starts at the superlative level, which leaves it nowhere to go, and its terms of reference on "great" are both vague and inconsistent. That's nit-picking. These five books are all treasure troves and musts for the collectors of significant works.

Fish of the Year

Pinky for avoiding capture again: this great beast must be over 50lb now. Sally the Carp for similar reasons. The inhabitants of that famous Colne Valley no publicity water which has now produced four different forties. They're getting bigger. Yatesy's record is beginning to look like a realistic target all of a sudden.

R.I.P. of the Year

Two of the Carp Catchers Club members (sic) have sadly left us in the last twelve months, 'B.B.' and Pat Russell. In addition the likable John Sidley and Brian Godfrey have been taken from us at far too young an age. Rest in peace all of you and thanks for the inspiration and pleasure you have given.

On the waters front Longfield has gone, Rodney Meadow has gone, Duncan's Mid-Northants has gone – all within a twelve month period. Thanks for the memories from all concerned.

Angler of the Year

Haven't there been some results? Bruce Ashby, Max Cottis, Albert Romp, Tony Moore, then the string of biggies from you-know-where. The record books are being rewritten by the day and statistician Chris Ball is working flat out to keep up with the changing forties list. And what about Skid? Started the season trying to get over 25 and couldn't catch anything under it! Rod predicted Scaley wouldn't be out this year, so Skid had it three times. We'll give this award to old timer Skid, because he's a lovely fella, he's got a lovely wife, and he catches big fish from Rod's water.

Slide Show of the Year

Albert Romp, who is now as funny publicly as he's always been privately, which is going some.

Richard Skidmore – angler of the year but not appreciated in parts of Lincolnshire.

Carp Organisation of the Year

All of them for just being there through difficult times, but especially the Carp Anglers Association for being courageous, decisive – and surviving.

Lager Lout of the Year

Fierce competition as usual with Smithy exporting his enormous capacity for falling over. Impressive collective displays at NASA and the Carp Society conferences. Difficult to select an individual winner seeing Fred J. insists that he's given up drinking, so we'll give this award to the impressive bacchanalian threesome of the Converter, Disgusting and metal Micky. They really have supped some stuff this year – and have managed to stay half nice with it. Very, very nice even. Mind you, once you've been down to Zyg's Paradise and watched Zyg in action you realise that everyone else is playing at it.

Smithy – has now exported his great capacity for falling over.

Michelin Man of the Year Award

It's been a year of inflation right across the board, both fiscally and fleshily. The editor got huge, but claims he's got it under control (does that mean he's wearing a corset?). Bamford's got bigger; so have Alf Romp, and Paul Selman, and a thousand others whose main exercise is lifting a glass from bar to mouth level. To our mind the most impressive growth has been shown by lovely Micky Sly who can't think of anything better to do with his vast wealth than pour it down his throat. All that weight being piled on and Big Bill Baitmaker is in the running for Slimmer of the Year - talking of which...

Slimmer of the Year Award

Have you seen the new look Derek Stritton? He's lost $2^{1}/_{2}$ stone in the last few months, which means he must have been as wide as he is tall before emaciation set in.

Derek Stritton. Slimmer of the Year. Now taller than his circumference.

Finest Example to the Youth of Today Award

Ritchie McDonald who has behaved impeccably and impressively through difficult times.

Main Man McDonald. Ritchie in action.

Whinger of the Year Award

Ritchie McDonald following last year's Headbanger Award.

Bait of the Year

Richworth Birdfood boilies. They caught at least three forties this year to our certain knowledge.

Editorial Slip of the Year

Carpworld, in which Roy Stallard's review informed the readership that Jack Simpson's long range rods will cast in excess of 30 yards! Obviously it should have read 300 yards.

Misinformation of the Year

Leading qualifier is a certain Drennan Award winning capture which had two extra thirties added to the actual total, and had two sessions rolled into one for added credibility. Probably a misunderstanding over the phone lines. Alternatively the landing of a catfish by Des Taylor which Des knew nothing about. Alternatively the landing of a thirty pound common in the North West which the captor later knew nothing about.

Hypocrite of the Year

All those south west carp men who have joined a three acre syndicate lake rumoured to contain an imported biggie. Like we've always said, when big carp are around principles fly out of the window.

Video Star of the Year Award

We'd love to give this to our Birch Grove duo of Paisley and Lilley, but there's a limit to how far we dare carry nepotism. Mary Paisley developed her own fan club among the Birch Grove viewers (but not with the Birch Grove anglers!) but gets the chop for the reason given above. Vic Bellars nearly got it for his stunning performance opposite the extraordinary Andy Nicholson, but we don't think "39 something" should be given that "Call it forty" bit – not in public, anyway. We almost gave this award to our hero Kev for starring in four videos and managing to come across as a really nice guy in the process. But the final vote goes to Lockie. Wait till you see him in the Bait video. The man's a star!

Video star Lockie.

Saga of the Year

The strange case of Darenth Paul, who carries all before him on an escalating tide of aggro and violence, and seems to move further and further up the Leisure Sport ladder in the process. You know what they say: it's not what you know, but who you know. Pity the Sidcup Assassin isn't still fishing Darenth...

Rig of the Year

Five ounce round leads. We're still trying to figure out how the Famous Five (approximately) managed to incorporate these leads into their floater fishing, which seemed to be their main method of catching this last year.

Man of the Year

Almost Roger Smith – again. He gets more and more impressive in his increasing scruffiness and postured eccentricity. His greatest exploit this last year was returning to England from Holland via Belgium. Having discovered the continent he now spends not only his summers there, but his weekends, too. But there's only one serious contender for this award, and that's the great Fred J. Taylor. In his seventy third year and he's still keeping up with lads a third of his age, doing more fishing than most, some drinking, can talk Alan Young under the table, and is one of the greatest ambassadors abroad that angling's ever had. The man is mega in every sense of the word.

Questionable Decision Award

NASA's decision to include the capture of Martin Guy's 48lb common on their big carp list. Now we're not trying to resurrect this vexatious issue, but sooner or later someone will have to answer this question. In the face of the revelations from Alan Smith and Robin Monday how come Martin has consistently declined to give a date of capture for the 48lb fish? Such a date might slip the memory of some people, but Martin? Look at the recent Coarse Angler articles regarding Martin's exceptional 9 weeks plus in 1990. Each capture had a visit number against it, and a date, and in most cases a time. The 48lb common the year before? Still no date, despite requests, both public and private, for this rather vital snippet of information. Are NASA's terms of reference of acceptance really that slipshod that they will accept an undated capture and give the fish precedence over Walker's great common in the big carp lists? We maintain that in the light of the doubts cast on the whereabouts of capture of Martin's fish it is up to him to give added substance to the capture if he wishes it to be accepted. We have never said Martin did not catch the fish in this country. We have maintained that as there is evidence to the contrary Martin must provide further evidence. It is not as though those casting doubts on the fish's authenticity are men of no substance. The esteem in which they are held in the specialist ranks is at least equal to the respect Martin's name carries.

Faux Pas of the Year Award

Lovable naughty Nev in Specialist Angler. Was it really very bright of a Daiwa consultant to state that a two hundred pound rod is a waste of time, when Daiwa was in the process of launching such a beast?

TEAM
DAIWA

Lovable Nev. Could make the Faux Pas Award his own with a bit more practise.

Madness of the Year Award

Have you looked at what's happening on the tackle front? Is it really any wonder that there is so much tackle thieving going on. Cop for this. It's now possible to pay up to £230 for a carp rod, and if it does the job the lads want it to do then they'll have three lying in the rests. 690 sovs. The rests? Two hundred quid's worth of stainless. 200 sovs. Three of the ultimate long range reels at £160 each. Another 480 sovs. Buzzers, £80 each. Another £240. Line, indicators, isotopes, rod mats, extension lead, buzzer box. Say £50. Any good all that? £1660 of gear sitting there trying to catch fish. And have you noticed most carp men's cars? Certainly not worth that much, a lot of them.

Conference of the Year

It depends on how you measure the success of a conference, doesn't it? Last year's NASA Conference wasn't too bright, but it was very nice socially. The BCSG/CAA Wembley affair was somewhat lacking in atmosphere, and the bar just wasn't open for long enough at the Carp Society's NEC do in November. Best of the bunch? The Carp Society Dunstable Conference in April. Terrific entertainment, terrific atmosphere, good bar hours. Leave it there, Society. There isn't a better venue in the world.

Farewell of the Year

Peter Mohan departed the carp scene after over twenty years of heavy involvement. Peter founded the BCSG (with Eric Hodson), and the CAA, and ran both organisations until early last year. He was responsible for the publication of the first carp magazines, organised the first carp conferences, and was involved in the publication of a number of carp books, including three of his own. Although he wasn't everyone's cup of tea his contribution to the carp world was considerable and his name will always be linked to carp fishing. Peter's health suffered over the last couple of year's of his BCSG/CAA involvement and we wish him better health in the future.

Matchman of the Year Award

Undoubtedly Tom Pickering for taking his second day World Championship blank like a man and not making excuses – and in the process paying a lovely, touching tribute to the great Kevin Ashurst. We presume that Tom now appreciates better than most that it isn't politic to renege on deals with the Almighty!

Write Off of the Year

Would you believe it, Selman wrote off yet another set of wheels during this last year?! Mind you, those who've been unfortunate enough to travel with the Warrington Whinger are amazed he ever completes a journey without writing something or someone off. Fair do's though, our Paul had a very good reason for the latest write off. As he himself disarmingly informed us, he was pissed at the time.

Amazing Capture Award

Did you see that article in Carp Fisher 18 about the amazing non-capture at Harefield? Angler Martin Clarke hooked a fish, then lost it. Next thing he sees a fish beached on the other bank 100 yards away, so he goes round with his landing net and scoops it up. The fish weighs 34lb. Martin claims it. Don't know about that. Sounds a bit like Marcel's French biggie, except that that fish hadn't even beached itself: it just got scooped out of the weedbed where it was quietly lying up, minding its own business.

Stalker of the Year Award

When you've got a bloke as mega as Des Taylor around you've got to give him an award for something, just to encourage him to keep on being around. We weren't sure about his talents as a stalker from his video of that ilk, but this more recent shot from Cuttle Mill suggests that Des does at least understand something of the rudiments of stalking, even if he actually catches the stalked fish with the rod stuck eighteen feet in the air and a boat moored two feet from the bait.

Des Taylor – Stalker of the Year. In this dramatic picture Des is seen stalking a cup of coffee in Clive Gibbins' swim.

Man of the Future

Paul Selman. At last we have a circuit angler who is aware of the need for political representation at all levels. (Looking for the sting in the tail? There isn't one; the future is a serious business.)

Rob Maylin Award

Awarded annually to Rob Maylin for being Rob Maylin. How can anyone as nice as Rob be banned from so many waters?

Bailiff of the Year Award

The Welsh Water bailiff who numbered the notable scalp of John Lilley among his successful prosecutions for the year. Eat your heart out Mr Roberts.

Bum Bailiff of Any Year Award

Actually the year in question wasn't last year, but we really do think we should point out what you are up against when you have the misfortune to have Severn Trent's Mr. Roberts as your local bailiff. A couple of years back he prosecuted Dave "Kosher" Glassman for fishing at twenty minutes to midnight on June 15th. The violation of Dave's privacy cost him over a hundred smackers. Mr. Roberts and his oppo tried to do Dave's mate further down the bank. His end tackle was hooked in the butt ring, but his *bombs were wet...* (Sounds like sufficient evidence to us, but the bailiffs let our man off with a severe warning as to his future conduct). Are these people real?

Wedding of the Year

NUTRABAITS
Price List
Order Form

Big Bill Bait Maker and Skid discuss business at Bill's wedding.

Confusion of the Year Award

For reasons that totally escape us we managed to get confused between Essex Alan and Essex John during 1990. The pictures below should clear the confusion.

Essex John, on a sponsored ride round Alderney.

Essex Alan. We daren't ask what he's doing.

The retreating figure is Knacker – who is retreating rapidly because he's just had a crab stuffed down his trousers! (Like you would).

Sadly, Doog was cut off in his prime as a Boyers' law enforcer. Here he's seen checking out the 20 yard rule on an overgrown part of the lake.

Solar Power

'Supreme' strength stainless set-up with Lite-Flo indicators.

Savay Seed Mixes and MixMaster additives.

Use 'Solar' products, and the only thing that'll be bending will be your rods! And it's happening more often than some anglers have been used to since switching to the 'Savay seed mixes' and more recently, combining them with the MixMaster additives, the successes have been phenomenal.

As the MixMasters have only been on general release since Christmas, I wouldn't like to guess how many waters will be 'turned over' on them in the coming months.

The MixMasters.

White Chocolate. Smells just like the Milky Bar Kid's fingers! *100ml £6.50. 500ml £25.00.*

Japanese Squid/Octopus Koi Rearer. As the name suggests, is used in the feeding of Koi carp. *100ml £8.90. 500ml £34.00.*

Golden Plum. With a hint of almond/marzipan about it. A busy water winner. *100ml £4.50. 500ml £15.00.*

Esterblend 12. Twelve fruit esters which do not boil out like alcohol based flavours. *100ml £4.90. 500ml £17.00.*

Stimulin Amino Compound. 18 amino acids with vitamins and minerals. *100ml £4.90. 500ml £17.00.*

Stimulin Amino Compound with Garlic. As above but with a mild garlic attractor. *100ml £4.90. 500ml £17.00.*

Liquid Candy Sweetener. Tastes like childrens sweet cigarettes to give the bait a completely different taste to anything currently being used. *100ml £8.90. 500ml £34.00.*

Powdered Candy Sweetener Enhancer. As liquid but with added flavour enhancers. *4oz £4.50. 1lb £15.00.*

Powdered White Chocolate. Same as liquid but, again with added enhancers. *4oz £4.90. 1lb £20.00.*

Fresh Fruit Powder Enhancer. Sharpens up the taste and smell of any fruity bait. *4oz £4.00. 1lb £13.00.*

N.B. All MixMasters carry mixing instructions including maximum and minimum d[illegible] optimum results.

What's New?

Lite-Flo indicators made from I.L.A. (intensified light absorbing) acrylic, and visible from 6 inches to 200 yards away! Now come in 3 sizes: 15mm Dia. (7 grams), 20mm Dia. (15 grams) and 25mm Dia. (24 grams) and in 4 colours – Blue, Green, Yellow and Red. All at £5.95 each.

There are three additions to the 'Supreme' stainless range, all of which are 'Solar' firsts.

Stainless Coin-slotted Opto Bolts and Nut Set. Domed Suregrip screw with a coin slot in the head, for extra tightening onto the fork. Coin also supplied! *£2.95 each.*

Stainless 'Lockey' Back Rests. U-shaped butt rest formed in stainless steel with a layer of foam to cushion and grip the rod. They can also be adjusted to clamp the rod in position when fishing snaggy swims. Complete with a stainless locking ring and rubber 'O' ring for alignment onto buzzer bar. The smartest back rest ever produced. *£3.95 each.*

Adjustable Bankstick Stabilizer. An updated version of our original design with an adjustable depth spike for extra grip in soft ground. *£6.95 each.*

'Polo' Sports Shirts. 3 button and collar type shirts with hand embroidered Solar logo. In 3 colours, Black, Royal Blue and Green. Large and Extra Large. *£9.95 each.*

All products available from 'Solar' stockists. Please contact us should you have any difficulty obtaining any items.

A new brochure is available with information on our full range of stainless products, baits, additives and articles. No charge, but please send a large S.A.E. Good luck.

Martin Locke

Savay Seed Mixes:	1 Kilo	3 Kilo's
Yellow	£6.95	£17.95
Red	£7.45	£18.95
Spice	£6.95	£17.95
Neptune	£6.45	£15.95
Quench	£6.95	£17.95
P&P	£2.50	£3.40

P&P on MixMasters 50p per 100ml/4oz. Three or more post free, or free when ordering with Savay Seed Mix. Postage on tackle items or shirts 50p any number of items. All orders sent back to you by return of post. Discounts on bulk orders, please contact us.

SOLAR TACKLE

35 Sutherland Road, Belvedere, Kent DA17 6JR. Tel: 081-311 3354.

WILLOW PARK

STOP
ALL PERSONS MUST
REPORT TO RECEPTION
BEFORE PASSING THIS POINT

My affection for Willow Park goes back to 1986 when I first fished the water as a guest of my friend, Andy Little.

I don't mind admitting that, at that time, I'd had a grueller of a winter on my local lake Drax and that fifteen weekend sessions produced only three chances and one fish! Cruel, cruel winter that it was, one had the audacity to cut me off on the ice. Thank you Lord!

However, things looked up, winter wise, at Willow with us averaging around a dozen chances a session (December-March). All nice, growing fish as well, mostly low doubles but some uppers and odd twenties. Since '86 I've fished the water sporadically – usually winter time and, as Tim would say, a good ego booster after horrific winters on Tilery, Drax, Three Lakes etc.

Just as Andy was kind enough to take me to the water, I've tried to 'follow on' by taking friends to the water to give them a taste of Willow Park action. The story, with pictures, that follows (à la Angler's Mail action replay sequence), is a typical session which we've enjoyed this winter on the water. This time my partner was BSCG founder and Profumo target, Eric Hodson, alias 'Uncle Backstop'.

Ladies and gentlemen, boys and girls, it's time for Willow Action.

Willow Park Fisheries is situated near Farnborough, Hants. and is owned by my good friend, John Raison. I would guess that, at a rough estimate, it's around 220 miles or three hours plus travelling distance away. Most of my sessions so far have been Friday to Sunday and in order to make sure we are at the fishery at first light, it means leaving home (or Sheffield) at 2.00 a.m. Sleep? Who needs it?

WINTER ACTION

A 1.30 a.m. rise saw me at Eric's by 2.00 a.m. and by 2.30 a.m. we were on the M1 and motoring. Not wishing to pay the extortionate service station prices, we had coffee and sandwiches in the car. Yorkshire thinking that boys! Unfortunately, a combination of too much coffee, a loaded car and inadequate suspension in the Golf had me dying for a pee with 15 miles to go. Caught between the need to relieve myself and the urge to get to the water, it was only willpower, gritting my teeth and a milk bottle (only joking) that got me there without a change of trousers.

5.30 a.m. we were at the front gates and, courtesy of John Raison, I have a gate key to let myself in. Fishing is normally 7.00 a.m.-7.00 p.m., but you can get night fishing permission from John at his discretion. Lights off, past Bert's caravan and we trundle past the little lake, between the windsurfing boards and the Bungalow bank.

Willow Park is around 12 acres in size, triangular in shape, with two bays round the headland. We've chosen the southern bank (Bungalow bank) and a wind from the west is pushing towards the peninsula area. Only one other angler on the water (headland) – things look good.

When we first fished the water, the top tactic was double baits on a 12" Dacron trace, 2oz fixed bombs and soft, anti-tangling tubing. Each year has seen the fish wise up somewhat and I've varied my tactics as the months roll on. A lot of this stems from Andy's teaching – on more than one occasion he's scored heavily on a change of tactics.

My current rig is a 15" hooklength made from 8lb Kryston Silkworm. I had shied off this for quite a while, but a good talk with 'The Voice' (Dave Chilton) had convinced me of its virtues and I haven't looked back since. Hook is a size 10 Middlesex Angling Centre Bent Hook. These are absolutely incredible hooks and I can't recommend them enough. Ultra

Sizzling bacon sarnies – before the snow came.

Julian Cundiff

sharp, strong - they even outfish my trusty Drennan 10's!

I've been working on a new rig for quite some time now – I've called it the 'fall-back hooker'. Without giving too much away at this stage, it involves putting a small split ring through the hook's eye and tying your hooklength to that rig. Tied correctly, it is a hell of a hooker and easily outscores a conventional bent hook set up. The hair is made from floss and I've dropped the use of tubing totally. We used stringers to avoid tangles and a 3oz bomb and bead completed the set up.

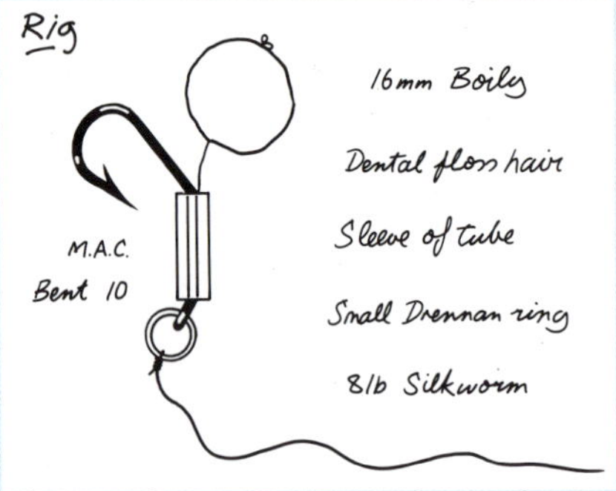
Rig
16mm Boily
Dental floss hair
Sleeve of tube
M.A.C.
Bent 10
Small Drennan ring
8lb Silkworm

I've had some really hectic sessions on the lake (20+ takes a night) so I always come prepared. Around 20 traces ready tied up on rig bins, hair stops cut, PVA separated and everything at hand. Be prepared; cold hands don't tie up good knots; tiredness leads to inefficiency and lost fish.

Having dabbled with ready mades on the lake for quite some time, I've now come up with a mix that I'm 100% happy with. Hell, it even outfished Richworth Tropicanos and Crafty Catcher Peanut Pros. No specific recipes lads, but it does include a base mix of Nutrabaits Enervite Gold, two low level flavours, an essential oil, colouring and powder sweetener. Together they've made a stunning combination.

Dave Chilton of Kryston fame had been good enough to provide Eric with some 'Ambio' and we were going to try it in the bait. It's received some incredible praise in the Press so we thought we'd give it a try. Boilies are normally banned at the venue, but John has lifted the ban between November and March to those who wish to day fish. Providing people behave sensibly, this will continue, however, I must state that this is only until late February and all fishing is at John's discretion.

My five trips, from November onwards, to the water have produced 84 carp, with my best session producing 27, most of which were doubles. The carp are well on the bait and, as the picture shows, they just can't get enough of it.

I'd only been chucked out an hour or two and I was away on my left

Can't get enough of it...

hand rod. However, it felt dodgy from the outset and after only a few seconds it was off. Blast – that happened the previous twice as well. First fish of each session lost – not good. Rebait, restringer and out it went to the 90 yard mark.

I wouldn't like to guess fish stocks at the water but it must be a hell of a lot. Fully scaled, perfect linears, commons, mirrors and odd leathers. All are in beautiful condition and scrap every inch to the bank. Best fish must be upper 20's and you've plenty of good back up fish as well.

12 noon and a single bleep had me over to the rods in a flash. Rod up and a protracted scrap saw Uncle Eric net a good fish for me. Here we go again!

A lot of people have asked for advice on winter fishing and I'd have to list it as Waters-Location-Organisation. So many people turn up to winter fish with no idea about the venue. You must plan in advance. Comfort is vital if you are to keep at it when temperatures drop below zero. Plenty of hot food, drink, thermal suits, two sleeping bags, hand towels and ground sheet, TV (!!??). You name it, I've got it. Never mind all those who criticise the TV owners amongst us – most of them give up about October. Oh, and yes I do have a television licence (honest!).

The day only produced one more chance to me and it turned remarkably cold. Fresh baits out before dark, everything checked for the night and it was time for tea. The weather forecast was daunting in the extreme. Heavy snow, gales, sleet, wind, the lot. God, that is going to be nice.

We'd just had tea when a single bleep gave Eric his first indication. A drop of the weighted needle and he was away. Again, a protracted fight and Eric was holding a 13lb+ mirror for the cameras. An absolute beauty, lots of scales and in pristine condition.

Runs had been fairly predictable over the past few weeks and I would expect action at noon, 4.00 p.m., 6.00 p.m., midnight and then 7.00 a.m. By 9.00 p.m. I'm up to five fish and then I suddenly hit what was obviously a better fish. This one was all over the place and we had to reel in the other rod to avoid a horrendous after dark tangle. Yes sir, a real beauty, 19.05 and in superb condition. Very pale, some lovely scales and it steamed in the cold night air. That was my best fish so far and as the boys say, "You're going to be famous". No doubt it will be one of 1991's 20's.

It had gone really cold now and it didn't look good at all. The wind shifted to over our backs but air temperatures were well down. Unhooking mats are compulsory on the fishery and mine had iced over already. Indeed, when Eric went to pick the net up, which was laid over the unhooking mat, they both came up together. Now that is the ultimate net-sling-mat combo!

Summer fishing at the venue produced absolute screamers; when we entered the era of 'cold weather carping' the situation changed almost totally. Half inch pulls, some drop backs and line tightens became the order of the day and I varied my tactics accordingly. The left hand rod was on a tight line to the lead with a heavy bobbin clipped 1" from the tip of the needle. The second rod was a light bobbin at the bottom of the needle; rod three - well, we'd better not discuss that one, had we?

My indicators are Delkims coupled with Nashy's 12 wheel paddles and Stevie Neville needles and bobbins. Each recast I clean the needle with a duster and check it for free running. Zenon Bojko wrote a brilliant article in Kevin's tackle annual on little tips like that – if you haven't got a copy, pick one up today.

12.15 a.m. and the left hand rod was away again – this time it was a stunning common of around 15lb or so. Not a scale out of place and hooked perfectly in the bottom lip. That was fish seven in sub-zero temperatures. That was a right result.

From around midnight onwards we had sleet and hailstones. Thankfully the indicators remained static and I had a good few hours' sleep. 7.00 a.m. and I was away in the land of nod when I thought I heard a voice in the background. Eric was away again and after paddling around in the mud I netted a pristine 13lb common for him. A totally mint condition carp and it didn't look as if it had seen a hook before. As if to celebrate the capture, a rainbow appeared above us to add colour to an otherwise bleak morning.

John Raison came down to see us with Tosh and Bert, the bailiffs. Fully 'tooled-up' the boys look the business and I wouldn't like to bend the rules on John's water! Hell, he's even promised to bring his daughter down to see me - what a nice chap!

Bert's been bailiffing the lakes for some years now and is due to retire this spring. A true gentleman in every sense of the word, nothing is too much trouble for him and we'll all miss him.

12 noon Saturday and it was very bleak all around us. Heavy snow had fallen all around the country and we were going to get it next. Birmingham was cut off, the M1 was closed and boy were we in the proverbial brown stuff. I thought TV was supposed to cheer you up, not depress you!

2.00 p.m. and a slow, stuttery run brought me to my senses. A quick slip on of the trainers and I was over to the rods. A funny bite this one, and no wonder. I eventually land the carp, which hadn't picked my hook up in its mouth at all. In its mouth is

I've got to drive home in this…

a rig attached to tubing and tied to the back of the tubing is a second rig (helicopter). Some misguided fool has been using a 2 hook rig and it's fouled my line so I can't count it. I carefully took one hook out of its mouth, one from its flank and untangle the whole mess. Enquiries revealed the owner of this rig – and he was also using four times the recommended flavour level in his bait. I won't name him but he knows and I hope he has learnt from this. High flavour levels (of solvents) are not necessary; they cause pain and discomfort to carp. When in doubt, leave it out please!!

It was starting to snow quite heavily now and, as usual, it was directly into my open bivvy door. Both Eric and I have Nashy 50" canvas bivvies, which are the only bivvies to use in winter. That's not blatant plugging of Kevin's gear (we both bought ours) it's just common sense. Sure, they may be heavier, but they are 100% waterproof, keep the wind out (or in, in my case!) and are very, very warm. Three years on and mine is still going strong – and I'm not exactly renowned for looking after my tackle. I've coupled mine with four storm rods, extra peg holes (thanks Julie), and a ground sheet. Unless you are 100% warm and well fed in winter you will not fish effectively. Spare clothes, hand towels (no rude thoughts please) and a lamp are essential.

Despite the bleak conditions I recast mine and Eric's rods, coupling all with three bait stringers. Contrary to popular thought, I've started to use the PVA doubled in winter; this makes sure the freebies stay attached to the hook when the carp tries a pick-up. They all go in together, the trace tightens up and due to its design, my 'fall back' rig hooks the carp.

It was absolutely horrendous out there now (6.00 p.m.). A combination of snow, sleet and gusting wind was battering the bivvy. Extension boxes are absolutely essential in this weather and a single bleep above my head from the box told me we were away again. On with the Gortex, slip on the boots and out into the storm. Christ, this was only a small one and it was coming in like a lamb. Bloody hell, it was a tench. Surely they don't feed in this weather? Yes they do! Do you know why tench have red eyes? It's because they are up all night, eating your boilies and tangling your hooklinks.

Rod rebaited (eventually) and it was back to bed once again. 10 minutes later I was away. (If that's a tench there's going to be trouble). It wasn't and a nice mirror was soon in the net. Despite yelling at Eric, he's either in the land of nod or more sensible. This one was worth a photo but I couldn't get the old bugger out of bed could I? I gave him the camera and allowed him to take the pics from inside his bivvy. These Minoltas (5000 i's) are superb cameras and,

Bleak house.

NO
FISHING

Eat your heart out, Rob Maylin!

providing you can press a button, you can't go wrong. Coupled with Fuji 100 slide film, results are consistently good.

Not surprisingly, the night was uneventful and a good night for kipping. 'Blind Date', 'Search for Spock' – good night and thank you.

7.00 a.m. and we were away again. Pushing back the flap an Arctic landscape appeared before me. I would guess we had had six inches of snow or more and still the Willow carp were having it. Bloody hell, that was cold - the reel was covered in snow, and so too were my hands.

"Not again" shouts Eric.

"Fraid so, Uncle Backstop – I can catch 'em".

This one kited all over the place and didn't want to come to Daddy. Our landing nets were frozen solid but a quick dip through the lake's ice softened them up a bit. Net down, rod up and fish in. Yes!!

We carried the carp to a suitable place and with blue hands I held her aloft. Nice – but not too many in this weather please. 90% of all takes have been slight tightens of the line – I wish I'd brought my Fox Swingers now. They are the ultimate twitch indicator, believe me.

Well, it had stopped snowing now so we thought we'd better pack up our tackle while we could. Bert's been down to see us and can't believe apprentice No. 1 has scored so well again. Purely luck I say. I had nine carp, one foul hooked, one tench and lost two in absolutely horrendous conditions. An excellent fishery indeed.

For many, the numbers of carp I have quoted make the fishery sound oh so easy. However, not so. It is quite possible to blank at the lake at this time of year if you follow bog standard carping techniques. Frequent fine tuning of my rigs (from trace lengths to indicator systems), an excellent bait, made better with Ambio, and a good knowledge of the lake have all contributed to the success rate.

No doubt many of you will wish to give the lake a try in the near future. All fishing is at John Raison's discretion and under his rules. Please ring before you turn up. No boilies after March. Unhooking mats are compulsory and night fishing only with permission.

To John Raison, Bert, Tosh and all the lads down there, thanks for some great times. See you soon.

P.S. Don't forget your daughter!

Chris

"CARPBUSTER BAITS"

Chris Haswell

'THE MENTAL SQUAD'

Nobby

Dave

Larry

Gary

Dougie

To give you a brief introduction to my range of baits and flavours I'd first like to say that in these times when there are so many different types of baits going in our lakes, I firmly believe that there are three main factors that go towards making a successful bait and they are: attractability, palatability, and above all digestibility and it is with this in mind that I have formulated three base mixes.

"THE MELLOW MIX" is a great all round mix, it rolls beautifully and is highly attractive to carp, add any of my flavours and you have a mix that will keep on working.

"THE FISH EXTRACT" is again one that rolls well and is also highly attractive to carp, I formulated this mix as an alternative to fish meals; it doesn't need any flavours or attractors but if you want to make it a bit different I recommend 5ml of our salmon oil to the pound mix.

The **"FACTOR SEVEN"** mix is without doubt the best mix I have used in recent years, I knew it would catch as soon as I let it out, but I was over the moon with the results. In my first year this mix accounted for over 100 twenties, around 16 thirties and god knows how many doubles, ranging from vast open pits to silty pools. It doesn't matter what the conditions have been like – freezing cold to blazing hot – provided the fish are feeding, this mix will keep on catching. 'THE MENTAL SQUAD' Specimen Group have used this mix exclusively and their results speak for themselves. I have had phone calls from various parts of the country and all are asking for more bait, *(reading between the lines some people are QUIETLY having it off on this mix).*

FLAVOURS	*100 ml*	*250 ml*	*500 ml*	*1000 ml*	*Inclusion rates per lb*
SWEET FIG	☐	☐	☐	☐	*5ml*
MELLOW BERRY	☐	☐	☐	☐	*6ml*
NUTTY SLACK	☐	☐	☐	☐	*5ml*
YELLOW PERIL	☐	☐	☐	☐	*5ml*
CITRUS	☐	☐	☐	☐	*5ml*
RED DEVIL	☐	☐	☐	☐	*5ml*
OLD ORIGINAL	☐	☐	☐	☐	*5ml*
CARRIBEAN COKE	☐	☐	☐	☐	*5ml*
ACTIVE ENZYME	☐	☐	☐	☐	*5ml*
STONEFRUIT	☐	☐	☐	☐	*5ml*
OLD FAITHFUL	☐	☐	☐	☐	*5ml*
BLOODSEED	☐	☐	☐	☐	*5ml*
*CARPBUSTER SPECIAL**	☐	☐	☐	☐	*10ml*
*SALMON SPECIAL**	☐	☐	☐	☐	*5ml*
*MALT SPECIAL**	☐	☐	☐	☐	*5ml*
CARPAMINO		☐	☐		*10-50ml*
SUPER SWEETENER	☐	☐			*5ml*

POSTAGE & PACKING

BASE MIXES

Up to 4lb **£2.50**
Up to 25lb **£5.50**
Up to 12lb **£3.30**
Over 25lb .... **P.O.A.**

FLAVOURS

Up to 1000ml **£1.25**

PRICES

BASE MIXES *per 5lb*

MELLOW MIX **£10.00**
FACTOR SEVEN **£14.95**
FISH EXTRACT **£12.00**

SPECIAL PRICES ON ORDERS OVER 20lb

FLAVOURS

Per 100ml **£5.00**
Per 250ml **£8.50**
Per 500ml **£15.00**
Per 1000ml **£28.00**

SPECIALS*

Per 100ml **£8.00**
Per 250ml **£16.00**
Per 500ml **£24.00**
Per 1000ml **£37.00**

SWEETENER

100ml **£4.25**
250ml **£9.50**

CARPAMINO

250ml **£5.25**
500ml **£9.50**

COLOURS *per 50g*

SUN ORANGE **£3.25**
BERRY RED **£3.25**
NUT BROWN **£3.25**
CITRUS YELLOW **£3.25**

ENHANCERS – SPICE & MILK/FRUIT ENHANCERS

LIQUID ENHANCER per 250ml **£9.00**
SWEET ENHANCER per 4oz tub **£5.00**

NUTRITIONAL MIXING OIL

Per 250ml **£4.00**

TIGHT LINES – *Chris Haswell*

25 Fox Lane, Keston, Kent BR2 6AL Tel: 0689 861567

Proprietor: Chris Haswell – formerly of Buttcracker Baits

Night closing in on the New Swim at the Mangrove.

BIG FISH SUMMER – 2

I'll explain the title. One of my chapters in "Big Carp" was titled Big Fish Summer. It was titled thus because it reflected my efforts to catch a big fish during the summer of 1989. The terms of reference for a "big carp" was one over 25lb, a weight I failed to achieve. (In fact I didn't do very well at all.) Then, on the last evening of our Shropshire summer, Mary caught a lovely mirror of 25lb 12oz from Birch Grove. All my efforts had been concentrated on the Mangrove, which had been unkind to say the least. No, unkind isn't quite the right word: unrewarding and frustrating, but that was because I was struggling with a change of method and a new bait. I was hoping for better things in the summer of 1990, and even kept a carp fishing journal for the first time ever.

I carp fish for pleasure, and I'm doubly lucky in having access to at least two waters I enjoy fishing, The Mangrove and Birch. The Mangrove

Evening on Birch Grove.

Tim Paisley

is a big fish water containing a number of thirty plus fish, only two of which come out with any regularity – Trio (a mid thirty common) and Scaley, a beautiful mirror. I've fished it since 1983 and at the start of the 1990 season I still hadn't caught a 25lb plus fish from the water. Set against the results of John Lilley and Roy Stallard that statistic looks a bit sick, but up to 1989 I hadn't put much time in on the water since 1984, when a 25 plus was still an exceptional fish. My struggles in 1989 showed me that I was not in tune with the fish of the Mangrove and I knew I would have to spend a lot more time there to come to terms with its lovely fish. On the other hand the great joy of carp fishing to me is just being there, so while I started last season half committed to a more intensive Mangrove campaign, a growing love of Birch, and thoughts of Mary's great fish, were always likely to erode that commitment.

What follows is, of necessity, a very abbreviated version of the events on the Mangrove and Birch during last summer. We'll start on the morning of the 15th of June. The work parties are behind us: a fair few pounds of HNV bait have found their way to the bottom of Birch Grove: the guests have been invited to the Opening of Season party at Birch, which just happened to be a wedding reception, too, Mary and I having been married on June the 14th...

Morning of 15th June – Birch Grove

"4.00 a.m. Cold, misty and fish showing in numbers over the baited area. Exciting prospect for Fred J. and Mary but will the carp continue to feed in that area? Didn't see any big fish. Is it possible to create an artificial feeding area for some of the fish but by no means all of them? Birch is only 5-6 acres so pulling them onto a baited area shouldn't be that difficult.

Pottering during the morning. Mary getting ready for the feast, me for the fishing. All day to set up in, but I had a feeling of panic that it wouldn't all be ready in time. Weather holding for the party and fish really flaunting themselves in the good weather. No spawning signs. Surely they haven't spawned out?

Arrivals: Ken and Carole (Townley) early afternoon. Fletch later. Fred J. and John at tea time. Steve, Ann and caravan early afternoon. Steady stream from the Mangrove – and elsewhere – through the evening. A lot of eating and drinking till the gathering thinned from ten onwards. Alan Young and Gary down from Ellesmere. Tony Baskeyfield, Bob Tapken, John Lilley,

"Mary's weekend" at Birch. We forgave her: after all it was her honeymoon!

Sweepy (John Ankers), Joe Bertram, Eka Green and Clive Gibbins from the Mangrove. Bill, Elsa, Rob and Angela from the family.

Incredibly, finally, half peace descended on the lake at 11.00 p.m., Fred retired at 11.30 p.m.

Then we fished."

Later

"Tired, but stayed awake through excitement. Action on the logs at 2.30. Went round to find Fletch holding the landing net and Steve the rod so presumed Steve had caught: it was a lovely 15lb common – very young looking. In fact Fletch had caught it – from the stream mouth, on a three year old Richworth!

Dawn opening morning. The fish are very quiet. Fred's up and at it and his baits are in position out on the baited area. Fish were all over the

place out there yesterday, but not a swirl today. Fletch and Steve are on the Logs, Fred in the Compound Swim, Mary on the left hand side of the cattle drink also fishing the baited area, with me on the right fishing across; John is in First Down in the trees, Ken and Carole fishing The Planks.

Fred wants to know when we can reasonably have our first drink of the day: managed to persuade him that it would be best if we waited till about 11.00 a.m. till we "just had one". Next fish to Mary at 7.00 am (17.12 mirror), then she's away again ten minutes later and lands a 15.08 mirror. Both fish to baits she cast out in the dark with no real idea of where they had gone. We had spread the free offerings over a wide area to keep the fish on the move."

That was a weekend of socialising, and definitely Mary's weekend in terms of fish catching. Fred J. and Ken Townley have both written about the session in Carpworld so I'll not add much to their splendid efforts. Micky Sly rolled up on Saturday afternoon and saw two twenty plus fish caught within ten minutes of arriving! John Mason landed a mirror of 23.08, which Mary followed ten minutes later with a mirror of 21.08. The fact that Mary had another twenty on the Sunday was an eye opener. There had been three twenties out of the water the previous summer, which had been matched in the opening weekend this time out. I had been going to pull of Birch after the weekend to fish the Mangrove for the rest of the week, but the pleasant social atmosphere and the spate of big fish contributed to a growing resistance to change lakes.

To put it another way, after the excesses of Sunday I was too ill to move. Now I'm not one to mix drinking and fishing, but Fred J.'s presence on occasions like opening weekend inevitably leads to us having "just the one". So we had "just the one" around Sunday dinner time to drink Fred's health and to wish him and John a safe journey. Unfortunately Fred left about a million gallons of home brewed wine, and Micky Sly insisted it was rude not to drink it. So I'm blaming Fred J. and Micky Sly for me not fishing the Mangrove that week, which was no hardship whatever.

It was a lovely week, and I had eight good fish, including three twenties, the first two of which were a brace of 24.04 mirror and 22.02 common on the Tuesday night. Ken and Carole had a rewarding session on the Planks, and all of a sudden the honeymoon was over and it was back to reality. We had a nice result but the fishing had been a little harder than I'd expected considering it was the first week of the season and the water had been heavily prebaited.

I made a note about bait and presentation in the journal. I was using the silt rig (that I'd been struggling to come to terms with in the "Big Carp" chapter), mainly because of the improved presentation over silt, but also because I wanted to use Kryston Multistrand, so needed the added anti-tangle advantages of this set up. To make doubly sure of no tangles I was also using the Kryston No Tangle gel, which is a brilliant concept and works marvelously well. I avoided the bent hook arrangement and went for Jim Gibbinson's Line Aligner rig, which served as a very efficient hooking arrangement throughout the summer. Jim has described this set up in detail on a couple of occasions and I really can recommend it. The only comment I would add to Jim's is that we use soft tubing to align the line and it seems to work just as well as the stiff tubing Jim suggests, and is easier to set up.

For bait I was on my preferred milk/egg protein HNV, but I'd boosted two of the Addit levels in an attempt to improve early season HNV results. Attract I'd left at the normal level, but I'd doubled up on Taste and Digest. Early results on Birch were encouraging so I decided to give the same bait a trial on the Mangrove. I can't remember why but we used different smells for the different waters. The Birch smell was a lovely blend of garlic, grapefruit, spearmint and peppermint oils, a mixture we called Garlic Mint. Although you are aware that there is garlic in there the mix doesn't have the anti social overtones one usually connects with this very effective oil. I used a different oil mix on the Mangrove, one I'd been toying with the previous season but hadn't settled my mind on. This one's called Scarborough Fayre, which should tell you what the component oils are – parsley, sage, rosemary and thyme. Both oil blends we used in conjunction with very low levels of the Nutrabaits' Sweet Spice glycerol based flavour, which we were field testing.

Mangrove 6th/7th/8th of July

I'd been putting some bait into the Mangrove, although I haven't got a great deal of confidence prebaiting this strange, lovely water. That's probably mental conditioning from when the eels were so active, but they were netted out in number during the close season of 1990, which may have made prebaiting much more viable. I'd put ten to fifteen mixes in by the time I came to fish the water in early July.

"Dropped Mary at Birch Friday afternoon and went off to set up at the Mangrove. Went across to the swim I used to call Sunset (variously called The Reverend's Retreat, Joe's and Fallen Tree) and felt at peace with the water straight away. Put a mix of bait out, set up camp, then went back to Birch for tea and to make sure Mary was installed for the night. Eric, Brian and Pete fishing Birch, which is fishing slow, but still producing good fish.

Back to Mangrove about seven. Roy, John and Bob fishing. Back across to Sunset (the swim the front cover of Carp Season was shot from). The swim covers the bay in the south east corner of the water. A potent combination of nature and working parties has thinned the trees, giving much greater access to the holding area to the right of the swim. The fish seem to move into the bay during the day, so the swim tends to fish at different times to other swims on the lake. Most swims don't produce after an hour or two into daylight; Sunset tends to fish from eight to eleven in the morning, although these are observations based on previous seasons' results and I didn't really know what to expect - other than a lot of waiting.

Put another half mix out, balanced the baits and settled in for the waiting game. Dark about ten. Just drinking my third coffee of the evening at about half past when I was away to a popped up bait fished in the middle of the bay. All runs are special; Mangrove runs doubly so. I could hardly breathe for anxiety playing that fish, but it wasn't particularly naughty. It swung left into the open water, almost made it into the pads but changed its made when I tried to help it into them, then let itself be netted at the first time of asking. Mirror – 22lb. I sacked it and sat up into the early hours with a big grin on my face.

I put another mix in during the night once I was fairly sure I wasn't going to get further action till morning. I woke with the light and conditions felt terrific, with a strong, warmish south westerly pushing straight into the bay I was fishing. I felt hopeful, but it was an optimism tinged with a realistic recollection of numerous other Mangrove mornings when the stone cold certainty of action to come had been totally misfounded. This time the water was doubly good to me and the middle rod steamed off at seven thirty. This one made the pads, but the hookhold was good and it came out without too much fuss. Mirror, 21lb. Bob Tapken made a good job of taking the pictures and I went back to Birch for breakfast a somewhat contented man. Mary had blanked (she paid a heavy price for her incredible start and didn't have another Birch fish till early August – which didn't bother

The swim I used to call Sunset, variously called Reverend's Retreat, Joe's and Fallen Tree.

her one bit).

The next two nights were gale lashed, with the wind howling into my corner, but the temperature had dropped and conditions didn't feel as carpy as on the first night. I spend as much time as I can out of the bivvy, even during the night, just listening for sounds of fish, and over the next two nights most of the fish movement was round to my left, in the area of the New Swim. One of these sounds was an event, one of those occurrences that convince us of the presence of the odd monster in the Mangrove. The sound came borne on the wind, and it was the sound of a massive fish trying to jump out of the water and not quite making it. It was dark, and it was a sound of a moment, but it was a huge sound. It made such an impression on me that I almost moved swim there and then, but a moment's reflection reminded me that I was in that swim because I'd been influenced by the number of big fish sightings in the bay to my right. This monster could well be on its way to my baits!

If it was it didn't let me know. The three day session produced one other fish, a mirror of 14.00lb at 5.00 a.m. on the third morning. I left, determined to spend all of my Mangrove time fishing the swim I'd been in,or the New Swim a hundred and fifty yards to my left."

First night in and a brace of 20's! This is the last at 22lb...

Mangrove Second Session – 12/14th July

The sound of that fish got to me and I was back on the Thursday evening, well wound up for a session in the New Swim. This is a platform that was erected during the last close season, giving close range access to an area of the water previously unfished. The journal started the morning after arrival.

"Setting up took from eight o'clock to quarter to twelve last night. Erecting a bivvy silently on a wooden platform is a delicate slow motion operation and that's why it took so long. These Mangrove platforms look a bit Fred Carnoe's, but the mere's banks change each year, and the platforms have to be rebuilt to suit the changed topography. This one is new and requires some modernising to make it entirely suitable. We could do with some form of covering, but the ideal – Astroturf – is expensive and could only be used if the platforms were permanent."

First Day

"Nicked an extra night to make a four night session. Had to be in the New Swim after hearing that fish – and the choice looked right when I got there. Warm northerly pushing straight into the swim. Tony Baskeyfield the only angler on the water when I got here: he's in Stoney's. He'd taken three fish in one night, then had three blank nights, including a blank day and night in Lightning Tree. I'm not organised for the trip and I've brought just about everything into the swim with me. Last minute rushing round doesn't lead to good planning.

Woke at first light – and went back to sleep. Woke with a start from a dream filled sleep shortly after. The buzzers must have woken me this time; nothing had moved (no indicator movement), but the right hand rod tip was knocking. By the time I got to it it had stopped. Fished on until three, including a long coffee session with Tony who seemed a bit disillusioned with the fishing and his own company. Lost all the end tackle on one rod when I had a mid line pike bite off: this is a bad area for that.

Two more bits of action later when both hook baits were picked up within ten minutes of each other but no run developed. Pulled off about three to go to Birch to see Baz and the Seal family. Mary arrived late (having got lost en route – which is the equivalent of saying it gets light in the morning), but my delay in getting back to the Mangrove meant I saw young Ben Seal land a mirror of 21.04. Carrying some spawn but a big looking fish."

Second Day – Sunday 15th July

"Quarter to five and I've just made the first cup of coffee of the morning. It's cool with the sun coming over my right shoulder from the south east. I haven't heard any action anywhere on the lake but I'll be surprised if there hasn't been. This is a nice time of day in this swim. I would have thought that there should be night potential but this is the best time with hopes of a take up until nine or ten o'clock.

I'm sitting on the floor of the bivvy writing this. I'm close to the fish and when you are bivvied on a platform you have to do everything noiselessly. Fish were moving over the beds of bait last evening but there's little movement of any sort at the moment. A fish has just swirled in the pads close to the right hand bait but it didn't look carpy. I've got the usual nagging doubts about the presentation of the baits after eight hours in the water, but I'm becoming much less fussy about precise balance – especially over seeds – so I'll sit it out awhile until the first light

A good sequence of Baz playing and landing a single figure fish, then John caught a lovely 17.10 from the far corner swim. Good angling.

potential is exhausted.

For the minute I'll simply drink coffee and reflect how lucky I am to be savouring the familiar normality of just another Mangrove dawn. Pigeons, moorhens, coots, ducks, reed warblers, peace and some numbers of large carp currently pretending they don't live here.

Half five. I brought the margin bait in to check it – and it was still balanced. The longer boiling period seems to have worked out. Can't I be dumb at times?

There's a lovely peach coloured sky to the right where the sun is in the process of rising. I can't get a satisfactory shot of the occurrence from this swim, which probably won't stop me trying. No. I'll just sit it out with the coffees and the reed warblers and the waiting.

Compared to yesterday morning the lake's very slow to start moving. The cold night after the very hot day must have done that. The pike are active just off the pads but I've seen no movement I could be sure is from carp yet. Looked across to Reed Warblers and John was recasting. That almost certainly means he's had a fish.

Six thirty and Tony in Stoney's has just had a screaming run - and landed the fish after a frantic looking ten minute battle. I think it was snagged at some stage of the fight. Tony's waited over three days for that fish so he'll be a bit happier now. It looks as though some of the fish have moved down to the west end of the lake on the changing wind. John might not have had a fish. He keeps reeling in and recasting so perhaps he's having problems with coots.

The fish must have moved down the lake in numbers. Four anglers in this half with no action between them. Tony's fish weighed 29.04; a glorious chunk of a mirror. John's had five runs; landed two and lost three."

"Scorching hot day on Birch. No fish overnight but taking floater during the day. Lost one in the snag tree. Got a good photo sequence of Baz landing a single figure fish, then John caught a lovely 17.10 from the far corner swim. Good angling."

Sunday Morning

"The beauty of the dawns and the joy of the bird song are losing their impact as the total lack of action continues. Mary says I've no patience! I think the session is a one-off. This south-easter is an unusual

Tony Baskeyfield's fish weighed 29.04; a glorious chunk of a mirror.

one: the only swim it really helps is Reed Warblers – and that's where the action is. Difficult session to read. I'll just put it down as one of those things and keep working at it.

John really is on top of what he's doing in that swim but he's worked long and hard at it – and he's suffered a four day blank this season: spending time here is still an important part of the equation. It's difficult to be objective through the early morning mist of anticlimax and disappointment. A run now would startle me!

5.55 The rising sun has just hit Eka's luminous red socks. Joe is packing up and they've not taken any pictures, so we're suffering together.

6.45 Have so far had visits from a squirrel, a toad and a wren this morning. No carp. Fact is the carp are still coming from the spawning areas. In a season when there hasn't been a proper spawning the fish seem to take a long time to disperse.

7.20 John has had another fish. Joe had a run but I think he must have lost it. I've just had a couple of violent knocks on the left hand rod tip (one of the open water baits). Clouding up now after a very clear, sunny morning.

8.10 Another knock on the left hand rod.

8.15 Screaming run for Joe, but he lost the fish."

"I was going to fish Sunday night but decided against. Too much to do with Carpworld to complete and the Hungary trip to prepare for. In addition the session didn't feel quite right.

Elliott (Symak) and party arrived at Birch while Baz was still there. John and I had done some work on the snag to the right of First Down. John home. Us home. The Elliott team set up ready to tear the lake apart! I don't think that will happen to the water again for a while."

The next session didn't feel right, either, mainly because the water was busy and I couldn't get anywhere near fish. I fished Friday and Saturday nights.

Sunday 5th August

"Woke up well pissed off with carp fishing. My confidence is plummeting good style here. I think I'll get off onto Rod's water for a couple of sessions just for the change – or start fishing Bottom of the Field or Royal Box just for more enjoyment.

Got up eventually and changed / checked out the hook baits. I'm not on top of what I'm doing and last week was just too hot to sort it all out. I'm fishing the Swamp (the swim of that name which was the Double Swim in Carp Season) and I don't think I've ever caught a fish from here. This weekend doesn't look like changing that statistic. Not big fish conditions, I guess. There have been fish in front of me over the baits. They were there last evening but this morning is wild and cool.

Is that the back of the heat wave? Don't know whether to fish tonight or not."

"Decided to have a relaxing night and day at Birch, just fishing with Mary. Very keen to get some impression of the effectiveness of the bait. Set up at Birch. Maurice and company on the road for two; Alan Young by four.

Mary fishing the stream mouth and the back corner. She had a run almost straight away after casting out. Two more runs during the afternoon, but all three fish lost. The fish seem to be concentrated down the far end so three runs in an afternoon and evening was a good result. Losses down to knot giving under heavy pressure; line ditto; hook pulling from fish which made a snag.

No action during the night."

Monday 6th August

"What a lovely relaxed day's fishing. Kept switching the position of the baits to try and find action but everything quiet. Fish still showing no interest in baits out in the main lake: what action there is is still only from the margins.

Spent the afternoon stalking. Watched Mary hook and play a fish while I was at the far end of the lake. Got round in time to net the fish for her but she could have managed it on her own, I think. Run from the stream mouth at about 3.15 p.m.. Mirror of 20.04 on the garlic mint HNV. Looked like a fish both Carole and I had caught from the Planks early in the season.

NUTRABAITS

She could have landed it on her own, I think. Mary with the mirror of 20.04.

Fished on till 8.00 p.m. Somehow knew I was going to get action and it came at about 6.30 p.m. Lovely common of 20.10. A lovely, golden, big framed fish with plenty of scope for growth.

Packed up to leave at 8.00pm. Nice day's fishing."

Nice day's fishng rounded off by a golden common of 20.10.

Mangrove, 6th September

"Writing this at 1.00 am in the middle of a gale lashed night on the Mangrove. The wind is ferocious and I'm fully exposed to it on the platform of the New Swim on the tree line of the south bank. I got down just after six and just managed to get set up in the daylight. The wind was strongish then but I managed to get the bivvy up and "home" sorted out. I was asleep by ten but the rising wind woke me at eleven and I've been sitting up drinking coffee since, cringing in the face of the tearing wind and hoping the the bivvy will hold out. The battering it's getting is frightening but it's well battened down.

The baiting situation isn't really satisfactory but the stringers of chopped baits are out amongst a scattering of boilies. The wind is too strong and too cool to be encouraging fish-wise, but on the other hand the conditions are so extreme that one take from a biggie may be on the cards. Seven years on and I think this is the first time I've fished the Mangrove in September. This would be exciting if it wasn't so worrying, but the wind must start to abate some time. Just a warm, moderate wind would be a result. I should catch fish from this session if conditions will just be on my side. Light out and ride the storm. 1.00 am onwards. Big fish time in my mind for the next few hours. Am I due a big fish from here or what? (That's a bit over the top but it's that sort of night folks!)

8.40 am The storm eased a bit and I managed some sleep. Still wild but not as frightening. Some signs of fish moving fifty yards out across to my right so I've cast a stringer out there. Not too far from the baited area. I do feel I'm in the right place, which is reassuring. Not expecting any action now but it's not beyond the realms of possibility. There's a big flock of seagulls on the water, which is rare.

9.30am. Mirror 21.04.

A wind-blown 25.14. Happy with that.

10.30 am Exhilarating now. Thank you Mangrove. Two twenties in half an hour – both mirrors, both coming to the rod I switched from the left to the right. 9.30 am; mirror 21.04. 10.00 am; mirror 25.14. Joy, joy. Wind very strong again now with some fine rain in the air. Trying to make a coffee but the carp keep interrupting.

11.30 am Mirror 17.10.

Struggled to take the pictures by tripod and remote control, using the motor wind for the first time. Can only hope."

Monday, 10th September 1990

Monday morning on the Mangrove now. Clear, bitterly cold night again with no action. Slept from half nine to half six. First coffee has just gone down. Thick mist, which is frustrating because there are fish moving and I can't see where. Clive and Eric are on the water, Clive in Stoney's and Eric in Sunset. I'm fishing till dinner time (mid dayish). Woke up with the usual end of session dread of going back into the world. Mist is starting to clear and I'm going to have another coffee. Traffic in the distance, Canadas sounding off, a bit of small fish movement starting up. This is life – and wife Mary would agree with that!

Noon Monday About to start packing up. No action to the rods. A fish has shown 60-70 yards out on the line of the edge of the clump of big trees. Reeled in a rod, stringered and put it out there – or thereabouts. The rods have got another hour while I stow the gear. I can recall just two last minute fish in all the sessions I've ever fished so I'm hoping rather hopeful.

Always finishing a session feels like the end of the world. What a lovely result though!"

The fishing wasn't over, but the summer was – and I'd finally got my Mangrove twenty five plus. Those three fish were my last from the Mangrove during the summer and autumn but there are a couple of further entries in the journal which are worth recording here. I was back in Sunset for a stormy three night session ending on Tuesday the 25th of September.

Saturday, 22nd September

"Half seven and almost dark. I'm writing this by torchlight. The swallows are still here – which surprises me a bit. The martins seem to have gone. 'B.B.' died last week and I thought of him as I watched the swallows and the gathering autumn this afternoon."

Monday morning, 4.00 am

"Good sleep, if a bit fitful. I was lying half asleep just now when there was a monumental "swirl" – a half crash, half swirl – down the margins to my right, in the area of the right hand baits. I can't describe how huge that fish sounded. That's twice this season I've heard the sound of a massive fish. Was it coincidence that it was in the area of the baits? I was lovely and warm and have a few more hours of sleep in me but I'd better be alert for this monster.

Conditions are superb. The sky's clear now but there's been heavy rain on and off. I'm quite happy with the baiting situation. Kettle's on but daylight's two and a half hours away. There's a limit to how many of these long dark nights I can put up with."

In terms of fishing the Mangrove I put up with just one more – the next night. The summer had gone and although we can now fish the season through on the water it is a place I associate with summer, greenery, short nights and reed warblers going about their family business. And having mentioned 'B.B.' and my thoughts of him during that last session I will lay the summer to rest by quoting from his "Confessions" chapter "The Last Day of the Season":

"My rods are laid up in their cases, my tackle put away, the summer has gone. But summer days will come again, and yet again, and if I am spared I will be there once more, beside the pools I know and love, listening to the cooing of wood pigeons as yet unborn, smelling the wild sweet water as it smokes in the summer dawn. Being an habitual carp fisher I am content to wait. After all, waiting is part of the game, I am well used to it."

Rest in peace.

FACT FILE...

Set-up: Silt rig. I struggled to come to terms with the set-up the previous summer and it cost me fish. Alan Tomkins suggests that the line damage I was suffering could have been caused by mussels clamping on the line – and he could be right.

Hook length: I used Kryston Multistrand hooklengths for almost all my fishing. It's very tough for its suppleness and the new No-Tangle Gel makes tangles a thing of the past.

Hooking: I used Jim Gibbinson's Line Aligner Rig (Carpworld 9) and pulled out of one fish all season, that was a Cuttle Mill biggie that picked up the second line and partly opened the hook. Thanks Jim.

ORGANISATIONS

OF INTEREST TO CARP ANGLERS

NATIONAL ASSOCIATION OF SPECIALIST ANGLERS

THE NATIONAL ASSOCIATION OF SPECIALIST ANGLERS – Actually started life, in 1965, as the National Association of Specialist Groups (N.A.S.G.) and has had a somewhat chequered history. In 1980/81 the organisation changed its name to reflect its intention to represent the individual to a greater extent. At the same time it improved its organisational abilities and its image. Aimed at anglers who have an interest in big fish it has catered well for the carp angler, even if it appears to be going through a bit of a sticky patch at the moment. It issues two colour magazines a year (Specialist Angler), various bulletins and holds a two day conference each year as well as a number of regional meetings. This year is the Group's Silver Jubilee and a celebratory conference was held at Loughborough.

SUBSCRIPTIONS

Membership is open to all at the following prices:
Adults – £12.00 (£1 joining fee)
OAP/Junior – £6.00

Specialist Angler
The Magazine of the National Association of Specialist Anglers
ISSUE NUMBER 16 - AUTUMN 1990 — £3.
Top names writing in this special issue include:
GRAHAM MARSDEN
PHIL SMITH
MARTIN GAY
NEVILLE FICKLING
GEORGE SHARMAN
ARCHIE BRADDOCK
PETER STONE
SILVER JUBILEE EDITION 1965 1990

NASA OFFICIALS

PRESIDENT
Ken Sutton, 19 Lilley Street, Long Bennington, Newark, Notts.

LIFE MEMBERS
Eric Hodson, 45 Long Croft Road, Dronfield Woodhouse, Sheffield
– Des Taylor, 5 Delemere Road, Meadow Rise, Worc.
– Bruno Broughton, 27 Ashworth Avenue, Ruddington, Notts.

HONORARY VICE-PRESIDENT
Fred J. Taylor

CHAIRMAN
Phil Smith, 155 Nunts Lane, Coventry

GENERAL SECRETARY
Brian Crawford, 6 Holmer Lane, Stirchley, Telford, Shropshire.

EDITOR
Gordon Chell, 11 Yew Tree Avenue, North Anston, Sheffield.

MEMBERSHIP
Kathy Fickling, Kilgarth, 27 Lodge Lane, Upton, Gainsborough.

POLITICS
Keith Barker, 89 Winsor Rd, Carlton-in-Lindrick, Worksop, Notts.

PUBLICATIONS
Ken Bundred, 9 Ruskin Avenue, Syston, Leics.

PRODUCTS
Dave Moore, 118 Silverdale Road, Ecclesall, Sheffield.

JUNIORS
Geoff Latham, 26 North Road, Chadwell Heath, Romford, Essex

CONSULTATIVE
Andy Dalby, 2 Mowbray Crescent, Seacroft, Leeds.

CONFERENCE
Geoff Parkinson, 30 Chequers Avenue, Lancaster, Lancs.
– Dave Lumb, 12 Wilson Close, Tarleton, Preston, Lancs.

PUBLICITY
Kevin Stephenson

BRITISH CARP STUDY GROUP

THE BRITISH CARP STUDY GROUP – The B.C.S.G. was founded in June 1969 by Eric Hodson, of Sheffield, and Peter Mohan, of Bristol.

From its initial 24 founder members there have been up to 250 members although, in latter years, it has been in the doldrums. With the retirement of Peter Mohan new officers are attempting to give it a new lease of life. Unlike the other two carp Groups, the B.C.S.G. has a somewhat elitist attitude to membership. Prospective members must have had ten years experience and a personal recommendation by an existing member is advantageous. Many applicants are rejected, however, once accepted membership is for life.

Application details are available from: Jim Hindle, 21 Palace Street, Bolton, Lancs. BO1 2DR

The B.C.S.G. produce their own magazine (Carp), and several annuals have appeared over the years. It has its own conference and meetings.

B.C.S.G. OFFICIALS

EDITOR
Alec Welland, 66 Waterford Park, Radstock, Bath.

CHAIRMAN
Peter Frost

SECRETARY
Jim Hindle, 21 Palace Street, Bolton, Lancs.

ASSISTANT SECRETARY
Kevin Maddocks, Withy Pool, Henlow Camp, Beds.

GRAPHICS
Len Gurd, Linear House, 2 Northcroft, Stenley Lodge, Milton Keynes.

CARP ANGLERS ASSOCIATION

THE CARP ANGLERS ASSOCIATION (C.A.A.) – Formed in March 1975, although the idea was first broached in 1974. Its inaugural meeting took place at Billing Aquadrome and the organisation has had up to 5000 members. Since the retirement of founder Peter Mohan in 1990 it has come under new leadership, and has undergone a major revamping of its aims and officials. The group publishes 2 colour magazines a year (The Carp Catcher), 4 newsletters (Margins), holds a large conference in May every year and oversees many regional meetings. Membership is open to all at the following rates:

SUBSCRIPTIONS

Adults – £11.00 per year
Juniors – £6.00 per year
Disabled – £5.00 per year

OFFICIALS

CHAIRMAN – Kevin Maddocks, Withy Pool, Henlow Camp, Beds. SG16 6EA
SECRETARY – John Gaze, 18 Downsview Road, Swindon, Wilts. SN3 1NT
PUBLICITY – Paul Nichols, 21 Sutton Court, Sutton Court Road, Chiswick, London
ADVERTISING – Sue Gaze, 18 Downsview Road, Swindon, Wilts. SN3 1NT
MAGAZINES/BOOKS – Dave Chilton, 7 Barnfield Drive, West Houghton, Bolton, Lancs.
EUROPEAN CO-ORDINATOR – Paul Van Den Beld, Bartokwegg 44, 1323 TB, Almere-Stad, Netherlands
BRANCH SEC. CO-ORDINATOR – Peter Sturges, 39 Lawson St., Kettering, Nothants.
EDITOR – Alec Welland, 66 Waterford Park, Radstock, Bath
JUNIOR ORGANISER – Clive Williams, 16 Owl Beech Place, Horsham, W.Sussex
CONFERENCE – Bryan Jarrett, Hinders, 169 Ermin St., Stratton St., Margaret, Swindon
TREASURER – Alan Parberry, 38 Kings Ave., Higham Ferrers, Northants.

REGIONAL ORGANISERS

AUSTRALIA – J.P.Thomas, 7 Carramar St., Mornington 3931, Victoria, Australia
AUSTRIA – Kurt Grabmeyer, Angelsportgerate, Handelsgesellschaft m.b.H., Rauscherstrasse 7, 1200 Vienna, Austria
BELGIUM – Stefan Michiels, Duivenstraat 59, 2580 Mechelen, Belgium
BIRMINGHAM – vacant
BRISTOL – Nigel Cobham (Telephone 0272-600397).
CAMBRIDGE – Peter Sturges, 39 Lawson Street, Kettering, Northants. (Tel. 0536 84996 - after 6pm)
CANADA – Roy L. Cummings, 15-1220 Royal York Road, London Ontario, Canada N6H 3Z9
CHILTERN – Rob Maylin, 65 The Quantocks, Flitwick, Beds.
COLNE VALLEY – David Greenwood, 59 Fairfolds, Garston, Watford, Herts. W02 4TN (Tel. 0923-678084)
DENMARK – Thomas Vedel, Holmeparken 37, DK-2830, Virum, Denmark
DEVON & CORNWALL – Zyg Gregorek, The Gables, Winsford, Halwill, Beaworthy, Devon
ESSEX – vacant (For meetings contact P. Collins, Lea Valley)
FRANCE – Didier Cottin, P.B. 2306180, Auribeau, France
FRANCE – Jean-Marie Devergnies, Nord-Loisirs, 2 Porte de Valencienne 59570 Bavay, France (Tel. 27-669679)
GLOUCESTER – Keith Griffiths and John Hobbs, 67, Woodlands Green, Upton-St Leonards, Gloucester. (Telephone 0452-613666).
GREECE – Nestor Koloros, 31 Venizelou St., GR 50100, Kozani, Greece
Kent – Kevin Goldberg, Wincheap Angling Centre, 72 Wincheap, Canterbury, Kent (Tel. 0227-456841)
LEA VALLEY – Pat Collins, 25 Chingdale Road, Chingford, London E4 6HZ (Tel. 01-524-0947)
MILTON KEYNES – Colin Maclean, 422 Whaddon Way, Bletchley, Milton Keynes MK3 7LA (Tel. 0908-368220)
NETHERLANDS – Paul Van den Beld, Bartokweg 44, 1323 TB AlmereStad, Nederlands (Tel. 01031-3240-61593)
NORFOLK/SUFFOLK – Cliff Roberts, 37 Fleetdyke Drive, Oulton Broad, Lowestoft, Suffolk NR33 9HB (Tel. 0502-569907)
NORTHAMPTON – Russ Labrum, 85 St. Leonards Rd., Far Cotton, Northampton
NORTHAMPTON – Allan Parbury, 38 Kings Avenue, Higham Ferrers, Northants.
NORTH MIDLANDS – John Callaghan, 4 Newlands Ave., Boughton, Newark, Notts. (Tel. Mansfield 861101)
NORTH WEST – Geoff Hayes, 73 Racecourse Rd., Wilmslow, Cheshire (Tel. 0625-520061)
NORTH WEST – Clive Kenyon, 3 Hillfield Rd., Little Sutton, Merseyside L66 1JA
NORTH WALES – Roger Thompson, Llyn-y-Gors, Llandegfan, Menai Bridge, Anglesey, Gwynedd, Wales LL99 5PN (Tel. 0246 -713410)
NORTH YORKSHIRE – vacant
NORWAY – Rune Johansen, Tandbergvm 61, 1927 Ranasfoss, Norway
PORTSMOUTH & DIST. – Mick Blandford, The Bungalow, The Futchers School, Drayton Lane, Drayton, Portsmouth PO6 1BS
SOMERSET – Paul White, 18 North Villas, Dene Road, Norton Fitzwarren, Taunton, Somerset TM 1DQ (Tel. 0823-433007)
SOUTH WALES – John Clarke and Mark Holt, 12 West Rd., Monkswood, Usk, Gwent NP5 lQR (Tel. 0493-28636)
SPAIN – Norman A. Smith, Villa Maureen, Avenida Mara Villas, Arroyo de la Miel, Benalmadena, Malaga, Spain
SURREY – Mike Starkey, 47 Keens Lane, Worplesdon, Guildford, Surrey (Tel. 0483-234414)
SUSSEX – Clive Williams, 16 Owl Beech Piace, Horsham, W. Sussex (Tel. Horsham 211109)
SUSSEX – Kevin Rayner, 8 Owl Beech Place, Horsham, W. Sussex (Tel. Horsham 41376)
SWEDEN – Eric Sandall, Stallvagen 13-103, S-352 52 Vaxjo, Sweden
SWINDON – Steve Cole, 3 Edwards College, South Cerney, Cirencester, Glos. (Tel. 0285-860967)
SWINDON – Tom Banks, Cotswold Angling, Kennedys Garden Centre, Hyde Rd., Kingsdown, Swindon SN2 6SE (Tel. 0793-721173)
U.S.A. – Bill Dowler, 52 River Drive, Titusville, New Jersey, NJ 08568, USA (Tel. 609-737-3493)
U.S.A. – Frank Bailey, 3338 Creek Valley Drive, Smyrna, Georgia 30082. USA
U.S.A. – Dan Gergerich, 1952A Provenchere Place, St. Louis MO 63118
U.S.A. – Andrew J. Holt, 3855 Bledsoe Ave., Los Angeles, CA 90066. USA
U.S.A. – Pat McNally, 7913 Ness Rd., PR #1 La Porte City, Iowa 50654, USA
WESSEX – John Aplin, 1 Athelstan Rd., Dorchester, Dorset (Tel. Dorchester 66500)
WEST COUNTY – Alec Welland, 66 Waterford Park, Radstock, Bath, Avon (Tel. 0761-34792)
WEST COUNTY – Nigel Cobham, 22A Memorial Rd., Hanham, Bristol BS15 JA (Tel. 0272-600397)
WEST GERMANY – Deiter Dorr, Alt-Auringen 16, 6200 Wiesbaden-Auringen, West Germany (Tel. 06127-62246)
WEST SUSSEX COASTAL REGION – Mark Hall, Flat 2, 31 South Terrace, Littlehampton, W. Sussex (Tel. 0903-713255)
WEST SUSSEX COASTAL REGION – Simon Lee, 73B Havelock Rd., Bognor Regis, W. Sussex PO21 2HB (Tel. 0243-824608)

THE CARP SOCIETY

THE CARP SOCIETY – Formed in May 1981 by Tim Paisley, Greg. Fletcher and George Sharman with the help of many others. Dedicated to the promotion of carp and carp fishing within certain ethical standards. Has a membership of around 5000 and produces two colour magazines a year (Carp Fisher). In addition it issues four newsletters, organises two conferences (in May and November) and supports countless regional meetings.

SUBSCRIPTIONS

Membership is open to all at the following subscriptions:
Adults – £13.00 per year
Juniors – £8.50 per year
Disabled – £9.00 per year

For further details write (enclosing a S.A.E.) to: Vic Cranfield, The Carp Society Administrator, 33 Covert Road, Hainault, Ilford, Essex IG6 3AZ

OFFICIALS

PRESIDENT – Roger Smith, 31 Willowmead, Hereford
VICE-PRESIDENTS – Chris Yates, Park View, Tollard Royal, Salisbury, Wilts.
– Ritchie MacDonald, 24 Mitchells Row, Richmond, Surrey
– George Sharman, 109 Middlewood Road, Sheffield S6 4H
CHAIRMAN – Mike Kavanagh, 33 Tiverton Grove, Harold Hill, Romford, Essex
GENERAL SECRETARY – Paul Selman, 60 Dover Road, Latchford, Warrington, Cheshire
MANAGING EDITOR – Tim Paisley, 1 Grosvenor Square, Sheffield, S2 4MS
FEATURES EDITOR – Julian Cundiff, 37 Oaklands, Camblesforth, Selby, Yorkshire
ADVERTISING – Jim Twitchett, 13 Broad Oaks, Epping Essex
REGIONAL CO-ORDINATOR – Andy Buff, 20 Longford, Yate, Bristol
PUBLICITY – Maurice Steeles, P.O. Box 54, Northolt, Middlesex
PUBLICATIONS – Dennis Johncock, PO Box 153, 52 Station Rd., West Drayton, Middsx.
AGENCIES – Micky Sly, 47 Millfield, New Ash Green, Dartford, Kent
POLITICS – Annop Kapitan – 14 Nursery Park, Ashington, Northumberland
CONFERENCE – Dave Curtis, 315 Windrush. Highworth, Swindon, Wilts.
JUNIOR FISH-INS – Alan Atkins, 31 Eastbourne Ave, Symonds Green, Stevenage, Herts.
REDMIRE POOL – Les Bamford, PO Box 1805, London
FRENCH CARP SOCIETY – M. Michel Thirot, 11 Rue Francois, Cherreau, 45720 Coullons, France.

REGIONAL ORGANISERS

COLNE VALLEY –Dougal Gray and Ian Hill, Flat 5, Kingsend, Ruislip, Middx. (Tel. 081-866-5284)
NORTH WILTS – Dave Curtis and Stuart Barnett ,315 Windrush, Highworth, Nr. Swindon,Wilts. SN6 7EE (Tel 0793-764163 and 0793-766365)
CHESHIRE, LANCS. & GRT. MANCHESTER – Paul Selman and Ian Ashworth, 60 Dover Road, Latchford, Warrington, Cheshire WA4 1NB
CENTRAL LONDON – Michael Walton, Gary Dawson and Tim Keane, 157b Prince of Wales Road, London NW5 3PY (Tel. 071-267-9629)
NORTHANTS. & LEICESTER – Dave Hurst, 3 Kingsley Close, Narborough, Leicester (Tel. 0533-750180)
DONCASTER – P.J. Webb and Rob Fryer, 50 Grange Ave., Hatfield, Doncaster DN7 6RE (Tel. 0302-841855)
WEST YORKSHIRE – Steve Akeroyd, 61 Carrbridge Drive, Cookridge, Leeds LS16 7LB (Tel. 0532-676151)
NORTH STAFFS. & SHROPSHIRE – Tony Baskeyfield, 556 Dividy Road, Bucknall, Stoke-on-Trent ST2 OAF (Tel. 0538-750446)
KENT & SOUTH EAST LONDON – Lee Jackson and Richard Lovett, 55 The Hollies, Gravesend, Kent DA12 5ER (Tel. 0474-320368)
YORKS. & NORTH DERBYS, – Tim Paisley, Jim Fielding and Richard Skidmore, Angling Publications, 1 Grosvenor Square, Sheffield S2 4MS (Tel. 0742-580812)
NORWICH – Dave Plummer, Norwich Angling Centre, 476 Sprowston Road, Norwich, Norfolk NR3 4DY
HERTFORDSHIRE – Alan Atkins, Steve Covell and Gary Lambert, 31 Eastbourne Avenue, Symonds Green, Stevenage, Herts.
READING – Roger and Gary Lambden, 88 Bruce Road, Woodle, Nr. Reading, Berks.
ESSEX – John Meacham and Andy Khakoo, 92 Neil Armstrong Way, Eastwood, Leigh-on-Sea, Essex
WALES – Tony Keoghane, 1 Farmville Road, Cardiff, South Wales CF2 2JN (Tel. 0222-460053)
WEST MIDLANDS – Baz Griffiths and Don Jones, 1 Fosseway Drive, Erdington, Birmingham B23 5LD (Tel. 021-350-6563 and 021-351-5970)
HANTS. DORSET & SOUTH WILTS. – Stuart Glover and Mike Barry, 74 Tam Drive, Creekmore Village, Poole, Dorset BH17 7DQ
MERSEYSIDE – Alan Young and Dave Glassman, 32 Argyle Road, Garston, Liverpool L16 8NW (Tel. 051-427-8675 and 051-722-2129)
MIDLANDS EAST – June and Graham Reedman, and John Dean, 65 Mary Street, Kirkby-in-Ashfield, Nottingham NG17 7JS (Tel. 0623-757645)
SURREY – Tony Arbery and Peter Collins, 7 Romney Close, Ashford, Middlesex, TW15 IEE (Tel. 0932-220920)
WEST COUNTRY – Andy Buff and Steve Gratton, 20 Longford, Yate, Bristol BS17 4JL (Tel. 0454-324397)
EAST LONDON & ESSEX – Lee Servis, Danny Regan and Maurice van Praagh, 113 Haldane Road, East Ham, London E6 3JL (Tel. 081-552-3795)
CAMBRIDGESHIRE – Alan Fleming and Andrew Chambers, 10 Drake Road, Eaton Socon, Huntingdon, Cambs. PE19 3HS (Tel. 0480-213664)
CHILTERN – Stuart Ewins and Mark Anderson, 41 Churchfield Road, Houghton Regis, Dunstable, Beds. (Tel. 0582-862833)
DEVON & CORNWALL – Ken and Carole Townley, 12A Place Road, Fowey, Cornwall.
GLOUCS., HEREFORD & WORCS. – Ken Tremayne, 11 Woodland Rise, Lydney, Glouc. GL15 5LH (Tel. 0594-841968)
GT. YARMOUTH – vacant
HOLLAND – Ton Kapoen and Joop van Loenen, Donkersloot 26, 2953 XB Alblasserdam, Holland
NORTH HUMBERSIDE – Clive Gibbins and Brian Skoyles, 140 Moorhouse Road, Hull, Yorkshire
NORTH EAST – vacant
ISLE OF WIGHT – Anthony Sylvester, 'Inglewood', Old Park Road, St. Lawrence, Isle of Wight
SCOTLAND – Michael Heath and David Matthew, 178 Portobello High Street, Edinburgh EH15 1DA
SUSSEX – Dave Burstow and Carl Small, 15 Bennetts Road, Horsham, Sussex RH13 5JX (Tel. 0403-56881)
SOUTH KENT – Tim Ford and Jason Lonton, 29 Benstead, Washford Farm Estate, Ashford, Kent TN23 2YQ
LINCOLNSHIRE – Paul Chandler and Rod Hutchinson, 42 Sandringham Drive, Louth, Lincs. (Tel. 0507-601064)
FRANCE – Thierry Fontaine and Bernard Rivaux, 41 Rue de L'Abbe, Gaudry, 45250 Briare, France
GERMANY – Ian Collins, Mainstrasse 119, 6050 Offenbach, Germany

PUBLICATIONS

OF SPECIAL INTEREST TO CARP ANGLERS

CARP BOOKS, AND BOOKS PROVIDING A SPECIAL CONTRIBUTION TO CARP FISHING

Books marked with an asterisk are out of print but can sometimes be obtained from secondhand book dealers. The year of first publication is given. A rough guide to their price is given but this is dependent upon condition and whether, or not, it is a first, or subsequent, issue. Books without an asterisk should still be in print and the publisher's name is given.

1. **The Fisherman's Bedside Book** – B.B. (Denys Watkins-Pitchford) [1945]* £30
2. **Be Quiet and Go a-Angling** – Michael Traherne (Denys Watkins-Pitchford) [1949]* £70
3. **Confessions of a Carp Fisher** – B.B. [1950]* £60
4. **Confessions of a Carp Fisher** – B.B. [1983, Witherby]
5. **Drop Me a Line** – Maurice Ingham & Richard Walker [1953]* £70-100
6. **Drop Me a Line** – Maurice Ingham & Richard Walker [1990, Witherby]
7. **Still-Water Angling** – Richard Walker [1953]* £60-70
8. **Still-Water Angling** – Richard Walker [1975, David & Charles]
9. **Carp – How to Catch Them** – D.L. Steuart [1955]* £7
10. **A Carp Water** – B.B. [1958]* £70
11. **Carp Fishing** – Richard Walker [1960]* £15
12. **The Art of Carp and Tench Fishing** – John Nixon & Ian Gillespie [1965]* £10
13. **The Whopper** – B.B. [1967]* £60
14. **Carp** – James A. Gibbinson [1968]* £40
15. **All About Carp Fishing** – Peter Mohan [1970]* £25
16. **Carp for Everyone** – Peter Mohan [1972]* £30
17. **Quest for Carp** – Jack Hilton [1972]* £20
18. **Cypry – The Story of a Carp** – Peter Mohan [1973]* £30
19. **Carp, Carp, Carp – 1st BCSG Annual** [1973]* £60
20. **Carp** – Jim Gibbinson [1974]* £8
21. **Catch More Carp** – Jack Hilton [1974]* £5
22. **The Second Carp Study Group Book** [1975]*
23. **The Third Carp Study Group Book** [1980]*
24. **200 Carp Tips** – Dick Langhenkel & Nico De Boer [1980]*
25. **Carp and the Carp Angler** – George Sharman [1980]*
26. **Rod Hutchinson's Carp Book** [1981]*
27. **Carp Fever** – Kevin Maddocks [1981, Beekay]
28. **Backwater** – Richard Digance [1982]*
29. **The Fourth British Carp Study Group Book** [1983]
30. **The Carp Strikes Back** – Rod Hutchinson [1983, Wonderdog]
31. **Redmire Pool** – Kevin Clifford & Len Arbery [1984, Beekay]
32. **In Pursuit of Carp and Catfish** – Kevin Maddocks [1986, Beekay]
34. **Carp Fishing** – Tony Whieldon [1986, Ward Lock]
35. **The Beekay Guide to Carp Waters** [1986]*
36. **Carp, The Quest for the Queen** – John Bailey & Martyn Page [1986]*
37. **Casting at the Sun** – Chris Yates [1986]*
38. **Angler's Mail Guide to Big Carp Fishing** – Andy Little [1988, Hamlyn]
39. **Tiger Bay** – Rob Maylin [1988, Beekay]
40. **Carp Fishing** – Tim Paisley [1988, Crowood]
41. **Carp Season** – Tim Paisley [1988, Angling Publications]
42. **Carp Now and Then** – Rod Hutchinson [1988, Beekay]
43. **Beekay Guide to 450 Carp Waters** [1988, Beekay]
44. **Dick Walker... A Memoir** – various authors [1988, The Carp Society]
45. **Fox Pool** – Rob Maylin [1988,Bountyhunter]
46. **For the Love of Carp** – Carp Society authors [1989, Carp Society]
47. **An Introduction to Carp Fishing** – David Batten [1989, Crowood]
48. **Master Fisherman... Carp** – Kevin Clifford [1989, Crowood]
49. **Big Water Carp** – Jim Gibbinson [1989, Beekay]
50. **Carp... Successful Angling** – Rob Maylin [1990, Beekay]
51. **Big Carp** – Tim Paisley [1990, Crowood]
52. **Carp, The Quest for the Queen/ Revised Edition** – John Bailey & Martin Page [1990, Crowood]
53. **Go Fishing for Carp** – Graeme Pullen [1990, Oxford Illustrated]
54. **Carp in Focus** – various authors [1990. Angling Publications]
55. **Let's Start** – Stillwater Carp [1990, Crowood]

SECONDHAND FISHING BOOK DEALERS:

E. Chalmers Hallam, 9 Post Office Lane, St. Ives, Ringwood, Hants. BH24 2PG (0425-470060)
Coch-y-Bonddu Books, Penegoes, Machynlleth, Powys. (0654-2837)
Phillip M. Hopper, 119 Grove Road, Chadwell Heath, Essex RM6 4PE (081-598-9999)
Yesterday Tackle, 42 Clingan Road, Southbourne, Bournemouth, Dorset BH6 5PZ (0202-476586)
Wigley Books, Stoke Bliss, Tenbury Wells, Worcestershire WR15 8QH (088-54-286)
John & Judith Head, The Barn Book Supply, 88 Crane Street, Salisbury, Wilts. (0722-327767)
Bob Butuex, 179 Billet Road, Walthamstow, London E17 5HG (081-527-1058)
J. C. Furniss, Crossway House, Torthorwald, Dumfries DG13PT (0387-75624)

CARP AND THE CARP ANGLER
GEORGE SHARMAN
CARP AND THE CARP ANGLER
GEORGE SHARMAN

MAGAZINES & NEWSPAPERS

I suppose for many of us, reading about carp fishing can be almost as enjoyable as catching them. Yet there will never really be a substitute for the adrenalin of the 'real thing'. But isn't it great to be able to seek inspiration and instruction from the multitude of magazines and books available today. Kevin has covered the books so here is a guide to the periodicals which are aimed at, or substantially include, features of interest to carp anglers. Indeed, many of our popular Carpworld writers appear, or have appeared, in most of these papers; which include Jim Gibbinson, Harry Haskell, Ken Townley, Chris Ball, Tony Davies-Patrick, Tim Paisley, Julian Cundiff, Paul Klinkenborg, Kevin Nash, Mike Wilson, and Allan Tomkins.

ANGLER'S MAIL – Editor: Roy Westwood, Kings Reach Tower, Stamford Street, London SE1 9LS (Tel. 071-261-5980) Weekly, price 60p, contains news, features and Andy Little's 'Carp World'.

ANGLING TIMES – Editor: Neil Pope, Bretton Court, Peterborough, PE3 8DZ (Tel. 0733-266222) Weekly, price 55p, contains news, features and occasional carp articles)

CARP FISHER – Editor: Tim Paisley, The Carp Society, 33 Hainault Road, Ilford, Essex IG6 3AZ (Tel. 081-551-8250) Price £3.75, available biannual in many tackle shops and at conference. Free to Carp Society members. Totally devoted to carp.

CARP CATCHER – Editor: Alec Welland, The Carp Anglers Association, 18 Downsview Road, Swindon, Wilts. SN3 1NT (Tel. 0793-537317) Magazine of the C.A.A. and free to members. Published bi-yearly. Occasionally on sale at conferences and meetings. Totally devoted to carp.

CARP – Editor: Alec Welland, The British Carp Study Group, 21 Palace Street, Bolton, Lancs. BO1 2DR Magazine of the B.C.S.G. and available only to members. Occasionally yearbooks produced and sold.

CYPRINEWS – Editor: Paul Selman, 60 Dover Road, Latchford, Warrington, Cheshire WA4 1NB (Tel. 0925-54952) News magazine of The Carp Society. Published quarterly and free to members. Not for sale to the general public.

MARGINS – Editor: Alec Welland, 66 Waterford Park, Radstock, Bath, Avon (Tel. 0761-34792) News magazine of The Carp Anglers Association. Published quarterly and free to C.A.A. members).

CARPWORLD – Editor: Tim Paisley, Angling Publications, 1 Grosvenor Square, Sheffield S2 4MS (Tel. 0742-582728) Comprehensive magazine devoted entirely to all aspect of carp fishing. Price £2.95 and available in newsagents, many tackle shops and by subscription. Published bi-monthly.

Carpworld
Price £2.95
Oct/Nov 1990
Bi-Monthly
No. 11
HOVER BAITS
THE SECRET IS OUT
INSIDE THIS ISSUE

BIG FISH WORLD – Editor: Kevin Clifford, Sandholme Grange, Newport, Nr. Brough, North Humberside HU15 2QG (Tel. 0430-440624) Big fish magazine which has a good carp fishing content. Price for this quarterly magazine is £2.95. Available from newsagents, tackle shops or subscription from Angling Publications, 1 Grosvenor Square, Sheffield S2 4MS.

SPECIALIST ANGLER – Editor: Gordon Chell, 11 Yew Tree Avenue, North Anston, Sheffield S31 7EW (Tel. 0909-563173) The magazine of The National Association of Specialist Anglers. Generally contains a good carp content. Price £3.95 or free to N.A.S.A. members. Available from selected tackle shops. Published bi-yearly.

COARSE ANGLER – Editor: Colin Dyson, PO Box 657, Sheffield, S10 1AT (Tel. 0742-304038) Monthly magazine which usually has a good carp content, depending on the time of year. Price £1.40, available from newsagents or subscription.

COARSE
fisherman
APRIL 1991 £1.70
MAHSEER for MEMSAHIB
In pursuit of the world's noblest fish
Joy Hurst
CLOSE SEASON CARPING
ANGLING PHOTOGRAPHY
New series on how to take better angling pictures
Kevin Smith
TAKING ON THE BEST
The AEC Matchgroup take on the best teams in the south
John Wright
FREE
COBRA
COMPETITION

COARSE FISHERMAN – Editor: Simon Roff, Metrocrest Ltd., 67 Tyrell Street, Leicester LE3 5SB (Tel. 0533-511277) Monthly publication which generally contains two, or more, features about carp fishing. Price £1.70 available from newsagents or subscription.

DAVID HALL'S COARSE FISHING – Editor: David Hall, 60 Hillmorton Road, Rugby, Warks. CV22 5AF (Tel. 0788-535218) Monthly publication dealing with all aspects of coarse fishing but usually contains one, or two, carp features. Price £1.70, available from newsagents or by subscription.

COARSE FISHING TODAY – Editor: Neil Pope, Bretton Court, Bretton Centre, Peterborough, PE3 8DZ (Tel. 0733-264666) Bi-monthly magazine which usually contains two, or more, carp articles. Price £2.00, generally available from newsagents.

STRIKE – Editor: Graeme Pullen, 17 Fleet Road, Fleet, Hants. (Tel. 0252-615360) Magazine dealing with all types of fishing. An occasional feature on carp. Price £1.75.

BIG CARP – Rob Maylin's new bi-monthly magazine dedicated to carp fishing. Price £3.75 from selected tackle shops or by subscription from Rob Maylin, 65, The Quantocks, Flitwick, Beds.

1990 30lb+ CAPTURES

We accept that this lIST will be nothing like a complete record of all the 30lb+ fish caught during the 12 months under review, but we can only publish information that is known to us – with apologies to those not included.

WEIGHT	TYPE	CAPTOR	LOCATION	MONTH
33-10	mirror	Andy Martin	Yateley Car Park	January
30-8	mirror	Mark Jones	Hyde Lane, Bucks.	January
40-8	mirror	Kevin Maddocks	Mid-Northants.	January
33-10	common	Martin French (15)	Sutton-on-Hone	January
40-0	mirror	Steve Gombocz	Mid-Northants.	February
36-8	leather	Robin Dix	Mid-Northants.	February
33-0	mirror	Andy Wiggins	Darenth	February
30-1	common	Kevin Bell	Oxfordshire pit	February
30-8	mirror	Paul Fox	Patshull Pool	February
33-4	mirror	David Balaam	Waveney Valley D lake	March
32-8	mirror	Martin Seymour	Essex lake	March
31-4	mirror	Mark Jones	Hyde Lane, Bucks.	March
30-10	mirror	Bob Tapken	Hyde Lane, Bucks.	March
30-4		Sid Farrance	Southern Pit	March
34-0	mirror	Martin Locke	Savay lake	March
33-10	mirror	Mick Bolt	Kent lake	March
31-8	mirror	Paul Brooks	Savay lake	March
30-10	leather	Roger Hawkins	Savay lake	March
30-12	mirror	Roger Hawkins	Savay lake	March
33-10	mirror	Dave Woods	Savay lake	March
33-0	mirror	Neil Pancholi	West Drayton	March
32-8	mirror	Steve Last	Waveney Valley E lake	March
36-0	mirror	Jason Brown	Darenth	March
33-4	mirror	Peter Broxup	Savay lake	March
32-12		Brian Murray	Brooklands	
30-8	common	Gary Thatcher	Sutton-at-Hone	
35-12	mirror	Andy Buff	Gloucestershire	March
30-8	mirror	Steve Allen	Norfolk	March
30-2	mirror	Tony Childerhouse	Norfolk	March
33-9	mirror	David Woodley (15)	North Kent	March
36-8	mirror	Ritchie McDonald	Yateley Lily Lake	March
35-0	mirror	Kevin Maddocks	Withy Pool	March
30-2	leather	Terry Pettybridge	Yateley Car Park	March
34-2	mirror	Michael Leach (16)	Exeter Canal	June
38-8	mirror	Andy Charles	Leisure Sport's Horton Fishery	June
32-4	mirror	Andy Charles	Horton Fishery	June
33-8	mirror	Richard Skidmore	Hutchy's	June
31-0	mirror	Rod Hutchinson	Hutchy's	June
38-4	leather	Neil Warner	Mid-Northants Fishery	June
35 1	common	Malcolm Downs	School Pool, Faversham	June
36-12	mirror	Andy Buff	Gloucestershire lake	June
34-8	mirror	Ron Buss	Langmans Lake, Send	June
42-0	mirror	Max Cottis	Savay Lake	June
45-4	mirror	Albert Romp	Savay Lake	June
44-0	mirror	Steve Burgess	Leisure Sport's Horton Fishery	June
41-0	mirror	Peter Wilson	Withy Pool	June
41-12	mirror	Alan Taylor	Mid-Northants Fishery	June
42-8	mirror	Bob Copeland	Harrow	June
35-4	mirror	Lee Travers	Waveney Valley	June
34-0	mirror	Clive Schooley	Darenth	June
30-4	mirror	Clive Schooley	Darenth	June
34-0	mirror	Paul Hunt	Darenth	June
33-0	common	Jim Wilson	Suffolk Stour at Nayland weir	July
36-12	mirror	Nick Peat	Yateley Car Park	July
31-0	mirror	Mick Leonard	Hamphire syndicate	July
30-14	mirror	Rob Pickering	Cambridgeshire stillwater	July
31-2	common	Neville Fickling	Nottinghamshire gravel pit	July
32-12	mirror	Steve Reeve	Savay Lake	July
34-12		Kenny Gates	Essex lake	July
32-8	mirror	John Ankers	Mangrove	July
32-8	mirror	Dave Phillips	Mangrove	July
31-2	mirror	Clive Jackson	Midlands lake	July
33-8	mirror	Steve Newman	Horton Fishery	July

Rod Hutchinson. 31.00 mirror. June.

Dave Lawrence. 33.06.

Zyg Gregorek. 30.06 mirror.

WEIGHT	TYPE	CAPTOR	LOCATION	MONTH
33-8	mirror	Andy Charles	Horton Fishery	July
40-4	mirror	Dave Willett	Mid-Northants Fishery	July
30-12	mirror	Ian Turner	Essex lake	July
34-0	mirror	Dave Miller	Darenth	July
34-7	mirror	Paul Cambray	Horton Fishery	July
34-1	mirror	Chris Bullimore	Homersfield	July
33-4	mirror	Paul Wells	Cambs. lake	July
30-8	mirror	Barry Middleton	Darenth	July
36-8	mirror	Chris Ladds	Harefield	July
40-8	mirror	Dave Compstone	Wraysbury	July
32-0	mirror	Pete Springate	Wraysbury	July
30-14	mirror	Nigel Millband	Gunthorpe Br/R.Trent	July
45-8	mirror	Tony Moore	Yateley North Lake	July
33-3	common	Ken Thorpe	Redesmere	July
32-8	mirror	Tony Long	Harefield Fishery	July
33-8	mirror	Chas Newman	Farlow Lake	July
34-8	mirror	Paul Atoni	Surrey gravel pit	July
35-1		Joe Holdsworth	Horton Fishery	July
34-0		Mick Daley	Surrey pit	July
30-12	mirror	Paul Selman	Darenth	Aug
31-8	mirror	Paul Goodey	Kent stillwater	Aug
32-0	mirror	Terry O'Brian	Savay Lake	Aug
32-8	mirror	Shaun Harrison	Bleasby	Aug
32-8	mirror	Peter Springate	Wraysbury	Aug
35-0	common	John Lilley	Mangrove	Aug
34-6	mirror	Cliff Fox	Savay Lake	Aug
33-6	mirror	Ronald Key	Horton Lake	Aug
32-12	mirror	Cliff Honeysett	Kent	Aug
34-12	mirror	Mike Willmott	Ashlea Pool	Aug
31-2	mirror	Stephen Weir	Sussex	Aug
42-12	mirror	Bernard Blight	Horton Lake	Aug
33-0	mirror	Sandra Blight	Horton Lake	Aug
38-8	mirror	Albert Romp	Savay Lake	Aug
30-12	mirror	Keith Sullivan	Yateley	Aug
33-6	mirror	Ron Key	Horton Pool	Aug
34-0	mirror	Paul Hunt	Essex stillwater	Aug
33-3	mirror	Robert Loadwick	Chapel Lakeside Park	Aug
35-2	mirror	Mike Willmott	Ashlea Pool	Aug
32-8	mirror	Joe Bertram	Mangrove	Aug
34-0	mirror	Eddie Lancaster	Harefield Fishery	Aug
33-8	mirror	Dougie Jones	Darenth	Aug
31-8	mirror	Phil Hughesdon	Darenth	Aug
30-3		Danny Regan	North Kent lake	Aug
36-8	mirror	Bernie Stamp	Savay Lake	Aug
34-6	common	Mick Allen	Honeycroft Fisheries	Aug
33-6	mirror	Mick Hatchman	Savay Lake	Aug
31-14		Gary Fletcher	Kent lake	Aug
30-10		Neil Warner	Northants. pit	Aug
30-0	mirror	Peter Broxup	Savay Lake	Aug
37-4	mirror	Bruce Ashby	Savay Lake	Aug
37-8	mirror	Dave Smith	Leics. stillwater	Aug
32-8	mirror	Alan Thompson	Leics. stillwater	Aug
38-0	mirror	Andrew Downes	Burghfield	Aug
30-10	mirror	Neil Warner	Northamptonshire pit	Aug
30-0	mirror	Phil Cousins	Withy Pool	Aug
33-8	mirror	Mark Dean	Darenth	Sept
39-8	mirror	John O'driscoll	Midlands lake	Sept
35-8	mirror	Keith Selleck	Savay Lake	Sept
34-8	mirror	Keith O'Connor	Savay Lake	Sept
32-12	mirror	Paul Mepham	Farlows Lake	Sept
35-4	mirror	Albert Romp	Savay Lake	Sept
30-4	mirror	John Holmes	Savay Lake	Sept
30-12	mirror	Dave Grout	Waveney valley lake	Sept
31-8		Matthew Lee	Essex lake	Sept
31-8		Clive Bates	Bedfordshire lake	Sept
30-12	mirror	Richard Tring	Withy Pool	Sept
30-2	mirror	Frank Matthews	Darenth Lake	Sept
30-2		George Beasley	Colne Valley	Sept
36-8	mirror	Richard Skidmore	Hutchy's	Sept
30-4	mirror	Cyril Hares	Cuttle Mill	Sept
34-0	mirror	Mick Sutton	Southern pit	Sept
32-12	mirror	Clive Rigby	Savay Lake	Sept
32-0	mirror	Bernie Heerey	Savay Lake	Sept
40-8	mirror	Geoff Ball	Horton Fishery	Sept
36-2		John Baldry	Yateley	Sept
35-8		Phil Cousins	Withy Pool	Sept

Dougie Jones. 33.08. August.

Gary Harrow. Darenth 32.00.

Richard Skidmore. 36.08. September.

WEIGHT	TYPE	CAPTOR	LOCATION	MONTH
34-4	mirror	Stuart Gillham	Harefield Pit	Sept
33-6	mirror	Steve Allcott	Johnson's	Sept
32-12	mirror	Bob Merritt	Surrey lake	Sept
32-2		Mark Stewart	Norfolk lake	Sept
31-12		Malcolm Binstead	Essex lake	Sept
30-12		Dave Grout	Wensum lake	Sept
30-8	common	John Freeman	Midlands lake	Sept
30-1	mirror	Ronnie Barnes	Darenth	Sept
30-8	mirror	Max Cottis	Savay Lake	Sept
31-12	leather	Malcolm Binstead	Essex stillwater	Sept
40-2	mirror	Allan Partridge	Harrow	Sept
34-12	mirror	Dave Thorpe	Midland syndicate	Sept
31-4	common	Alan Fewkes	Nottinghamshire lake	Sept
34-4	mirror	Rob Still	Harefield Pit	Sept
33-8		Scott McBride	North Kent lake	Sept
32-4	mirror	Graham Clarke	Canterbury	Sept
31-12		John Casey	Private lake	Sept
31-8	mirror	Bernie Stamp	Savay Lake	Sept
31-4		Craig O'Brian	Midlands lake	Sept
30-1	mirror	Adam Rogers	Kent pit	Sept
30-0	mirror	Percy Moss	Buckshole Reservoir	Sept
33-2	mirror	Eddie Dodd	Kent lake	Sept
32-0	common	David Spinks	Southern gravel pit	Sept
31-0	common	John Noon	Church Pit	Sept
33-0	mirror	Dave Smith	Hertfordshire lake	Sept
32-4	mirror	Darren Spicer	Hertfordshire lake	Sept
36-8	mirror	Tim Hodges	Harefield Lake	Sept
34-4	mirror	Rob Still	Harefield Lake	Sept
34-0	mirror	Jim Bayliss	Homersfield Lkae	Sept
33-4	mirror	David Courtenay	Harefield Lake	Sept
31-8	mirror	John Mason	Hertfordshire lake	Sept
31-4		Roy Ecob	Leics. lake	Sept
30-14	mirror	Daniel Cox	Darenth	Sept
34-12	mirror	Joe Bertram	Mangrove	Sept
33-6	mirror	Martin Atkinson	Nottinghamshire lake	Oct
33-8	mirror	Scott McBride	Kent lake	Oct
31-8	mirror	Clive Bates	Beds. stillwater	Oct
30-14	mirror	Daniel Cox	Darenth	Oct
39-14	mirror	Allan Parbery	Mid-Northants. Fishery	Oct
39-0	mirror	Robert Coote	Withy Pool	Oct
35-12	mirror	Peter Springate	Wraysbury	Oct
33-0	mirror	Phil Cousins	Withy Pool	Oct
30-8	mirror	Phil Cousins	Withy Pool	Oct
31-5		Mark Marsons	Southern pit	Oct
32-12	mirror	Cliff Honeysett	Kent lake	Oct
37-8	mirror	John Hampton	Horton Fishery	Oct
32-8	common	John Philip	Warmwell Leisure Lake	Oct
37-14		David Elford	Kingsweir	Oct
33-12	mirror	Stephen Galliver	Horton Lake	Oct
33-12		Adam Rogers	Essex pit	Oct
30-14		Paul Henson	Kent lake	Oct
30-6	mirror	Rob Hill	Harefield	Oct
36-12	mirror	Tony Cheadle	Harefield	Oct
34-2	mirror	Dave McAllister	Hyde Lane, Bucks.	Oct
30 0	common	Rob Hales	Patshull Pool	Oct
36-6	mirror	John Mason	Hertfordshire stillwater	Oct
30-4	mirror	Terry O'Brien	Savay Lake	Oct
30-10	mirror	Cliff Honeysett	Kent lake	Oct
33-6	mirror	Rob Hill	Harefield	Nov
43-1	mirror	Peter Bond	Yateley Lily Lake	Nov
37-8	mirror	John Hampton	Horton	Nov
33-5	mirror	Stephen Swinyard	Darenth	Nov
31-6	mirror	Ashley Mount	Waveney Valley	Nov
33-0	mirror	Neil Cottam	Southern England	Nov
35-10	mirror	Keith Sullivan	Yateley	Nov
31-8	mirror	Jeff Hall	Darenth	Nov
30-8	mirror	Barry Griffiths	Patshull Pool	Nov
31-12	mirror	Larry Watson	Darenth	Nov
35-4	mirror	Tony Olivo	Darenth	Nov
35-12	mirror	Mark Henderson	Darenth	Nov
33-4		Alan Burchell	Kent lake	Nov
31-12		Scott Jaeger	Warmwell	Nov
30-4	mirror	Graham Clarke	Kent lake	Nov
35-4	mirror	John Harry	Savay Lake	Dec
33-0		Dougie Jones	Darenth	Dec
31-11		David Edwards	Kent lake	Dec

Richworth

Albert Romp. 39.04 mirror.

TEAM
DAIWA

Nev Fickling. 31.06 common.

Derek Stritton. 33.08.

YEARBOOK'S

One of the country's best all-round specialist anglers who works for a well-known Midlands' tackle dealer. Name the angler and the dealer.

DAIWA SPONSORED CARPWORLD QUIZ

Thanks to the generosity of DAIWA, we are able to offer prizes to the value of £1000 in our Special Carpworld Yearbook Quiz. Further details of the prizes will be appearing in each issue of Carpworld magazine. Thanks DAIWA.

The rules for entering the Quiz are as follows:

1. **Closing date is 31st December 1991.**
2. **One entry per person.**
3. **Answer questions clearly.**
4. **Any enquiries to the compilers of the quiz will mean disqualification.**
5. **The decisions of the Organisers will be final.**
6. **All entries to Angling Publications at the address shown on Page 1.**
7. **Results will be announced in the first Carpworld of 1992.**

Tackle consultant, leading carp angler and a regular contributor to Anglers Mail. Name his column.

One man and his dog. Name them both.

A famous angler with a famous fish. Name both.

What is the exact weight of the biggest carp this man has caught?

Two well-known Stoke anglers and a national angling figure enjoying the festive season. Name all three.

An initiation ceremony at a west country venue. Name the club.

ORD 345X
4WD

Same venue. Name the tippler.

MATCH THE CARP TO THE FISHERY

1. Sally	A. Redmire
2. Trio	B. Harefield
3. Raspberry	C. School Pool
4. Heather	D. Yateley North Lake
5. Nelson	E. Waveney
6. Parrot	F. Hutchy's
7. Big Scale	G. Savay
8. Basil	H. Yateley Car Park Lake
9. She	I. Mangrove
10. Minty	J. Horton

MATCH THE ANGLER TO BAIT

1. Chris Haswell	A. Maestro
2. Albert Romp	B. Lucebaits
3. Ken Townley	C. Prime Attraction
4. Geoff. Bowers	D. Carpbuster
5. Martin Kowal	E. Nutrabaits
6. Alan Clarke	F. Richworth
7. Alan Parberry	G. Premier
8. Martin Locke	H. S.B.S.
9. Nev. Fickling	I. Catchum
10. Rob Maylin	J. Solar Baits

WELL-KNOWN CARP ANGLERS' NICKNAMES

Match the angler to his nickname

1. Lee Jackson	A. The Captain
2. Bruce Ashby	B. Big Boy
3. Keith Selleck	C. Jock
4. Tim Paisley	D. Uncle Back-Stop
5. Peter Wright	E. Bubbles
6. Rod Hutchinson	F. Little 'Un
7. Kevin Maddocks	G. Python
8. Richard Skidmore	H. Grim Pastry
9. Lloyd Bent	I. Chinese Ace
10. Alan Taylor	J. Gerry Cottage
11. Brian Hankins	K. Red Hopkinson
12. Ian Booker	L. Big Foot
13. Martin Locke	M. Gino
14. John Pooler	N. Curly
15. Bob Baker	O. Disco Dancer
16. Mike Hatchman	P. J.J.
17. Andrew Downes	Q. Lucky
18. Rob Maylin	R. Pee-Wee
19. Eric Hodson	S. The Brain
20. Peter Mohan	T. Maestro

SPECIAL QUIZ

GENERAL KNOWLEDGE

1. In 1953 only one carp over 20lb. was caught in Britain. Who caught it?
2. Who formed the British Carp Study Group in 1969?
3. What year was the Carp Society formed?
4. What was Dick Walker's middle name?
5. Name the year when Chris Yates first met Rod Hutchinson.
6. Who was claimed by the angling press to be the first angler to catch 100 'doubles' in a season?
7. Jack Hilton first met Tom Mintram where?
8. Name the year that the Carp Catchers Club was formed.
9. Which manufacturers of hooks produces the 'Grey Shadow' treatment?
10. What is the connection between Jack Hilton's first carp over 10lb. and Kevin Maddocks?
11. Which famous water connects Dick Walker and Rob Maylin?
12. At what weight did Angling Times initially report Dick Walker's record carp in September 1952?
13. Which two anglers are credited with inventing the 'hair-rig'?
14. Who was the first angler to catch two carp over 20lb. in a season?
15. What is the connection between Valerie Noyce, the 2nd woman to catch a 20lb. carp, and one of the previous questions?
16. What was the real name of the rod maker who first commercially produced the MkIV rod?
17. Name the famous water which was bailiffed by Reg Philpot?
18. Which water relates to "the Night of the Beer Barrels"?

Name the anglers and the venue.

A very special occasion. Name the young man who was the reason for it.

GUESS THE YEAR

1. What year was Redmire Pool stocked with carp?
2. When was the Carp Society formed?
3. When did the last issue of Fishing magazine appear?
4. In what year did Jack Hilton catch a 28lb. carp from Ashlea?
5. Successful carp angler Kathleen Holmes married someone who wrote a book about carp. When was it first published?
6. In what year did Maurice Ingham first fish with Dick Walker?
7. What year was it when Peter Springate fished at Yeoveney and stunned us all?
8. When was Rod Hutchinson's first carp book published?
9. What year saw Chris Yates fish the first week at Redmire?
10. Name the year that Woldale was first stocked with carp?

Another very special occasion – at Dunstable in 1988. In honour of whom?

Name the water and the angler in the bivvy entrance. Why are the two linked at the date of writing this? (March 1991).

GUESS THE WEIGHT

1. What did Dick Walker's second biggest carp actually weigh?
2. A mother and son once regularly fished a famous carp fishery. What was the weight of their most significant carp?
3. Roy Johnson once held the Kent carp record, what did the fish weigh?
4. A big carp was once connected with Robinson Crusoe. What was its reported weight?
5. Give the weight of the biggest carp caught in the North-West of England?
6. What was the weight of a Cheshire carp that helped to make someone publicly eat their words?
7. Research chemist Mike Smith once held a famous fishery carp record. What did the fish weigh?
8. What was the weight of Clarrissa when she died?
9. What was the 2nd largest carp caught from Cheshunt Reservoir prior to the 2nd World War?
10. What did Ted Brown's largest carp from Mapperley weigh?

The Carpworld Yearbook Quiz has been compiled by Kevin Clifford, Julian Cundiff and Tim Paisley. All entries will be checked by them and their decisions about the correctness of the entries, and decisions regarding the allocation of the prizes will be final.

NORTH

30/32 NORTHGATE,
NEWARK
NOTTS.
TEL: (0636) 611622
Shop and Mail Order

HOOK UM

Specialist Tackle and Bait

FORMERLY CATCHUM RETAIL • NEW PROPRIETORS GARY & AMANDA BAYES

SOUTH

FARLOWS LAKE,
FORD LANE, IVOR,
BUCKINGHAMSHIRE
Shop only • Situated next to Cafe and Bar on the Heron Point at Farlows. 10 minutes from either M40 or M4 Junctions of the M25.

England's premier carp bait and tackle supplier. Tackle and bait by all the top names. Efficient mail order service. Extensive stocks at Newark and Farlow, why not pop in and see us at Farlows in the close season. Not only can you see the latest in carp tackle, have a meal in the cafe and pint in the bar, you can fish as well – close season fishing for carp to over 30lbs!

INTRODUCING OUR NEW RANGE OF RODS:

The Sabre II and the Horizon II. England's most popular carp rods are now, thanks to new hi-tech fibres, even better still.

SABRE Mk. II

	Blank	Finished Rod
11' 2lb	**£70.50**	**£107.30**
12' 3lb	**£74.60**	**£114.43**
12' 2¼lb	**£76.60**	**£117.50**
13' 2¼lb	**£86.85**	**£132.80**

HORIZON Mk. II

	Blank	Finished Rod
12' 2¾lb	**£79.70**	**£122.60**
13' 3lb	**£86.85**	**£132.85**

SABRE Mk. II ER *(EXTREME RANGE)*

	Blank	Finished Rod
12' 2¼lb	**£110.35**	**£168.60**
12' 2½lb	**£113.40**	**£173.70**
13' 2¾lb	**£120.55**	**£194.15**

HORIZON Mk. II ER *(EXTREME RANGE)*

	Blank	Finished Rod
12' 2¾lb	**£113.40**	**£173.70**
13' 3lb	**£126.70**	**£194.15**

HORIZON ER

	Blank	Finished Rod
12' 2¾lb	**£113.40**	**£173.70**
13' 3lb	**£86.85**	**£132.85**

HORIZON Mk. II ER
The rod they are all talking about. The ultimate casting machine, and yet it is a forgiving fishing tool.
Coupled with a SS3000, Zen Bojko cast over 190 yds. Already we have orders for over 200 rods. Zen's got one, Phil Harper's got one, everyone else wants one. Long range fishing, can't reach 'em? You can bet the man with the HorizonII ER will. Amorphous high technology, this blank is a genuine exclusive to Hookum.

DAIWA SS3000

Imported from Japan after extensive field testing by Kevin Nash the ultimate long range reel. Long taper solid polished alloy spool, five ball bearings, unique line guard system. The casting reel as used by Rob Maylin and Kevin Nash.

PRICE **£153.25**

DAIWA SENSITRON

The first bite alarm with variable sensitivity and unique memory system eliminating false indication in wind. If your carp are picking up and ejecting on the spot the Sensitron will nale 'em. The best indicator to date.

PRICE **£71.50**

Daiwa

HOOKER PURSUIT

Brilliant new product from Kevin Nash. Surely the ultimate carp angler's rucksack. Too many features to mention – you must see it to believe it. Simply the best.

PRICE **£99.10**

THE NASH OVAL BROLLY

Now established as the No. 1 carp angler's brolly. Simply nothing else will take the abuse. The strongest brolly available that fully covers the angler's bedchair.

Oval Brolly	**£88.10**
Oval brolly with brollywrap spec.	**£170.85**
Oval mini side	**£29.20**
Oval brollywrap special	**£68.95**
Oval overwrap	**£88.12**

NASH 50" BIVVIES

50" Brollywrap	**£38.80**
50" Brolly overwrap Mk. II	**£78.50**

COLEMAN STOVES

Double burner, unleaded	**£58.10**
Single multi-fuel 8000 btu	**£57.35**

K.J.B.

2 Rod Pod	**£61.25**
3 Rod Pod	**£66.35**
3 Rod Special	**£71.25**
New long bait gun	**£35.70**

BULK BAITS

When I worked for Catchum developing their top range of baits I must have mixed hundreds of tons of bait over the years and talked to hundreds of anglers about bait. I even had the time to occasionally get out and catch a few on the baits myself.

From all that experience came a simple philosophy. Forget all the bullshit you read, the best baits are the simplest, and neither do you need a second mortgage to be able to afford the best fish catchers. But why are Hookum baits exceptionally cheap? Simple. I can now buy the highest quality ingredients from the most reputable suppliers at the same rate per 25k as I used to buy 1 tonne lots – mix them and sell direct to you.

FISHMEAL BASE
The same mix that did the damage last year for the lads on Catchum at Harefield. This six slaughtered the hardest waters and goes on an on. The results actually improve second and third season.
15 kilo **£40.35** 1 kilo **£3.10**

SPICY FISH
The fish meal base with added spices and birdfoods. An instant bait. Because of its obvious pulling power, not as long term as the fish base but it will cane any water for a season.
15 kilo **£46.41** 1 kilo **£3.55**

SEAFOOD SALMON MIX
Probably all round the most consistant instant fish catcher ever developed. Based on the old seafood recipe which has undoubtably caught more big fish around the world than any other bait.
15 kilo **£64.37** 1 kilo **£5.10**

RED BIRD FOOD
The original mix of bird foods: Robin Red etc., that is still used by many top names today and still catching just as many fish as alternative baits.
15 kilo **£49.55** 1 kilo **£3.80**

YELLOW BIRD FOOD
A "feed back mix", it's improved every season. It's like using a different bait every season. More sophisticated than the red mix with added vitamins and flavour enhancers.
15 kilo **£56.20** 1 kilo **£4.40**

BOILIE MIX
Well balanced, excellent for baiting or pump the flavour levels up and use as an instant. Excellent flavour retention for long sessions.
15 kilo **£38.30** 1 kilo **£2.96**

PROTEIN MIX
Well balanced combination of all a carp's requirements. Based on milk proteins with added vitamins, minerals, fats etc. The ultimate long term bait at sensible money.
15 kilo **£96.40** 1 kilo **£7.38**

RIVER MIX SWEET, RIVER MIX FISH
A successful recipe that takes the Trent apart. If you're fishing a river this is the kiddie! Come to think of it it's probably a darn good lake mix as well!
15 kilo **£27.10** 1 kilo **£2.10**

• • • • • • • • • • • • • • **ACCESS AND VISA TELEPHONE ORDERS TAKEN** • • • • • • • • • • • • • • •

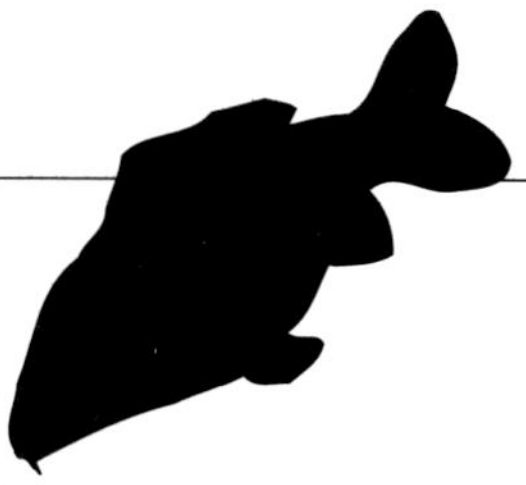

CARP ON VIDEO

It's strange to think that, despite the recent glut of video releases, only two, or three, years ago videos about carp were almost unheard of. I say "almost" as some videos did exist. Old C.A.A./B.C.S.G. members cannot fail to remember Roy Johnson's carp film, Kevin Maddocks' Northants. record or, dare I say it, Peter Mohan's comic, Ashlea affair. From there we saw some amateur attempts by Chris Ball and crew. Taped excepts from London T.V. (Five O'Clock Show – Yateley Monster Show) were also banded about. Personally, I preferred the private 'Making of the Yateley Monster Show'. Those classic words from Terry Whitley, "I can't believe my luck" (said in a broad, cockney dialect) were a show-stopper. Terry mate, I can tell you, neither could Chris Ball, Robin Dix, Andy Little etc!

Nowadays, the close season carp viewing isn't just restricted to the chosen few as it is possible to buy, or hire, a variety of videos about carp, made by a variety of anglers. Below is a list of those presently available and where to obtain them. For many of us it will be the nearest we get to a forty pounder!

CARP IN SESSION PART 1 – John Lilley and Tim Paisley at Shropshire's Birch Grove, with guest appearances from Mary Paisley, Steve Colclough and Ray Stone. Ninety minutes long, costing £14.95 from Angling Publications. Also available from selected tackle shops.

CARP IN SESSION PART 2 – John and Tim conclude the Birch Grove session with a number of twenty pounders. Another enthralling ninety minutes for £14.95. Available from Angling Publications, 1 Grosvenor Square, Sheffield S2 4MS or specialist tackle shops.

CARP FEVER 1 – 'The Revolution' with Kevin Maddock. You witness carp to 35lb. and an overview of Kevin's contribution to carp fishing. More than 60 minutes long, it costs £14.99 from Beekay Publishers.

CARP FEVER 2 – 'Rigs & Baits' with Kevin. This time carp to over 20lb. are caught and you are entertained by an interview with Duncan Kay. Again, over 60 minutes for £14.99 from BeeKay Publishers.

CARP FEVER 3 – 'Baits & Rigs' again with Kevin Maddock. More carp to over 20lb., are caught. The same length as the previous tapes at the same price. Beekay Publishers, Withy Pool, Henlow Camp, Beds. SG16 6EA and selected tackle shops, including mail order.

FISHING AT CASSIEN – This is part of the Bob Church Video series. Cassien experts, Phil Smith and Joe Taylor, take us through 60 minutes of instruction and advice on how to succeed at the 'Big Pond'. Lots of 'mind-blowing' trophy shots. Available from specialist tackle shops and mail order.

CARP FISHING – This video covers a light-hearted session at the famous Mid-Northants. Fishery with Duncan Kay and Ian Heaps. The video lasts for about 60 minutes and costs £14.95. It is available from Walker's of Trowell, Nottingham Road, Trowell, Notts. (Tel. 0602-301816)

CARP FISHING WITH DES TAYLOR – The ebullient Des with his own brand of carp fishing. Lots of instruction and plenty of action at Cuttle Mill. Price is a very reasonable £9.95 for over 60 minutes worth. Available from David Hall's Coarse Fishing, 60 Hillmorton Road, Rugby, Warks. CV22 5AF (Tel. 0788-535218)

STALKING CARP WITH DES TAYLOR – Again filmed at Cuttle Mill, angling's answer to Chubby Brown talks his way through 60 minutes of advice and tips on stalking carp. Plenty of explosive action. Available, as above, from Clean River Video Productions, David Hall's Coarse Fishing.

CARP FISHING AT SALAGOU – This video is another in the Bob Church series and again features the dynamic duo of Phil Smith and Joe Taylor. Loads of carp, as might be expected from last year's most productive water. An hour long tape it can be obtained from Phil Smith, 155 Nunns Lane, Coventry, CV6 4GJ (Tel. 0203-687780) or selected tackle outlets.

CARP FISHING WITH JOHN WILSON – If you enjoyed John in his T.V. series then this one is for you. Covering 30 minutes of carp fishing in addition to another 30 minutes devoted to a separate species. This footage is taken directly from his popular T.V. programme. Cost is a modest £9.99 and it is widely available, including many tackle shops.

CARP FISHING IN THE CANARIES – Released by the Norwich Angling Centre and featuring Dave Plummer and special guest Kevin Nash. It represents a complete guide to fishing in the Canaries and costs £14.99 for 60 minutes.

FRENCH CARP FISHING WITH DAVE PLUMMER – Another release from the same stable. This one covers French carp fishing on the well-known River Lot and Lake Cassien. An hour long tape costing £14.99 and available from the Norwich Angling Centre, 476 Sprowston Road, Norwich, Norfolk NR3 4DY (Tel. 0603-400757)

RIVER LOT CARP FISHING PART 1 – A 70 minute tape of action on the River Lot with Mick Hall and friends. Lots of action interspersed with instruction. Price £14.99

RIVER LOT CARP FISHING PART 2 – More from Mick Hall and friends, including some 'whackers' from large French stillwaters. 70 minutes for £14.99. Available from Mick Hall Videos. (Tel: 01-805-8763).

WRAYSBURY CARP AND LONGFIELD LUNKERS – Chris Ball's video of carp to 40lb. 'on the top' and on the bank. The tape runs for 60 minutes and costs £12.99 from The Carp Society, PO Box 153, 52 Station Road, West Drayton, Middx. UB7 8QN

LONGFIELD, THE NETTING – Vic Gillings and Steve McNeill present the netting of Longfield and the subsequent stocking of Horton. An hour long video available from the Carp Society (see above). Price £11.99

RICHWORTH VIDEO 1 (BAITS) – An hour long look at boiled baits plus lots of action and still shots of big carp.

RICHWORTH VIDEO 2 (TACKLE & TECHNIQUES) – Another hour long tape this time looking at tackle needed for carp fishing.

RICHWORTH VIDEO 3 (PRESENTATION) – This one covers carp rigs and presentation. Again 60 minutes.

RICHWORTH VIDEO 4 (SESSION) – Clive Diedrich and Malcolm Winkworth fish a session at the famous Cutt Mill. 60 minutes of action. All the Richworth videos were filmed in the early 1980's and are in places somewhat dated. The sessions took place at Cutt Mill and The Conservative Club water. These tapes are not now commercially available but copies are still occasionally available at specific fishing tackle outlets or can be hired from certain video shops.

CANARY CARPIN' – A ninety minute video featuring Kevin Nash and Gary Bayes fishing at Embalze de Chira in the Canary Islands. A complete guide detailing travelling, baits, rigs, location etc. Professionally produced coverage of carp weighing over 30lb. Price £15.95 from Carp Vision, 2, Poplars Close, Alresford, Colchester, Essex. CO7 8BH (postage free).

LE CARPING – A complete guide to fishing in France and featuring Andy Little. This ninety minute long tape deals with passports, travel, baits, rigs, rules, tactics etc; in fact, it covers all you need to know about French carping. Included on the video are mirrors to 42lb., and commons to 33lb. 6oz. Highly recommended. Price £14.95 including postage. Available from Zed Epsilon, Video Presentation, Discovery House, Southgate Street, Gloucs. GL1 1EX.

CARP BAITS – A 90 minute look at the whole spectrum of carp baits through the eyes of Tim Paisley, Andy Little, John Lilley, Martin Locke, Bill Cottam, Alan Parbury, Kevin Crawley and Clive Gibbins. Price £15.95 from tackle shops.

CARP IN WINTER – Still at the editing stage, this excellent film covers winter carping in Devon, Essex, Hampshire, the Midlands and Shropshire. The anglers include Fred J. Taylor, Tim Paisley, Andy Little, Derek Stritton, Julian Cundiff, Alan Young, and the waters are Cuttle Mill, Anglers Paradise, Birch Grove, Willow Park, and an unidentified Essex venue. A surprising number of carp got caught. Watch Carpworld for further details.

Undoubtedly, the interest in carp videos is on the increase and availability and choice should develop to meet it; but, be warned that the majority of commercial videos, and all the private videos that I am aware of, are only available on the V.H.S. format. If you go abroad to France, or the Low Countries, you may see various carp videos on sale. The Mahin Brothers have one out, so does Sensas. However, whilst they do play on our video systems they only produce black and white images. Furthermore, American videos don't work at all. Privately produced vidoes are available from a number of individuals and certainly worth looking out for are the following: 'Making a Yateley Monster Show', 'Trent & Kent Carping' and 'Whitley Tours Parts 1 and 2'.

Zenon Bojko

What possessed me to chose 'Tackle Box' , as opposed to 'Long Range Fishing', when asked by Julian to do a piece for the Annual.

My tackle box is grey and it's got things in it. There, easier than I thought. Now for Long Range Fishing....

When I spoke to Julian on the phone, and read out the masterpiece, he went quiet for a moment. "Well, we were hoping for a bit more than that Zen, like what type of hooks you use and so on. We'll pay you too," said the rather distraught voice on the other end. "You've just talked me into it," I replied.

The bulk of my bits and pieces are stored in the largest size 'Stewart' tackle box, available from practically every tackle shop throughout the country, at about £5. Some are coloured with clear lids which soon become scratched, so I prefer the grey ones.

A few years ago I stopped fishing for a while and gave my tackle box to a friend. Being unable to wrest it back I was forced to buy another, plus its contents. I knew exactly what I needed and drew up a long list of items – hooks, swivels, beads etc. I know it doesn't look much when you lift the lid but the lot added up to £120. You don't notice it when you're building the contents up over a period of time, but I must admit I was taken aback when I had to fork the cash out.

The first job I did on arriving home with the box was to cut half a section out of one of the two biggest compartments. This allows my Effgeeco hook wallet to fit and, although these are no longer generally available, I still had a few as I bought several some time ago. In these I store pre-tied hooklengths, attached to swivels. The hooklengths for my 'helicopter' rigs, which use swivel beads, makes it difficult to close the wallet so I store these in plastic packets – (4 to 6 hooklinks per packet). Then I cut a small piece of card and write down the hook size and length of hooklink. All of my rigs are tied at home, under no pressure thereby giving plenty of attention to detail. My son, Rael, and I get a little system going between us. I tie the rigs to the hooks and then the hooks to the Gamabraid. Then, whilst I start of the next one, Rael slides on a one inch length of silicon rubber and ties the hooklength to the swivel, or swivel bead, at the desired length. Also in the hook wallet I keep my club permits and rod licences.

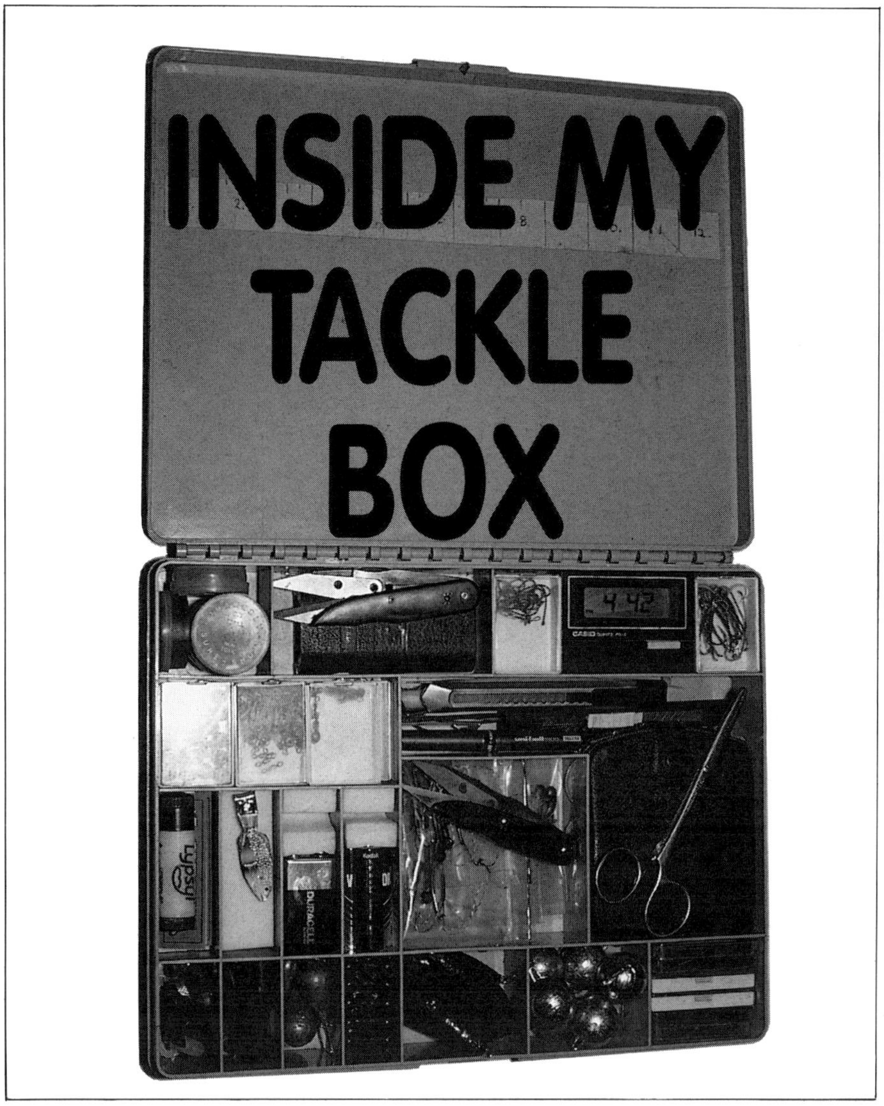
INSIDE MY
TACKLE
BOX

The Stewart Box – Zenon's choice for all his bits and pieces.

The next job with the box is to make the longest (top) compartment into three sections. For this I cannibalise one of my old, broken boxes or get hold of some plastic sheet and cut it to size. The pieces are then glued into place, in the top section. The smallest one contains five tubs of split-shot (Swan, A.A.A., B.B., No.1, and No.4), the next section holds a small torch, plastic 'snippers' (these are much easier to use than scissors and are generally available), a small screwdriver and spanners (one for the Coleman and the others for my reels). The last section contains ten plastic boxes, with sliding lids, which contain my hooks. They consist of black Gamakatsu's, Drennan Lure hooks, Mustad S.S. hooks and fine wire

Kamasan's. This section of the box also holds my alarm clock, which just so happens to fit perfectly (from Dixons costing £8).

The section below this is my 'oddments' section, containing 'snap-off' carp knives, (needed to cut the Gamabraid and shape the base of our candles to fit into the candle-holders. Rael uses his to cut everything, including his fingers. Silly boy! Next is a flat 'Swiss' file, which is not used much nowadays with chemically sharpened hooks which, when blunt, are discarded. There is also a plastic hook-tie gadget (for Rael's float fishing), crochet hooks for baiting up and rig tying, a small knife (for opening cans etc.) and disgorgers. In fact I sort all the long, thin items into this section.

The next compartment also contains those super, little, plastic boxes that I use for my hooks; these, however, are used for holding beads, swivel-clips, swivels, swivel beads, leger beads, Drennan rings and one inch lengths of silicon tubing (used to shield swivels). The small compartments are used for a multitude of handy bits and pieces, such as spare batteries for the new Sensitrons and torches, ether-foam (which can be used for a wide variety of purposes, such as spacers in the tackle box or rig foam, or even butt-foam. Under the strips of ether-foam I keep some elastic bands which I use to keep the rods together when broken down. Another compartment holds spare thumb screws, monkey-pin 'pips', torch bulbs and spare tip-rings (just in case). The next section holds back-leads; mine start from oz. to 2oz. I've found the heavier ones are best. The last, small, compartment contains even more beads, as I now get through twice as many using the 'helicopter' rigs. The next two compartments hold a few, of the many, 4oz. leads I carry with me. The first holds Roger and Kerry's highly fashionable round leads (please note that these are made without attached swivels which greatly enhance the object of the exercise, which is to bring the hooklength closer to the lead). Roger did mention that his leads are only obtainable from most leading tackle shops, NOT from him. Unfortunately, these round leads, due to their non-aerodynamic shape, are somewhat lacking when it comes to long-range fishing. In this area I use the highly popular long-range leads also made by Roger and Kerry. These Zipp style leads are perfect for both accuracy and distance.

The last compartment holds, again, even more beads, silicon tube and two flip top boxes. In these are some large hooks I'm presently playing around with.

Finally, in the back cover itself I keep a few spare blades for my carp knives and a large assortment of sewing needles, which have come in handy on countless occasions. A pair of 5in. forceps completes the contents of my tackle box.

I have another, smaller container, of my own design, which I call "my baiting-up box." This again has a hinged lid, but is much deeper so as to hold a plastic bag full of pop-ups. I also carry a tub of tungsten putty and two tubs of split-shot (A.A.A. and B.B.) for bulk weighting. The putty is used for fine tuning, either moulded around the split-shot or, more often than not, when using a bent hook or long-shanked hook. In these circumstances I mould the putty around the eye of the hook which throws things out of balance on rejection of the bait. Little things like that can make a lot of difference and result in a few extra fish on the bank, perhaps even that "big 'un" we're all after. There is another one of my favourite slide-top, plastic boxes, this one holds my boilie-stops, a dental floss dispenser (un-waxed, for tying on pop-ups or boilies) and a packet of

Useful additions to any tackle box

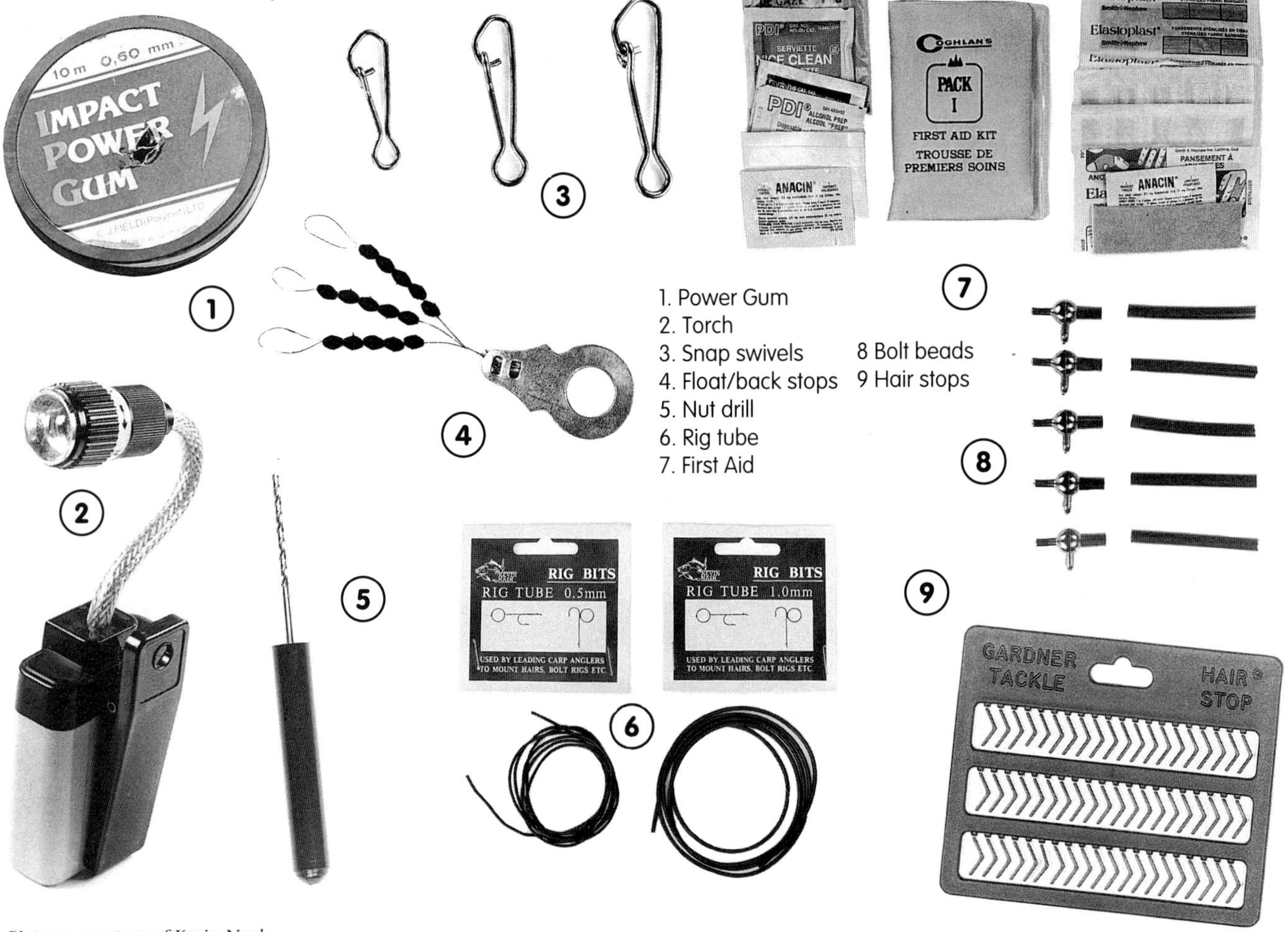
IMPACT POWER GUM
10 m 0,60 mm
FIRST AID KIT
TROUSSE DE PREMIERS SOINS
ANACIN
Elastoplast
RIG BITS
RIG TUBE 0.5mm
RIG TUBE 1.0mm
USED BY LEADING CARP ANGLERS TO MOUNT HAIRS, BOLT RIGS ETC.
GARDNER TACKLE
HAIR STOP
1. Power Gum
2. Torch
3. Snap swivels
4. Float/back stops
5. Nut drill
6. Rig tube
7. First Aid
8 Bolt beads
9 Hair stops

Pictures courtesy of Kevin Nash.

P.V.A. tape for stringers. In fact, my tape is rolled up like a carpet and then cut into four equal sized rolls with a Stanley knife. This is a lot more economical, and a damn sight easier, than trying to cut strips off using scissors. Speaking of scissors, I have another pair of snippers for trimming the dental floss. The lid of the box has two ether-foam strips, superglued to the inside about 3in. apart. These have slits cut into them to hold my baiting needles, crochet hooks, nut drills etc.

Finally, the last item of tackle is a plastic tube, with a cap at either end, that contains my anti-tangle tubes. It holds about thirty of them.

My spare spools, and spools of Gamabraid, are kept in reel cases and in a side pocket of the back-pack. Another pocket holds a host of 4oz. leads. I also have a Tupperware box in the boot of the car with a whole load more leads, plus spare catapult elastic, plumbing floats, matches, flints, plasters, in fact everything I think I might ever need for long sessions. If asked what was my most useful item of tackle I'd have to say my soap and towel – I'd never be without them.

Zenon certainly knows how to use his tackle. On the right he is pictured returning his second forty pound plus fish!

STILL CARP

Believe it or not, 1990 marked the start of the 4th Decade I've been seriously chasing these creatures called carp. That sounds a long time but I'm young really! Mind you I've always said, "You're as young as the woman you feel."

In the early part of the year carp anglers everywhere read of the closure of Longfield, the top carp water in Middlesex. This meant one of the most famous waters in modern carp fishing history was going to be the scene of intense activity, as the plan was to move the huge carp present. You may have already read Longfield Remembered, the three-part serial that I undertook in Carpworld. Why I re-tell this tale is because it dominated my free time, and a good deal of my thoughts, as time slipped away from the end of the season into the spring. What fishing I had done had been a little at Yateley and a few visits to Willow Park. Although I had nothing to report at Yateley, except a pair of bream, I did witness the Match Lake's first authentic thirty pounder. A super fish this, just like the ones we had been catching, except bigger! The Willow Park sessions were by contrast good: this water is now coming of age with some great looking and growing carp.

The close season is a time when non-angling people think that the fisherman is a home loving, decorating and gardening person! We know different, don't we? The close season is, for me, one of the best times of the angling calendar. We need this break, let alone the fish and the bankside. To us carp anglers it means so many things, tackle renovation, bait making, maybe a trip abroad, finding out about new waters and clubs to join.

This last close season was a bit too short for my liking. The reason was I had to work abroad for the greater part of May and missed some great trout fishing that my friends Jan and Andy experienced. Besides double-figured rainbows, Andy managed also a big 'Lake' salmon as well. All on the finest of hookpoint leaders, just 3lb. line!

I did get away to Grande Canary and fish for the De Chira carp but, although I came away with some fish under my belt, none were of notable size. However, I did get a great suntan! Space doesn't allow me to say too much about this trip and I've written an account of the visit in Coarse Fisherman.

"One thing on my mind – Wraysbury". Chris with a Wraysbury floater-caught twenty from a previous season.

We started in this country with the tremendous hot weather in May and, upon my return from the continent, only one thing was on my mind – Wraysbury. I don't think there will ever be a time when I won't be at Wraysbury in the close season. It has such a strong appeal to me, not just because I've managed to catch a few of its inhabitants, but because no one knows for sure just what's swimming around in its acres of water.

There is a tale I'll tell you one day of a fish that two, highly respected carp anglers once spied that will blow you away. Only recently I had chance to talk with one of them – I'd heard the original version in a crowded pub at the time. As we talked his eyes and voice seemed to lose track of what he was relating – such was the lasting effect of the sight of that carp. The incident happen almost ten years ago now.

I'm often asked whether, after all the looking and searching I've done at Wraysbury these last few years, I've chanced upon a 'super whopper'. In truth, although I've seen big carp, and a handful were very big, only one or two were in the 'thirty-five pound' range. That is of course huge, but maybe Wraysbury is going to surprise us all in time to come with something really special. I certainly hope so for, if we know everything about the waters and every fish in them (and this has happened on many waters), then I feel that one of the main reasons we all go fishing, the mystery, is largely lost. I'm far from being the only carp angler who thinks like this these days. Having fished a great many waters over the years containing carp, never knowing what was swimming out there was half the fun. And, more importantly, the mystery kept my mind and imagination on a high. It's all down to the 'unknown' element. It's so important.

Enough of me 'wittering' on, back to the fishing! Just a few days before the end of May and with the weather being prefect, I made that first visit to Wraysbury. Nothing had changed, the place was in its early summer glory and looked, smelt and felt right. Actually, one important thing was different, the water level. It was seriously down for the time of year and, as the summer unfolded, it

CRAZY

dropped as low as the 1976 level. On that first trip I found the carp, or I should say some of them. Being creatures of habit they tend to show in the same areas at the same time of the year. This last year was no different. As I rounded the corner on the north bank the unmistakable, shiny bump of a carp's back was visible lying only ten yards out from the bank. Creeping round to a well-known climbing tree I was soon aloft. What a sight! There, lying beneath my feet, were five of the highly prized Wraysbury carp. Strangely, they were all of the 'tubby' type – short, deep, almost black looking, lightly scaled mirrors. It was great to see them again, they all looked in superb condition. I guess they ranged in sizes from 20lb. plus to, maybe, within a pound or two of 30lb. I had bait with me, some Chum of course, and some boilies. With a gentle breeze blowing into this corner, it was a simple matter to 'catty' some Chum out upwind so that it would come naturally down, on the drift, to where the fish were. Several of these carp were on the move, yet all keeping in the general area. The Chum drifted slowly into position but brought no response from the carp. Then an exciting moment; out of my vision to the right a big carp cruised in almost unnoticed. This fish came straight up to the first piece of Chum in its path and engulfed it! How can that happen? Such queer fish these carp – that must have been the first bit of surface food it had seen for months. It went on to take several more mouthfuls before stopping for a breather, and crunching up his find!

This was a cracker of a fish, one I've seen before and, in contrast to the others, very long and beautifully coloured. Its body colour was a mixture of a deep, reddy/bronze hue with its fins being lightly tinged yellow, almost coral coloured. That's the kind of carp that would turn the head of any freshwater angler, let alone a carp angler. I would have thought it was close to, if not over, 30lb. in weight. What a fish, and taking Chum too!

Out went some more surface bait and soon it was back taking the Chum. However, this time its antics were encouraging the other carp into feeding too. In the end, and after a period of only 15 minutes, four out of the other five carp in the area were feeding on the Chum. In between this I managed to introduce some boilies and these were deposited on a gravel hump that was clear of weed. Guess what, the first fish to find them was the hungry surface feeder. It nosed down and polished off half a dozen in short order. To see it up-end, almost at my feet, and twist and turn on the bottom was a sight I only wish you could have seen. What fantastic creatures large carp are, especially when they are as beautiful as this one was.

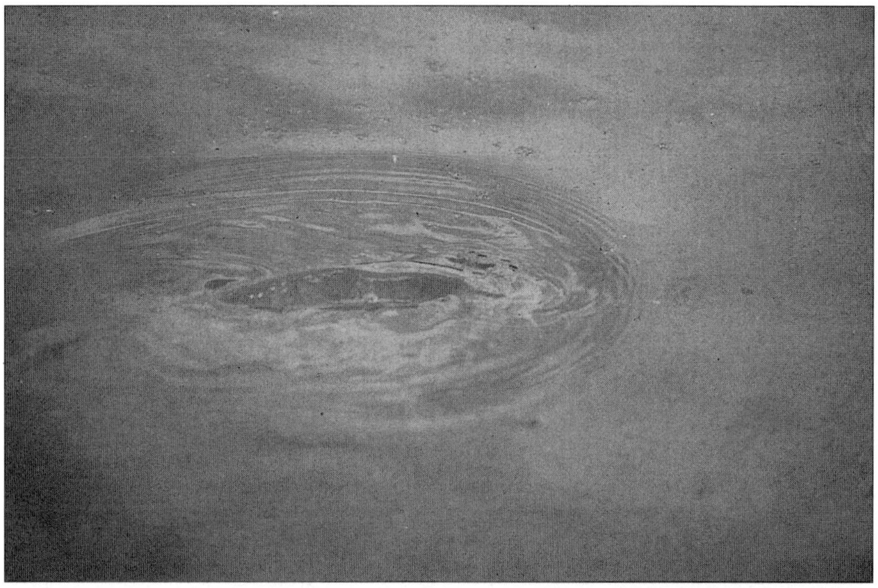

Chris Ball

I managed several more trips during the following few weeks but found generally the same carp, although every now and then there would be an occasional different one, including a definite thirty pounder.

For me this had been a fascinating period at this awe inspiring lake, but something was looming that was to make my days at Wraysbury numbered, for the time being anyway. What could that be I hear you ask? The answer – Savay. You see, with the demise of Longfield, which is near Wraysbury, my car was not pulling to the left so much as I sped around the M25 near Staines!

Floater fishing at this Redlands water was not a much practised art, and indications from my friends said now was the time to try. So Savay it would be; the Wraysbury carp would have to wait. You might think I'm mad, but investigations revealed that there was every chance of catching a whopper off the top at Savay, and I just had to have a try.

The difference between Savay and Wraysbury, is there are more carp and more anglers at Savay, plus it's further away from home. But for numbers of big carp, it can't be beaten. A lot of these are from the original Leney stock of the 1950's. "Long, lean fighting machines", as someone put it. Weed is a recent phenomenon at Savay and this had, without doubt, encouraged the fish onto the surface. This, coupled with the extremely hot weather we were experiencing, made sure they were nearly always on, or near the top, during those long summer months.

Early on, I concentrated on a swim that was enclosed by the considerable scum that the prevailing wind had piled up in one corner. The carp were in this stuff all right or, should I say, under it. My fishing resulted in several of the 'newer' stock fish taking a liking to Chum, but there were much bigger fish around that area and what might be lurking under the scum made me 'toss and turn' in bed at night. Yes, I still get that tremendously exciting feeling when I know big carp are around. I never connected with one in that area but, later, in another part of Savay I came close to landing one of the larger fish. Unfortunately, it weeded me after I'd hooked it fair and square. After heaving and pulling like crazy all I was left with was a huge ball of weed on the controller.

In the few weeks I fished at Savay I managed eight surface caught carp, including a couple of nice twenties. Mind you, there were several 30lb. plus fish caught off the surface at Savay during the summer, so it shows what's possible.

Just after this foray at Savay, I tried my surface approach at the Hampshire stillwater, Willow Park, run by John Raison, of Raison Bros. tackle shop. This is a super fishery that is up and coming. The carp are impressive looking and growing all the time. There are good fish in here, with a few around the 20lb. mark – some being commons! Besides this, there is a big head of doubles with many close to fifteen pounds.

It's good fishing that can be sometimes outstanding fishing. I hit the jackpot in two consecutive evening sessions, when a total of 24 carp to 19lb. were landed. The first evening I experimented using Kryston multi-strand as the floating hooklink. This proved quite deadly and fooled 16 carp! The following evening I tried one of my favourite rigs, the 'Suspender'; again another super session, with the remaining eight carp caught in a flurry of action that left me breathless. All these carp were caught 'on the cane'. That is, a little built-cane Mk.IV Avon carp rod that dates from the 1950's and an equally old, but perfectly usable, Ambidex No. 2. fixed spool reel. With no snags or weed present in Willow Pool this outfit was ideal for this kind of fishing. The signs look good here at 'Willow' for the years to come.

I also went back to fish another favourite water of mine in Hampshire, one that the Army controls. It was here, a few years ago, that I managed to catch on surface baits some big, beautiful, original Leney carp. But times had changed, and the areas I'd caught them from had now been cleared and were out of bounds. But, through some hard work, I managed to find the carp again. To my surprise the water seemed to have had some recent carp stockings, and it was these new fish that had become very keen on Chum. I saw, on a couple of occasions only, some of the awe inspiring, big, old Leney carp, but they would come nowhere near me! (can't really blame them!). However, I'll be back this coming year; I must catch one.

Suddenly it's winter-time again and the angling I've done so far is at Willow Pool. Now that the carp have settled into their winter rhythm of life you can fish at the peak time, thereby saving long periods sitting in freezing conditions. At present the best is 18lb. 8oz.

As you have just read, this season so far has NOT been a year of big fish for me. But, what the heck, I've had some great fishing. However, more importantly, I've known several times that I've got into some good situations, close to the big fish, and all I needed was a few seconds of that all important luck and the story could have been so different. I guess that's why I'll be back for more next year and I bet you'll be the same!

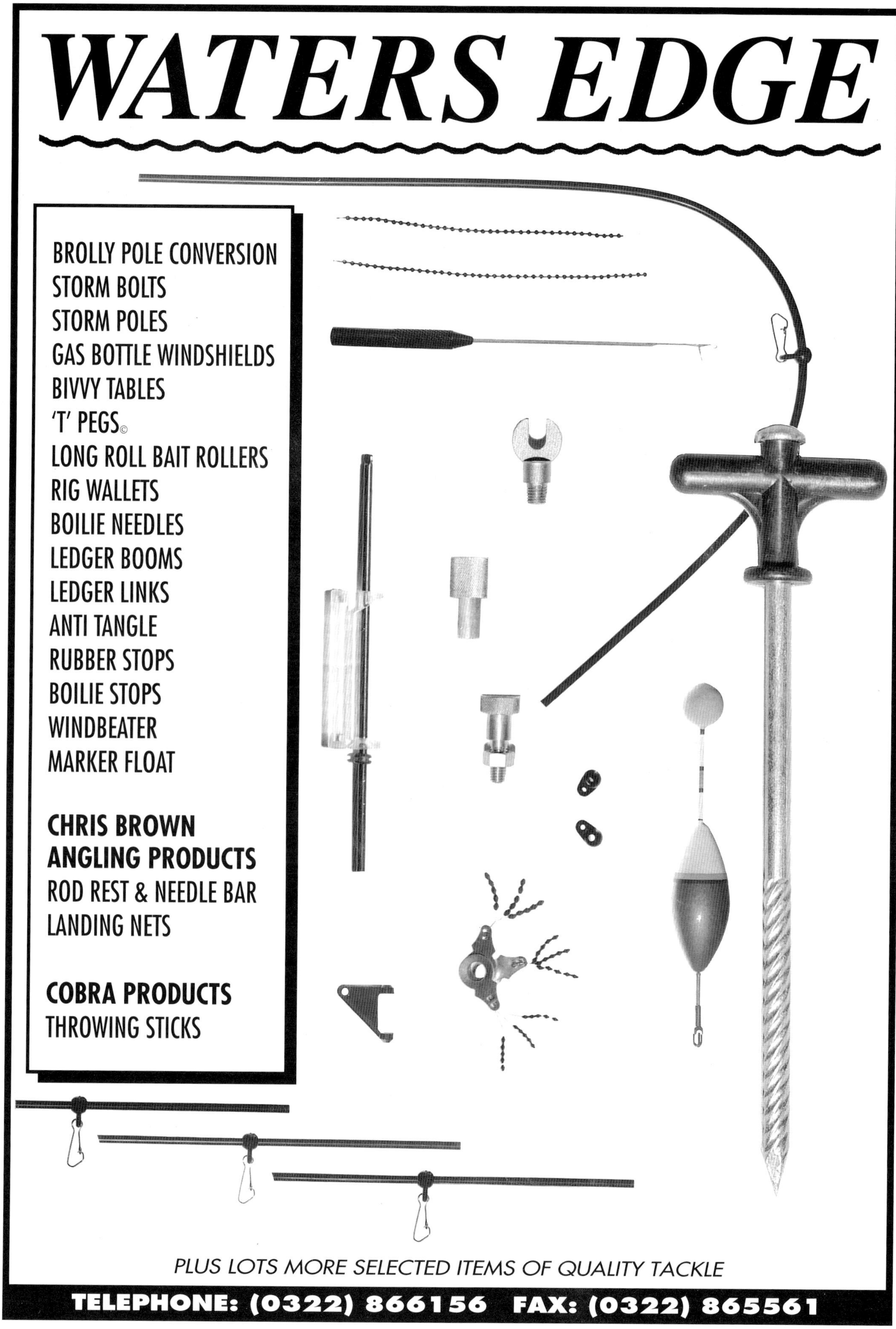
WATERS EDGE
BROLLY POLE CONVERSION
STORM BOLTS
STORM POLES
GAS BOTTLE WINDSHIELDS
BIVVY TABLES
'T' PEGS©
LONG ROLL BAIT ROLLERS
RIG WALLETS
BOILIE NEEDLES
LEDGER BOOMS
LEDGER LINKS
ANTI TANGLE
RUBBER STOPS
BOILIE STOPS
WINDBEATER
MARKER FLOAT
CHRIS BROWN ANGLING PRODUCTS
ROD REST & NEEDLE BAR
LANDING NETS
COBRA PRODUCTS
THROWING STICKS
PLUS LOTS MORE SELECTED ITEMS OF QUALITY TACKLE
TELEPHONE: (0322) 866156 FAX: (0322) 865561

INDEX OF TACKLE MANUFACTURERS
PUBLISHERS, VIDEO MAKERS, BAIT MAKERS etc.

ABU Garcia Ltd
Unit 5
Aston Way
Middlewich Motorway Estate
Middlewich
Cheshire
CW10 OHS
Rods, reels and accessories

Angling Publications
1 Grosvenor Square
Sheffield
S2 4MS
Books, magazines and videos

Aqua Products
18 Francis Street
Crewe
Cheshire
CW7 6HF
Bivvydomes

Avon Scale Co. Ltd
1 Claremont Street
Edmonton
London
N18 2PR
Weighing equipment

Barbour & Sons Ltd
J Simonside
South Shields
Tyne & Wear
NE34 9PD
Clothing

Beekay Publishers
Withy Pool
Bedford Road
Henlow Camp
Beds
SG16 6EA
Books and videos

Belstaff International Ltd
Caroline Street
Longton
Stoke on Trent
Staffs
ST3 1DD
Clothing

BiTech Viper Ltd
PO Box 928
Aylesford
Kent
ME20 6XF
Bite alarms

Brent (Hailsham) Ltd
156 Station Road
Hailsham
East Sussex
BN27 2SA
Fishing line

Bruce & Walker Ltd
Huntingdon Road
Upwood
Cambs
PE17 1QQ
Rods

Broadland Bait Launchers
Pruners
Coast Road
Bacton
Norfolk
NR12 OEY
Remote control boats

Carroll McManus Ltd
9 Sybron Way
Jarvis Brook
Crowborough
Sussex
Conoflex rod blanks

Carpbuster Baits
25 Fox Lane
Keston
Kent
BR2 6AL
Bait mixes and ingredients

Cascade Tackle
238 North Sherwood Street
Nottingham
NG1 3EN
PVA, hooks and accessories

Century Composites Ltd
58 Hutton Close
Crowther Industrial Estate
Washington
Tyne & Wear
NE38 OAH
Armalite rod blanks

Chubbs Ltd
132 White Lion Road
Little Chalfont
Amersham
Bucks
HP7 9NQ
Books

Church & Co Ltd
16 Lorne Road
Northampton
NN2 7EU
Clothing, rods, equipment and accessories

Cobra Products
73 Paines Lane
Pinner
Middx
HA5 3BX
Throwing sticks

Cotswold Baits
Kennedy Gardens
Hyde Road
Swindon
Bait ingredients and mixes

Crafty Catcher Products
28 The Cotes
Soham
Cambs
CB7 STU
Readymades, ingredients and mixes

DAM (UK) Ltd
29 Dunlop Road
Hunt End
Redditch
B97 5XP
Rods, reels, luggage and accessories

Daiwa Sports Ltd
Netherton Industrial Estate
Wishaw
Lanarks
ML2 OEY
Rods, reels, bite indicators and accessories

Dellareed Ltd
20 Eagal Hill
Ramsgate
Kent
CT11 7PY
Bite indicators

Delkim Products Ltd
4 Gold Street
Walgrave
Northamptonshire
NN6 9QE
Bite indicators and tackle accessories

Drennan International Ltd
Leopold Street Works
Oxford
OX4 1PJ
Rods, catapults and accessories

Edward Barder
The New Barn
North End
Nr. Newbury,
Berkshire
Hand made split cane rods

Essential Products
43 Alderny Road
Bridgewater
Somerset
TA6 5DA
Bivvy and brolly conversions and products

E.T. Fishing Products
Unit 72
French & Jupps Maltins
Ind. Estate
Stanstead Abbotts
Ware
Hert
SG12 6HG
Rig bits, bivvydome and accessories

Fordham & Wakefield
Kinvale
Third Street
Langton Green
Tunbridge Wells
Kent
TN3 OEN
Sportex rods and blanks

Fox International
Fowler Road
Hainault Industrial Estate
Hainault
Essex
IG6 3UT
Chairs, bedchairs, bite indicators and accessories

Bob Frost Tackle
23 Bath Street
Leamington Spa
Warks
CV31 3AE
Specialist tackle supplier

Gold Label Tackle
2c Beech Road
Erdington
Birmingham
B23 5QN
Specialist tackle supplier

Harrison Advanced Rods
107 Summers Road
Brunswick Business Park
Liverpool
L3 4BL
Rods and blanks

Ivel Trading Co
Ivel House
10 Sandpiper Close
Biggleswade
Beds
SG18 8DT
Rig bits and accessories

Kamasan Ltd
13a Old Mills Industrial Estate
Paulton
Bristol
BS18 5SU
Hooks

Geoff Kemp
Pilgrims Court
Days Lane
Pilgrims Hatch
Brentwood
Essex
Bait ingredients and flavours

Kent Particles
40 Borkwood Way
Orpington
Kent
Particles and seed baits

KJB
Crabtree Close
Fenton Industrial Estate
Stoke on Trent
Rod pods and accessories

Waters Edge (ex. Kingfisher)
36 Lombard Street
Horton Kirby
Kent
DA4 9DF
Brolly conversions, bait rollers and accessories

Kryston Advanced Angling Products
Bolton Enterprise Centre
Washington Street
Bolton
BL3 5EY
Hook length materials

Leeda Tackle Ltd
14-24 Cannon Street
Southampton
SO9 2RB
Mitchell reels

Lyons Tackle
Hollins Mill
Rochdale Road
Walsden
Todmorden
Silstar reels, rods and accessories

Mainstream (Midlands) Ltd
Unit 32
Anglesey Business Park
Littleworth Road
Hednesford
Cannock
Staffs
Clothing

Malthouse Productions
PO Box 36
Owestry
Shropshire
SY10 8ZZ
Videos

Marvic Worldwide Angling
5 London Road
Harleston
Norfolk
IP20 9BH
Floats, accessories and rig bits

Maxima Marketing Ltd
Glenlora
Lochwinnoch
Strathclyde
PA12 4DN
Fishing line

Magnum Stainless
14 Lyndhurst
Blackwater
Camberley
Surrey
Stainless rod rests, buzzer bar setups

M & B Products
37 Redlands Road
Enfield
Middlesex
EN3 5HN
Bait mixes, stainless steel products

Middy Tackle International Ltd
Unit 1
Draycott Mills
Market Street
Draycott
Derby
DE7 3NB
Floats, rig bits and accessories

Mustad & Son Ltd
2 Brindley Road
Southwest Industrial Estate
Peterlee
Co Durham
SR8 2LT
Hooks

Nash Tackle Ltd
34 Brook Road
Rayleigh
Essex
SS6 7XN
Bivvys, Brollies, luggage and accessories

Normark Support Ltd
Pottery Road
Bovey Tracey
Devon
TQ13 9DS
Rods, rings and accessories

North Western Blanks Ltd
Grimshaw Lane
Middleton
Manchester
M24 2AA
Rods, blanks and accessories

Norwich Angling Centre
476 Sprowston Road
Norwich
Norfolk
Specialist Tackle Shop and Rod builders

Nutrabaits
25-27 Fife Street
Wincobank
Sheffield
S9 1NN
Bait ingredients, mixes and flavours

Optix Ltd
Hobberend House
Main Street
Shadwell
Leeds
LS17 8JG
Sunglasses

Original Video Co
PO Box 885
Shenley Lodge
Milton Keynes
MK5 7YU
Videos

Partridge of Reddich
Mount Pleasant
Reddich
Worcestershire
B97 4JE
Hooks

Predator Baits
Cornsland
Hall Lane
Upminster
Essex
RM14 1TX
Bait

Premier Baits
15 Blenheim Close
Pysons Industrial Estate
Broadstairs
Kent
CT10 2YF
Bait mixes, ingredients and flavours

Reedwortley
c/o Daystate Ltd
Newcastle Street
Stone
Staffs
ST15 8JU
Boilie launcher

Redport Net Co. Ltd
94 East Street
Bridport
Dorset
DT6 3LL
Nets

Reuben Heaton Scales Ltd
The Square
Market Bosworth
Nuneaton
Warks
CV13 OLL
Scales

Richardson Angling Supplies
2 Barfields
Loughton
Essex
IG10 3JH
Ready made boilies

Roberts Fishing Tackle Developments
102 Minster Road
Westgate on Sea
Kent
CT8 8DG
Accessories and rig bits

Ryobi Masterline
Cotteswold Road
Tewkesbury
Glos
GL20 5DJ
Rods, reels and accessories

Rod Hutchinson's Fishing Developments
Redburne Road
Louth
Lincs
Readymades, ingredients, rods and accessories

Saccom Products
38 Kings Avenue
Higham Ferrers
Northants
NN9 8LA
Ready made boilies

Shakespeare Co. UK Ltd
PO Box 1
Broad Ground Road
Lakeside
Redditch
Worcs
B98 8NQ
Rods, reels and accessories

Shimano UK Ltd
Unit B2
Lakeside Technology Park
Pheonix Way
Swansea Enterprise Park
Llansamlet
Swansea
SA7 9EH
Rods, Reels and Clothing

Silverstream Films & TV Productions Ltd
4 South Parade
Seascale
Cumbria
CA20 1PZ
Videos

Simpson's of Turnford
1-2 Nunsbury Drive
Turnford
Hertfordshire
Rod builders

Solar Tackle
35 Sutherland Road
Belverdere
Kent
DA17 6JR
Bait ingredients, stainless accessories

Specialist Bait Supplies
7a Cooper Drive
Springwood Industrial Estate
Braintree
Essex
CM7 7RF
Ingredients, ready made boilies

Sporting Prints
11 Cherrywood Green
Bilston
West Midlands
WV14 6HL
Sweatshirts and T-shirts

Starmer Bait Supplies
9-11 Rutherford Close
Progress Road
Leigh on Sea
Essex
SS9 5LQ
Bait

Steade & Son Ltd
53 Cately Road
Darnall
Sheffield
S9 5JF
Umbrellas, bivvies, accessories

Stephens (Birmingham)
Beach Road
Sparkhill
Birmingham
B11 4QL
Clothing

Streamselect Ltd (Richworth Products)
Island Farm Avenue
West Molesy
Surrey
KT8 OUZ
Bait mixes, ready made boilies

Sundridge Tackle Ltd
Vicarage Lane
Hoo
Nr Rochester
Kent
ME3 9LW
Rods. bite alarms, accessories

Stalker Products
28 Whitehill Road
Brinsworth
Rotherham
S60 5HZ
Clothing

Tony Osborne
1 Morley Road,
Sutton,
Surrey
Particle and seed supplies

Tri-Cast Composite Tubes
Watson Rorks
Duke Street
Rochdale
Lancs
OL12 OLT
Rod blanks

Waterqueen UK Ltd
28 Tithe Barn Drive
Windsor Road
Bray
Berks
SL6 2DG
Fishing line

Whipp Rods
Unit 4
Lon Dewi Sant
Nefyn
Pwllheli
Gwynedd
LL53 6NY
Rod builders

Wychwood Tackle
Northwood Road
Windrush Industrial Park
Burford Road
Witney
Oxfordshire
Luggage

Zipp (Leatherbarrows)
196-198 Church Street
Urmston
Manchester
M31 1DX
Leads and rig bits

CARP FISHING IN EUROPE

To the best of our knowledge the two men from England best qualified to write from their own experiences about fishing in Europe are Tony Davies-Patrick, and the author of this article, Geoff Shaw. Geoff's pictures and words make it clear that he not only knows where to go, and how to get there, but how to catch them when he is there, too!

I've been fishing for carp over in Europe on a pretty regular basis since 1985; I've concentrated most of my efforts on France, a really beautiful country, full of mysterious, unexplored lakes and rivers, as yet unspoilt by hordes of anglers.

Some of the trips I have made have been of the pioneering sort; by that I mean there's been no real set plans, other than to fish interesting looking waters and, obviously, catch some carp. The waters were often chosen simply by looking for blue bits on the maps, then driving to them for a closer look.

My travels have taken me all over France and I've been lucky enough to have fished in some very beautiful and dramatic settings. Sometimes I've made the trips alone, but usually I go with a mate who also enjoys this type of carp fishing.

The whole thing seems to become

Geoff Shaw

an adventure from the moment I decide to go, the planning and organising, the navigating, the driving – I enjoy it all.

Investigating the potential of a new water can often prove to be difficult because of the limited time you have to find out as much as you can, as quickly as you can. Just talking to people on the bank can pay off and I always call in the local tackle shops. In some of the more remote areas, where there are no towns, cafes and bars are worth a visit.

Another thing that can really save a lot of time and which really comes into its own on the bigger waters, is a Fish Finder. At the moment I use an Eagle Ultra; it really can give you fast and accurate information about depths, bottom features, etc.

However, by far the best way to learn about a place is to fish it. This type of fishing can be incredibly exciting; being the first to fish a water, starting from scratch, not really knowing what's likely to happen when the buzzer goes off, these added elements seem to make the whole thing more intense.

This type of fishing can often be slow going, but if you are lucky enough to catch a fish or two, you feel as if the work has paid off and you have really achieved something.

This pioneering stuff obviously won't suit a lot of anglers who fish in France. If you only have a limited time in which to catch, say a couple of weeks a year, then trying to find new waters is not really going to be a good idea; sticking to one of the better known, established venues is a safer bet. Although these waters have had some angling pressure they still offer some very good fishing for those anglers who make the journey.

Carp fishing in France can often be unpredictable. On a lot of the waters, different factors come into play, things that are often outside the usual experience of most English carp anglers. I'll give some examples to try to illustrate the point.

Time of year is a very important factor when considering fishing in France. For instance, if you are fishing a lake that is part of a hydro system, then it is likely that, at certain times of the year, the water level will fluctuate. It may drop drastically for weeks on end; at other times, the water will be high. In either case, the place may become unfishable on some of the very large lakes with a relatively small head of carp. Location can become almost impossible except for the times when fish gather in shoals to spawn, or move over autumn feeding grounds.

In the summer months – July and August probably being the worst – the lakes in the hotter regions are used by thousands of holidaymakers for windsurfing, swimming, camping etc., and this again can make serious carp fishing impossible.

Lake Cassien spawning bay. Below: Geoff returning another whacker.

On a lot of waters, another thing you come up against is snags; some lakes can be full of tree stumps festooned with razor sharp zebra mussels or just have big sharp rocks lying around the bottom. Again, this can make the fishing really hard. Even when you've made every effort to combat these hassles, another factor that sometimes effects the fishing drastically, on the bigger waters usually, is getting to a swim. Often there is no way to drive down to the area you would like to fish; just getting yourself and all your gear to the swim can turn into a military operation involving co-ordinated route marches and boat manoeuvres; then there's the night fishing problem which, in my opinion, is the most important of all. I know plenty of waters in France that will only produce at night, so what I am saying is that life ain't all rises out there. However, if you're ready to face a few problems, a lot of the fishing is very different to the fishing in England.

Carp fishing in France isn't easy to describe; it really all depends on where you go. It's a big country, thousands of waters holding carp;the big rivers are full of them, the big hydro lakes, the small farm ponds - almost every type of water in France holds carp, so to generalise and say that carp fishing in France is like this or like that would be meaningless. Even if you are looking at fishing places that are green, have never seen a carp angler before, you still can't generalise. Each place will be different; the amount of natural food available, the number of carp present, other fish in the water, etc., etc. All these things will vary, so it follows that catching fish in some waters will be hard and in others it will be easy.

My advice, for what it is worth, to anybody contemplating their first trip out to France is don't expect an easy time of it. If you are going out to fish a water that is supposedly easy, don't believe it until you see it. Go with the right attitude, be ready to work hard at your fishing and be prepared to take a few knocks. Don't expect to catch loads of 20's and 30's, because you probably won't catch 'em!

The first trip you make may be a new experience, fishing wise, and if you've never been over to France before, then the whole thing is going to be new to you, so enjoy it all. If you have a bit of luck and a biggie gets your hook stuck in its mouth, great! Like most things in life, the more you do it, the easier it gets. After two or three trips you get a better idea as to what is going on, you suss out new and better places to fish, you meet people and they tell you things and you start catching more fish. The spectacular catches we read about in the mags are, sometimes, really the exception rather than the rule, so don't set your sights on that sort of stuff straight away.

I hope this article is not beginning to sound patronising, but I really think this needs to be said, because I speak to a lot of anglers who want to know about fishing in France and 90% of them seem to think that French carp are easy to catch. From what I've seen of it, probably 50% of anglers blank on their first trip, even when fishing the more productive venues which regularly throw up very big catches. Usually it's because they haven't put enough thought into the planning stages of their trip and when they arrive to fish their chosen water, they are ill equipped to tackle the place effectively and, in some cases, they are not even going to be in with a chance of a fish. Now I'm not slagging anybody off here, I was exactly the same when I first went out and I'm still making plenty of mistakes even now.

Last year, whilst fishing Lake Salagou, I met two separate parties of English anglers at the lake. Neither party had boats, enough bait, any knowledge of the layout of the lake and no knowledge of the horrendous mussel beds that cover most of the lake bottom. Basically, they hadn't done any homework at all on the place. One of the parties did manage to catch a few fish, but all the lads went home disappointed.

Anyway, I was asked by Julian to write this article and make some sort of guide to fishing in France. I don't think he wanted all this waffle, so I'd better get on with it. What I'll try to do is to give as much information as I can that may be of some help if you are planning on having a bash out in France. If you've already been, then you will know most of this stuff. If not, read on.

If you can turn up softly, with all the right stuff for the job, knowing as much as you possibly can about the place you intend to fish; if you've thought of every possible fishing situation that may arise and got it covered, then you are giving yourself the best chance you can and that's what you've got to do.

The first thing I would suggest is that you go with a good mate, rather than an acquaintance. Keep the party of anglers as small as possible; remember, a week or two living on the bank with someone really puts a strain on even the best of friendships and you don't want to spend your time arguing the toss with someone.

Decide where you want to fish. It's best to choose more than one venue so that you've got something to fall back on if your first choice doesn't work out. You've got to accumulate as much information as possible about the intended venue. Buy detailed maps of the area. If you can find other anglers that have already fished the water, then approach them, they may be willing to give you some help. Spend plenty of time thinking about the practical side of things; if you start to plan your trip say, 6 months in advance, then that should leave you ample time to sort things out.

PASSPORTS

A current passport is needed for entry into France. You can obtain a yearly one from the Post Office. It costs around £7.50 and you will need a couple of photos and some form of identification, i.e. birth certificate or medical card.

DRIVING

To drive in France you will need a current licence. If you decide to use your own vehicle, be sure it is going to be up to it. If you have any doubts, then forget it and make other arrangements. If you do use your own vehicle, get it serviced and thoroughly checked out; take a basic breakdown kit with you, some tools, spare fan belt, tyre foam is a good idea, a set of points, fuses, and so on. If you do break down in France you have to have one of those reflecting triangles to stick on the road to warn traffic, so this is where you start with your money.

Your lights must be adjusted for driving on the right – you can buy a kit for this conversion from any motor spares shop. It's a simple operation, just a case of sticking a bit of card over part of your lights – takes about a minute.

The French style of driving is aggressive, signals are used if only really necessary and they drive really fast, jostling for places in and out of small gaps; it takes a few days to get used to it, so be careful.

The auto routes are excellent. I prefer to plan my route before I go. Usually I choose auto routes. I like to travel at night wherever possible and it is definitely worth avoiding cities at rush hour time, which seems to be between 4.00 p.m. and 7.00 p.m. Paris and Lyon are the worst, even the ring roads and bypasses get very congested at these times. The smaller roads often look more direct but I've found that they are a lot slower because they pass through towns and villages and you end up stopping at traffic lights.

Petrol is a bit more expensive. I don't know the exact price at the moment, but to fill my car up in England costs £25, in France it costs about £30.

All the motorways are toll roads, which means you pay to use them. The cost obviously depends on how far you are travelling, to get right down south costs around £100 for the round trip. You pick up a ticket from the barrier as you enter the toll and the junction you leave determines how much you are charged. The motorways have a lot of service stations and the standard of food is good.

INSURANCE

Get yourself fixed up with good breakdown cover for your vehicle. This is a must – if you break down at 2.00 a.m. in the morning, in the middle of nowhere, with a head gasket blown or worse, you're going to be in trouble if you haven't got any. The AA offer a very comprehensive deal; you can take the policy out at the ferry port, usually they have an office in the reception area. Your vehicle must be under 10 years old and be in a reasonable condition to qualify for the basic insurance, other than that there are no real restrictions. Take all your documents along, i.e. insurance policy, log book, driving licence, MOT – obviously they must all be current. Fill out the form, part with your cash and you are away. It costs £24.50 for 1 to 15 days cover; £39.95 for 15 to 31 days cover. That's for a basic policy, if you pay a bit more you can have extra car hire allowance. You get a really good deal for your money; you are given vouchers which are for 'on the spot' type payments. They can be used to pay garages, car hire and there is even a repatriation voucher which is worth £300 and can be used towards the ferry ticket home.

If you break down, get to the nearest phone. You are given a free phone number to ring and this immediately puts you in contact with a friendly, English speaking AA operator. Give them all the relevant details and they will get someone out to help you, usually within the hour. If the worst comes to the worst and the car blows up, the AA will ship your car back home, charging only a small import tax, so all in all, it's a good deal.

It is best to get a Green Card, which is an international insurance document. This can be obtained from your insurance broker; prices vary but they are not too expensive – I think my last one was £30.

The DHSS have a form called he E111 (or something like that). If you complete this, it extends your National Health cover to France, meaning you don't have to pay medical fees if you get berry berry or whatever! A few years ago, a mate of mine ended up paying £60 for a tetanus jab, near Cassien, so as you see, medical stuff can be quite expensive. It's worth getting a policy to cover your tackle against loss, damage, theft, etc. You can pick a form up from your travel agents.

MAPS

You are going to need a good map for route planning, a Collins or AA atlas of France are well worth buying. They cost seven or eight quid, cover the whole of France and are reasonably detailed. I like to buy a detailed map of the particular water I intend to fish. I consider this very important, it can show access tracks, camp sites, river inlets, bridges etc., and to have a basic idea of the layout, especially it it's a big water, can save valuable time when you get there. The sort of detailed maps I find most suitable are called *Serie Orange, 1:50,000 1cm pour 500m.* They are actually French, but you can obtain them from Stanfords, 12-14, Long Acre, Covent Garden, London, WC2 E9LP, telephone 081 836 1321. Give them a ring or write to them and they will send you a catalogue.

FERRIES

It's a good idea to book ferries well in advance. Sealink and P&O operate from Dover to Calais, which seems to be the most popular crossing. It takes about one and a half hours. There's also a hovercraft service running, which is quicker but a bit more expensive.

The ferry costs vary considerably throughout the year, so visit your travel agents and pick up a couple of brochures. If you haven't been on a ferry before, it's worth taking some travel sickness pills.

Most places can be fished on an annual regional licence, which can be bought in every local tackle shop (usually they are around 100-250 francs). Be sure to make it clear that you only want to fish for carp, fill your name and address in as usual and that's it. Ask for a CARTE DE RECHE.

Say 100 francs is a tenner, then it's not hard to keep a check on what you are spending.

Above: Carp fishing French style, and below: the possible result.

FOOD & DRINK

You can get more or less the same stuff as at home basically, but generally it's a bit more expensive. Supermarkets are the best bet, their prices being reasonable. If you plan to cook for yourself, then it may work out cheaper to take your food with you and just buy bread, milk, that type of thing when you are in France. If you are going to one of the hotter regions, a cool box or fridge is essential.

If you don't mind spending a bit more on yourself, then eating out may suit you better. The French are renowned for their food and it is excellent. They love food and eating and the standard is really high. All the cafes and bars offer a basic meal of some sort; you can usually get a good meal for between 50 and 80 francs.

One thing worth mentioning, all meat is served rare in France, so if you order any kind or burger or steak, be sure to ask for it well done.

CAMPING

Camping in France is very popular and the sites are of a high standard. If you are fishing anywhere in France, I would think a nearby camp site would be easy to find. There are books that actually list the sites all over France, giving details of the facilities and these can be helpful. I've stayed on quite a few basic sites and never paid more than 35 francs a night, that charge being for one person and one bivvy. It is usual to leave a passport as security. When you check in at a camp site, get them to write down how much they are going to charge per night, as this saves any misunderstanding on settle up day. July to September is the busiest time on the sites.

It is obviously helpful if you can speak some French, even if is is only very basic. If you spend just a couple of weeks looking at a good phrase book before you go, it will make life a lot easier and a lot more enjoyable. The book I found the easiest to use is called 'Berlitz New Revised French for Travellers'.

NIGHT FISHING

Night fishing is illegal in France on most waters. There are a few exceptions, but 90% of the fishing is dawn till dusk only which, incidentally, is the same all over France.

There are places where some anglers do fish at night illegally, and the authorities do seem to tolerate it to a certain extent if the anglers are being discreet. However, if they receive any complaints from local fishermen about anglers fishing in the night, they are duty bound to investigate and will do so. If you are caught, your fate could be quite nasty. All your tackle, your car, or anything you've got with you when caught, can be confiscated. You may also end up appearing in court and perhaps shelling out a heavy fine. You may, on the other hand, only get a slap on the wrist – it all depends on your luck.

If you are thinking of night fishing in France, which I know some of you are, then be very, very careful.

Behaviour. Some of my French friends have asked me to mention a few things, if I get the opportunity, regarding our conduct in France. They ask if we could not leave shit all over the banks where we fish; could we stop threatening to, and I quote, "punch your f***ing French head in", if a zander angler, who has probably never seen a carp angler, unintentionally stops his boat over your baited area 100 yards out from the bank for a bit of live baiting. It happens. I've seen it more than once.

I know this only applies to about 1% of the anglers who do go out there, so to the other 99%, have some good fishing and enjoy yourself.

Oh yeh. I forgot to mention that the French people are really friendly and helpful.

LONG LIFE

I first started thinking seriously about dried baits when I was told by a Continental friend that he considered them superior to fresh-made baits. His enthusiasm for them was not influenced by their potential for longevity but, quite simply, because he considered them more effective. Obviously, I was interested in his reasoning but, to be honest, I was not and am not convinced that they are superior. What very definitely did interest me, though, was the fact that dried baits would presumably stay 'fresh' for long periods without there being any necessity to keep them chilled. For my normal day to day fishing the issue of bait freshness is not a problem because, not being a long-stint angler, I simply take a bag of frozen baits out of the freezer at the commencement of a trip and they remain in perfect condition for my usual day-sessions. If I am fishing overnight and into the next day I either take some baits in a vacuum flask or in a chilly-box with a couple of freezer-packs. The system works fine and generally suits my purposes admirably. But, now and again, I like to go for longer trips, maybe two or three days at a stretch; and for these longer trips, especially in very hot summer weather, neither flasks nor chilly-bins are really up to the job. And then there are the overseas trips; when I go to the Continent for a solid week's fishing there is no practical way of keeping baits fresh for the duration unless access to a freezer can be arranged. With this problem in mind my thoughts returned to my friend's dried baits. My lack of belief in their acceptability to carp was mitigated a little when I read Tony Davies-Patrick's comments about them – it seemed that he too rated them as not merely an alternative to fresh baits, but actually superior.

But, try as I may, I had a mental-block about their use – it seemed illogical that dried baits could be as effective as fresh-thawed or freshly made baits. But what about 'Munchies' and their ilk? They are dried 'baits', and they work well enough. And I recalled Tim Paisley writing that H.N.V. baits were at their most effective for their first 24 hours from thawing (or less in very warm conditions), but then became effective after about 72 hours providing no mould had appeared. Tim was not talking about dried baits as such – but then three-day old baits are not exactly fresh either, are they? So perhaps my obsession with ultra-freshness was only appropriate up to a point? Perhaps it only applied to fresh-made or fresh-thawed baits? Maybe it was inappropriate to apply it to baits per se?

Jim making bait on the bank during a long session. Is there an alternative other than freezing for the DIY boilie maker?

So with a trip to France in the offing I decided to dry a kilo, or so, of fish-meal/bird-food/milk-protein baits that had been flavoured with bun-spice. The weather was hot and sunny at the time so I put the baits in a mesh bag and hung them on a tree in my garden. They stayed there for three days, baking in the full force of the sun. It went very much against the grain I can tell you – up till then I had always taken great pains to keep my baits ultra-fresh, and here I was letting them broil in the midday sun! But I tried to rationalise what I was doing by telling myself that in many hot countries they keep fish 'fresh' by drying it in the sun; and when I was in Africa I ate some biltong, I think it was called, which was dried antelope meat.

After their period of drying, the boilies were rock-hard and biscuity. They smelled okay and looked okay – and when I dropped a few in water and left them for a few hours they reconstituted and, to be honest, struck me as being virtually identical to freshly-made baits.

I still was not convinced! Not until I caught a carp on them would I be able to accept that they were a viable alternative to fresh baits. So I took them to France and fished them on one rod. On the other two rods I used boilies that had been made fresh on the bank. That night (it was a privately owned water and I had permission from the owner to night-fish) I caught five carp – three on the fresh-made boilies, two on the dried ones. "Mmmmm, interesting!" I thought. I did not want to read too much into the distribution of captures, but it was fair to claim that the dried baits had at least held their own.

The next night I again used dried boilies on one rod and fresh-made baits on the other two. I had three carp that night two of them fell to the

BOILIES

dried baits.

"Mmmmm", I thought again, "VERY interesting!"

The first night could have been a fluke, but two nights on the trot... that was looking decidedly promising.

I had no further opportunity to try dried baits that trip for the simple reason that I had run out. But my confidence in their acceptability had moved a step or two in the right direction – but still there was a little 'maggot' in my brain that gnawed away at wholehearted belief in them. My doubts went something like this, "Okay, so they caught carp, they even held their own; more than held their own in fact, after all they were only used on one rod; but these were easy, naive carp (and, as everyone knows, all Continental carp are easy and naive!)... perhaps they would not work as well with really difficult fish..." Once that doubt had been sown there was no way I could have fished confidently and effectively in some of the very hard waters on which I spend a lot of my time.

So I decided to try another tack. I contacted several major food processing companies in the U.K. and asked for advice about the use of chemical preservatives. I had several, very interesting and helpful replies and the general consensus seemed to be that potassium sorbate was the most likely candidate. The level recommended was 1/1000 (1 gm. preservative to 1000 gm. bait-mix).

I made up an H.N.V./bird-food mix containing the preservative in the recommended proportion and first time out took a 25 lb. mirror on it.

"But what if that had been the first bait it picked up?" I asked myself. Did I really know that baits containing the preservative were palatable? Would carp eat such baits in quantity, I wondered?

I can fully understand that many of you reading this will be wondering what it takes to please me! My dried baits had worked from the outset, more than holding their own against fresh-made baits. My baits, containing one part to a thousand of potassium sorbate, had taken a mid-twenty (from a very difficult water too), first time of trying.

"Just stop whinging Gibbinson, and use the damn things, they obviously work."

Yes, I agree but...

The illogical nature of my lack of confidence in chemical preservatives is demonstrated by the fact that shop-bought, shelf-life baits contain potassium sorbate, and at five or six times the level at which I used it – and they catch plenty of carp. Obviously, therefore, there can be absolutely no doubt about the palatability of baits incorporating the stuff.

Which raises another point. Why all this agonising over dried and chemically preserved baits for long sessions and holiday trips? Why don't I do what most other anglers do and

26½lb mirror on fresh-thawed frozen bait – my usual choice.

Jim Gibbinson

simply use shelf-life baits?

I have always made my own baits. I have complete confidence in my fresh-made/fresh-frozen baits and, quite honestly, reckon them to be superior to any shop-bought alternatives. The fact that goodness-knows-how-many carp have fallen to shop-bought baits does absolutely nothing to convince me that they are anything other than a very poor second best. Whether or not that is a correct assessment, or even a fair assessment, I honestly do not know – we are not talking logic and practicalities here, we are talking serious issues of confidence; or rather the lack of it.

So I need to find a way of extending the effective life-span of my baits, but one that in no way diminishes their acceptability to carp. Maybe I have already found it, perhaps dried baits or chemically preserved baits are the answer and I only need to give them a period of sustained use to acquire the necessary confidence. Certainly I shall endeavour to psyche-up my determination and will try to give them a fair trial, on one rod at least. Early indications were undeniably promising and I would be a fool if I did not do a proper follow-up.

But my temperament is such that I have to keep 'worrying' at a problem until I become 100 per cent convinced that I have got it completely 'licked', so I experimented (albeit superficially) with another approach – the preservation of baits in oil. I first got this idea from my wife who, being born and bred in the south of Italy, was well acquainted with the whole concept of preserving foodstuffs in oil. When she suggested it to me I was a bit dubious; I thought the baits would go soggy, as with prolonged immersion in water, but I decided to give it a try anyway. A few H.N.V. baits were put in an empty Nescafe screw-top jar and covered with sesame seed oil – they were then put on an unused, high shelf in the kitchen and, frankly, forgotten. A couple of weeks later when I suddenly remembered them I retrieved the jar from the shelf and examined the contents. They were perfect! I imagine that the molecules of oil, being larger than those of water, did not permeate the boilies – but, whatever the reason, those boilies were as firm as when I first immersed them. They smelled okay too and, on cutting some open, I could find no evidence of decomposition. So I took the remainder on several successive fishing trips with the intention of trying them on the carp – but somehow never got round to it. So, preserved-in-oil baits remain untried, by me at least. But I am sure that they would prove acceptable to carp – they last well too; that particular batch must have been five or six weeks old by the time I decided that I was fed up with carrying them around and threw them away. And they were still in good condition.

But the method that interests me most is one that I have not yet tried: I am talking about irradiation. I am convinced that a combination of vacuum packing and irradiation will enable fresh-made baits to be preserved for up to a week, or so, with no detectable change in taste or flavour and with no significant decomposition – virtually indistinguishable from fresh made or fresh thawed baits, in fact.

So could irradiation be the answer I am looking for? I think it might be and I am currently investigating how I might arrange for a trial batch of baits to be treated – I have already sorted out the vacuum packing.

I realise that this article contains more questions than answers – but for those of us who like to make our own baits it is a subject that warrants some attention. With an increasing number of us trolling off to the Continent for our fishing, and for the session-men among us too, a really effective method of short-term bait preservation would be a boon.

If anyone has been working on this matter and has come up with a workable procedure I, for one, would love to hear about it. And I suspect that I will not be the only one.

Above: I think this is the $25^1/_2$ that took the potassium sorbate preserved bait.

Below: $24^1/_2$. Took the same bait as was tried with the preservative, but this time without the chemical.

SAVAY – THE FIRST SUMMER

Savay Lake is a mature gravel pit on the border of Hertfordshire and Buckinghamshire in the Colne Valley, owned by Redlands and run by fishery manager Peter Broxup. This 70 acre pit is now regarded as one, if not ***the***, premier carp fishery in the country. Over the years, it has played host to some of the country's leading carp anglers and has filled many a chapter in the best selling carp books we have seen.

In 1988, I was lucky enough to be offered a place in the syndicate, just before the start of the season, which, naturally, I jumped at, although I had already made my plans for that summer and Savay hadn't been part of them. I only fished the lake a couple of times in my first season, but it gave me a good insight into the water and a chance to get a feel for it.

The following season I decided to give carp fishing a rest in general. I felt I had lost my hunger and I was in danger of burning myself out; the challenge had gone out of it for me and I knew that unless I took a season off, I was likely to give up carp fishing altogether.

The break did me a power of good and come the start of this season I was like a dog on heat! June 15th saw the 'Toad Rota' congregating outside the main gate. As you would expect, most of the rota had turned out for the off; Bruce Ashby, Tony Hall and Carl were all there when I arrived. Shortly afterwards we were joined by Cliff Fox and Tottenham Bob, so after a quick chat a couple of us decided to get some eggs and bacon down our necks in preparation for the day.

Summer Savay. Below: Max's first Savay 30lb+ – 30lb 15oz.

Max Cottis

When we returned from breakfast, the numbers had grown, so when the gate was opened at midday, it was off for a walk around the lake for a look at some of the fancied pitches before meeting back in the car park to make our choices about which swim we intended to fish. The system run down at Savay is a simple one - first there, first choice!

When it came to the big 'make your mind up time' both my fancied choice of swims were taken, so I opted for the Reeds, a swim about half way down the canal bank. I figured that until I knew where the fish were, somewhere in the middle wasn't a bad place to start.

During the afternoon I saw a good fish poke its head out right over the back, a good sign, believe me. I set up, full of anticipation, waiting for the turn of midnight to cast out and start the new season. Well, to cut a long story short, three days came and went without even as much as a tench and doubts started to creep in about my choice of swim.

Simon Ball and Bernie Heerey were in the North Bay, one just to the right of Wilson's Island and the other in a new swim between Caldwells and Reagans. Both had seen some action; Bernie had lost a couple of fish and Simon had caught a fish of 23lb. Spending some time observing the bay, it became apparent that there were a few fish in the weed, so I asked Simon if he would mind if I moved into Caldwells. He had no objection, so I asked Bernie and he didn't mind either, so off I went to pack up my gear and move swims. That night proved to be more of the same (fishless).

On Wednesday, I decided to wind in, go home and have a freshen up, top up the provisions and make some more bait. After a good meal (and watching the England game on television) I made my way back to the lake, arriving some time around eleven o' clock at night. A quick word with Simon about the day's events and he informed me that there had been several fish showing, one of them a real 'whacker', which had rolled over my baited area during the afternoon but, being the gentleman he is, he had resisted the temptation to cast to it whilst I was away.

Filled with a new enthusiasm, I baited up and cast out three bait stringers, which were backed up by a hundred or so baits in the throwing stick. Rods out, I settled back on my bedchair when, almost immediately, I had a small lift on the left hand indicator. It stopped, then some minutes later it pulled slowly into the butt ring, only to drop back again. Simon strolled up to me to see what the couple of bleeps were all about, when it pulled back up again. I was

"I was lost for words" (claimed Max!). Savay's first forty – 42lb.

convinced that a tench had hung itself on, so I struck. I met with a heavy resistance; not one that powered off, just a dead weight.

After a short spell of pump and wind, still convinced that I had 5lb of tench and 50lb of weed on, the fish was beneath my feet. Simon turned on a dim torch towards the net where, to our surprise, there was no weed, just a large, fat carp wallowing in the margins. Simon netted it first time and it was only then that the weight of this fish became apparent. He struggled to lift it out of the water onto the unhooking mat, muttering something about having 'nine carat plums'.

At this point, I don't know who was more pleased, Simon or myself, for I was a little shell shocked and he kept slapping me on the back saying "Well done mate, what a whacker. I bet it was the fish I saw earlier, knew I should have cast to it." (His nickname is Motormouth).

Out came the Avon scales, so with the weigh sling wetted and the scales zeroed, we attempted to weigh her. At first, we thought she weighed in at around the low thirty mark, but this didn't seem right and on checking the coloured disc on the scales, we noticed that only half the red was showing. It had bottomed the 40lb Avons out.

I went down and woke 'Telecom' Steve (Reeve), knowing he had a pair of Reubon Heaton scales with him that went up to sixty pounds (ever the optimist). Steve and Pete (The Brain) both came up and weighed it for me. With several witnesses present, we agreed that the fish weighed in at 42lb exactly. I was lost for words. Savay's first forty!

The rest of the night went over my head a little. Steve went and fetched Peter Broxup (the Boss), John Harry (the Plum) and others from the syndicate to see the fish and take a few photos. For the remainder of the night I didn't sleep at all, the excitement had been too much.

As dawn broke, I had another take, this time a screamer. Straight away I knew this one was a carp. As I struck, the fish powered off to my right and Simon emerged from his bivvy, strolled up to see what all the noise was about and stood by my side whilst I played the fish. After five minutes or so, the fish rolled half way out for both of us to clearly see that it was a common. Looking at each other, we joked that it was probably 'Sally' (the country's most famous common carp).

Simon said "If that's her, you're going in".

To which I replied, "If that's Sally, once I've landed her, I will gladly jump in".

Unfortunately it was not (well, everyone is entitled to dream) and Simon netted a scale perfect, immaculate common of 17lb 4oz.

That was the end of the action for

The mirror of 25lb 4oz that took a liking to Chum Mixers.

me that week. Simon added another fish at 22lb 10oz and a smaller common and our rota finished on the Saturday lunchtime.

The following rota I was away in France with Lee Jackson, making a video for Malthouse, so I was unable to fish again until mid July.

By this time the hot weather had played havoc with the weed and many of the swims had changed quite dramatically from the opening week. The spots I had fished in Caldwells at the start had become unfishable, so I chose to fish the swim that Bernie had been in during opening week. Although there was a fair amount of weed in front of this swim, I did manage to find a clear channel leading up to a plateau some thirty yards out. I fancied this swim a lot as the weed offered the carp plenty of cover as well as giving me the chance to do a spot of floater fishing during the day.

The first day brought no action, although I saw several fish in the weed, a good sign, for I knew that there were at least some fish present and, with the weed, they were likely to remain there.

The second day the sun was out with a vengeance and the carp were soaking it up. I started trickling in some Chum, half a dozen here, half a dozen there, over the space of an hour or so, until I saw a good fish drift up and take two or three in a line with almost brash arrogance. Quickly joined by a couple of other fish, they were now taking the Chum as well, so I quickly set up a controller rig using a three foot nylon hooklength, coupled to eight inches of Multistrand, water knotted to the end and tied to a size 7 Owner.

Choosing my moment carefully, I flicked it out several feet past the feeding fish and gently drew it along into their path. Within seconds, one of the carp drifted up to my hookbait, opened its mouth and sucked it straight in. Result, a beautiful mirror of 25lb 4oz to get the session off to the right start. The rest of the day remained uneventful, so I changed back to the bottom baits for the night.

At six o' clock the following morning, I had a screaming take which immediately found sanctuary in the weed bed. Twenty minutes or so of trying to free it, proved useless and, not knowing whether or not the fish was still on, I was faced with two options; pull for a break or get the boat out. I set about getting hold of John Harry. He arrived and after some excellent manoeuvring, I was able to free the fish from the weed bed in which it was well and truly stuck. A swift net job by John (who, incidentally, doesn't need to see the fish, just smell it) and my first thirty from Savay was on the bank. At 30lb 15oz this lean, mean, muscle bound whacker really made my day.

Another floater caught fish of 20lb 3oz and a bottom caught fish of 27lb 1oz rounded off the session and sent me home with the feeling that I couldn't do anything wrong.

You know the feeling - just when you think you have got something 'sussed', you get kicked straight in the plums! - well, Savay invented it! The following rota I returned, with plans to take it apart (very naive I know) and guess what? I blanked! Even after several moves trying to get on fish, Savay had done what she is best at, bringing people back down to earth.

It was now mid August when I arrived for the start of the fifth rota, my fourth session. After a wander around, I decided to fish Andy's, the first swim on the canal bank. This is a very interesting swim and there are so many features in it, it can leave you in a dilemma as to just where to place your baits. Strategically, it is one of the best swims for it allows you to place your baits in two lines, one close to cover any fish that may move in or out of the North Bay, the second at distance, giving you a good chance of catching any fish that may be on

One of the nicest carp I've ever caught! Linear mirror, 30lb 8oz.

the move through to the shallows into the Cottage Bay. During the course of the week, I saw more fish showing in this swim than I had previously seen anywhere else on the lake, but whatever I tried, they didn't want to get their heads down. Several members on the rota told me that it was very common to see fish showing in Andy's, but not catch; more often than not they were 'on the move' through to the Cottage.

Finding it difficult to move off 'showing' fish, I persevered and on the last afternoon I got my reward, a plump mirror of 25lb 12oz, right out of the blue, just when I felt that it was all over.

The following session I was only able to do forty eight hours, so for convenience more than anything, Cliff Fox and I chose to fish the Cottage Bay, myself in the Rat Hole and Cliff on the Point. We saw several fish during the afternoon we arrived and put a fair amount of bait out, in the hope that it would bring them on and produce an early result. The first night produced a blank, until the morning, when I had a take, only to connect with a good fish that powered off some forty yards across the surface before slipping the hook.

The following morning produced a 22lb for Cliff and an 18lb 8oz for me before we had to make tracks home. Knowing that Simon was coming down the following day, I phoned him and told him to get himself in Rat Hole, as we felt that the fish were moving into the Cottage and they would probably be stacked up by the time he arrived. This he did and, just to prove us right, he took eight fish up to 31lb 4oz - now who had 'golden plums'?!!

The middle of September was to be my last visit down to Savay for the summer. Arriving at midday on the Sunday (when the rotas change over), I decided to give it my best shot in Andy's again. Cliff set up next door in the Root. We decided to pile in the bait in the hope that if any fish moved through we might have a chance of holding them for a while.

My first Savay Italian job – this one went 28lb 8oz.

The first couple of nights produced a couple of fish each, all small, but an encouraging sign nevertheless; then at 6.30 a.m. on the third morning when I had a belting take that resulted in my first Savay 'Italian' at 28lb 8oz. Around 9.00 p.m. that night, I was away again, this time striking into a fish that I had to give line to straight away. After five minutes or so, and just when I thought I was making some headway, the fish just fell off, some thirty yards out. To say I was gutted would have been an understatement. Never mind, it wasn't the first time and it probably won't be the last, so baiting up, using a three bait stringer, I recast back onto the spot that had produced the take and returned to my bed to ponder on what might have been.

At 3.30 a.m. the same rod rattled off again and this time I didn't make any mistakes. Ten minutes or so of rather careful fish playing saw one of the 'stockies' at 22lb safely in the net. A few photos (sacks are banned at Savay - and rightly so) and the fish was returned.

After sorting myself out, I returned to bed, happy as a 'pig that had just escaped the bacon slicer', looking forward to a good night's sleep.

At 7.00 a.m. the following morning I was once again disturbed by the sound of my Optonic. Was I dreaming or was this for real? Fifteen minutes later and Savay had given me one of the best looking fish I'd ever caught and my second thirty of the season to boot, with a 30lb 8oz linear mirror.

Apart from a smaller common later that morning, that concluded my first summer on Savay. I'd set out hoping to catch a handful of fish if I was lucky, instead it had given me my most enjoyable season to date, not only because of the fish I'd caught, but also the company I'd caught them in.

Thanks lads, long may it continue!

HOLIDAYS WITH CARP IN MIND

When you consider that the amount of time for fishing holidays is limited, it is important that the correct choice is made to suit the particular individual's requirements. Whether you are single, or married with a tribe of youngsters, there are holidays which fit the bill. You may well fancy a trip to the continent in search of that "fish-of-a-lifetime or alternatively you may want a quiet, relaxing holiday with the family with some easy carp fishing on the side. In the following feature we list a few of the carp fishing holidays available, along with their location and details of the facilities on offer. Choose carefully, have a great holiday but remember one thing – carp are carp, no matter where they are. It's up to you to catch them not the owner of the lake!

WAVENEY VALLEY LAKES
Wortwell, Harleston, Norfolk IP20 0EH
Tel: Homersfield (098686) 676

WAVENEY VALLEY LAKES

This complex of lakes is well known in the carp world and many famous anglers have fished there over the years. The site is ideal for a family holiday offering caravan and chalet accommodation in a pleasant rural situation. The small Norfolk village of Wortwell, where the Lakes are situated, lies between Harleston and Bungay on the main A143 trunk road. This road also leads to the coastal town of Lowestoft about 15 minutes away. To the north, within easy travelling distance, is Norwich and the Broads.

The 1989/90 season at Waveney Valley ended on a high note with a 33lb. 4oz. mirror carp from D Lake in the very last week of the season. This was the largest fish landed from the Lakes since the present owners acquisition of the complex in November 1988. The lake record now stands at 35lb 4oz.

C Lake produces a number of very good fish early every season, the best so far being a 32lb. 12oz. mirror. In 1990 three other thirties were also landed from C Lake during the season as well as numerous twenties and high doubles.

F Lake has started to produce the fish that the owners have always known were there, with several mid-twenties being landed and two very large upper twenties. The biggest of these weighed 28lb. 12oz., and we still believe that there are a couple more surprises in store!

G Lake still continues to be a summer favourite with many anglers and always fishes well during the early season. The largest fish from the lake this season was a 27lb. mirror, again caught during the summer. Basildon, Essex angler Mark Smith also landed eight different twenties, in a thirty fish haul during a two week spell in August.

B Lake houses the Carp Society caravan together with a number of private caravans and one holiday caravan. The largest fish landed has been a 27lb. 12oz. mirror. An encouraging note from B Lake was that the growth of a number of fish, introduced the previous year was

WAVENEY VALLEY LAKES
CARAVAN PARK
OFFICE & SHOP
SELF CATERING HOLIDAY CARAVANS
FOR HIRE
TOURING VANS & TENTS WELCOME
DAY LICENSES FOR FISHING
CAR PARK
SLOW - RUMBLES
10
MPH

quite remarkable, with an average increase of around 4lb.

A Lake, which is entirely private, produced fish up to 27lb. which is quite exceptional when you consider that it is no more than acre in size.

Two new fish were introduced into D Lake in the late autumn; the first at 28lb. 4oz., which incidentally was caught four weeks later at 29lb. 8oz., and the second at 29lb. 4oz.

During last year two new projects were completed. The first was the construction of a licensed bar which opened during October and proved a great success with the winter anglers. The second was the opening of a new office, which now enables the owners to give over the whole of the former office to a tackle and provisions shop. Over the last couple of years additional land has been purchased, adjacent to the complex, and the owners are now working with local conservation groups to establish a new fishing lake, of around four acres, and a bird sanctuary of ten acres to be completed by the end of 1992. Over the last couple of years, during the close season, the owners have travelled to France to fish a lake in the Dordogne region. Whilst they have never managed to land any of the really big carp that they have seen they have always caught a lot of fish up to 26lb., seven fish during a night being not uncommon. Because of the interest this has generated they have decided to organise a number of trips, throughout the season, for small groups of between four and six anglers. Whilst they cannot promise any fish of monster proportions they can assure anyone interested that they will catch carp and they will have a good time. The local food and wine is superb the people are very friendly and, yes, night fishing is permitted.

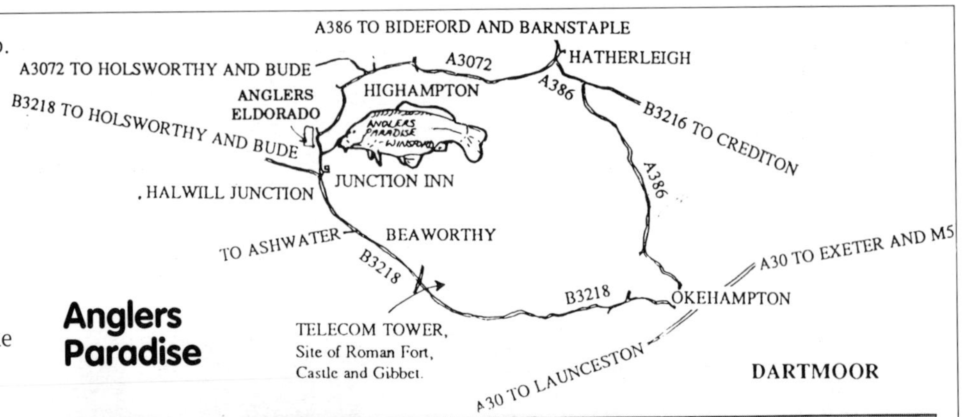
A386 TO BIDEFORD AND BARNSTAPLE
A3072 TO HOLSWORTHY AND BUDE
A3072
HATHERLEIGH
ANGLERS
ELDORADO
HIGHAMPTON
A386
B3216 TO CREDITON
B3218 TO HOLSWORTHY AND BUDE
JUNCTION INN
A386
. HALWILL JUNCTION
TO ASHWATER
BEAWORTHY
B3218
A30 TO EXETER AND M5
B3218
OKEHAMPTON
Anglers
Paradise
TELECOM TOWER,
Site of Roman Fort,
Castle and Gibbet.
A30 TO LAUNCESTON
DARTMOOR

ANGLERS PARADISE

Since it was opened for business in 1985 Anglers Paradise has become nationally known for its superb fishing, especially carp, and its Five Star luxury cottages and villas. Every year its reputation seems to grow, as more and more lakes are added, the carp get bigger and more and more holiday makers leave happy and content. A large proportion of Anglers Paradise's customers actually book their holiday for next year before they leave.

Zyg and Rose set out to make Anglers Paradise the sort of place they would like to go on holiday themselves and Zyg set out to make the fishing the kind he would enjoy. Judging from the comments in the visitors book and the angling press the Gregoreks have succeeded beyond their wildest expectations.

Zyg has used his fish farming expertise to good effect. There are now 9 fishing lakes at Anglers Paradise between 1 acre and $4^1/_2$ acres. Four of these lakes are carp lakes. The 'jewel in the estate' is the largest, the Main Carp Lake. It is teeming with large carp with a few golden tench and golden orfe. The first fish were stocked during October 1979 (biggest fish about $2^1/_2$ lb.). It now contains 165 carp, with an average size of about 16lb. and at least 30 around 20lb. to mid-twenties, with 47 golden tench to 5lb. and 35 golden orfe to 5lb.

Octopussy Lake is about $1^1/_2$ acres and has an 'Octopussy' island so that each angler can have his own bay and swim. It holds about 100 carp, mostly high singles and about 40 doubles, to upper doubles.

There is also the one acre Beginners Carp Lake, with over one thousand carp weighing up to double figures (most of the carp are between 1lb. and 4lb.). There is a walk-on-island and nobody who has spent a day on this lake has blanked.

Then there is the Specimen Lake which is about $1^1/_2$ acres in size and houses an 'aboriginal' shaped island, so six anglers can fish in comfort. When the lake was drained and enlarged, in January 1990, all the small fish were taken out except for about 20, or so, of the best looking fish which averaged about 2lb. These have been coming out in 1990 at between 6 and 9lb.! The 18 big fish are all good twenties, mostly upper twenties with about 5 thirties. The best recorded growth rate of one of the carp in 1990 was Jumbo, who was put back at 22lb. in January. Jumbo was then caught in March at 23lb., in June at 25lb. 4oz. and at the beginning of September weighing 29lb. 2oz. There are two carp in the Specimen Lake which came out during the January 1990 netting weighing over 27lb.! These two fish have never been caught on rod and line and have evaded capture during 1990. Zyg confidently predicts that in the next 3 to 4 years there will be several 40's in his waters! The maximum time allowed for any angler on this lake is two days and one night, and only six anglers per day. There is also a charge of £5 per day for fishing the Specimen Lake.

There are 5 other lakes at Anglers Paradise, full of exotic species. There is the Float Fishing Lake with a Z shaped walk-on-island. This fishery is teeming with golden tench, golden orfe, goldfish, crucians and koi. This is a very easy lake with guaranteed results if you spend a day here.

Then there is the Tench Lake, shaped like a tench and full of golden tench (to over 6lb.) and blue orfe. The Specimen Tench and Golden Orfe Lake has twenty golden tench between 4lb. and 7lb. and twenty golden orfe between 4lb. and 6 1b. Pixie Lake is about a third of an acre in size and is probably the easiest of all the lakes, full of goldfish, Shubumkins, golden rudd, golden orfe and golden tench to 3lb. There is also a Koi Lake with koi to double figures and it has a dragon raft.

There are no day tickets at Anglers Paradise and the only people who can fish are people staying at the holiday complex. There is a separate charge for the fishing. A budget ticket for six of the lakes, for the week, is only £25. This is for two rods each, in the Main Carp Lake and Octopussy, and one rod in the Beginners Carp Lake, Tench, Float and Pixie Lake.

There are 25 villas and cottages at Anglers Paradise designed to the highest standard, all fully fitted out with microwaves, ceramic hob cookers, colour T.V.'s, quality furniture, even carp shaped coffee tables. Some have whirlpool baths, leather Chesterfields, dishwashers, some have ornate four poster beds! All are tastefully decorated with sporting prints and split cane rods and other sporting paraphernalia. The accommodation is double glazed and with night storage heaters is very warm in winter.

The African Safari Bar is open every evening and decked out with African artefacts, including zebra, crocodile and leopard skins, animal horns, tribal carvings, spears and all sorts of things that Zyg picked up during his years in Africa. The tables are carved out in the shape of carp, as are the benches. There is also a games room with a pool table and video machines, a table tennis room, ship climbing frame, woodland sculpture walk and loads of other goodies.

All holiday makers are greeted personally, by either Zyg or Rose, and offered a glass of wine, the children a glass of lemonade, before they are escorted to their accommodation. With such delights and pleasures no wonder Anglers Paradise is always booked solid.

For an 18 page colour brochure please send a large stamped addressed envelope to: Zyg and Rose, Anglers Paradise, The Gables, Halwill Junction, Beaworthy, Devon EX21 5XT (Telephone Beaworthy (0409) 221559.

WYRESIDE LAKE FISHERIES

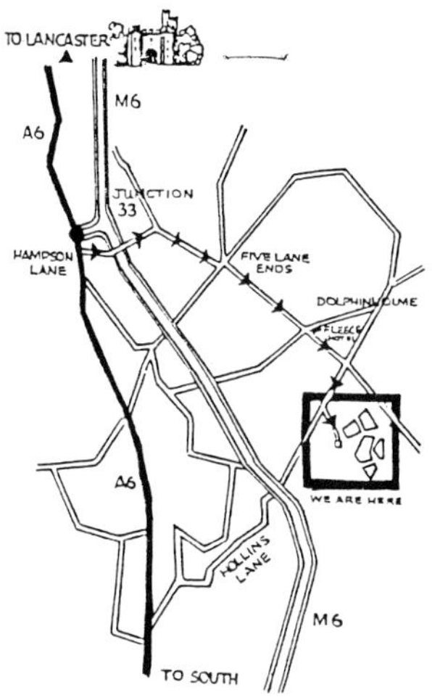
TO LANCASTER
M6
A6
JUNCTION 33
HAMPSON LANE
FIVE LANE ENDS
DOLPHINHOLME
WE ARE HERE
A6
HOLLINS LANE
M6
TO SOUTH

DIRECTIONS: Turn off A6 50 yards south of M6 Junction 33 Roundabout, onto HAMPSON LANE. Turn right at T junction & over two crossroads, past Fleece Inn. Turn right at next crossroads. Fishery entrance is 400 yards on the left.

Contact: Larry Fitzgerald at Wyreside Lakes Fishery, Sunnyside Farmhouse, Bay Horse, Nr. Lancaster for further details on: (0524) 792093.
For lodge brochures contact: Duchy of Lancaster, Estate Office, Forton, Preston PR3 0AD on: (0524) 791494. Eves/Wkds: 791830.

WYRESIDE LAKES FISHERIES

Despite the fact that they have virtually transformed the carp fishing scene in parts of the south, gravel pits still tend to be very thin on the ground in many other less fortunate areas. In the north west the relative scarcity of such waters has also tended to work against the angler in more ways than one. Not only are such venues rare, but even those few pits which do exist are often ruined for any serious sport, simply because they are almost invariably "shared" with other water users.

However, there is now at least one small complex of former gravel workings which are ideal for the north western angler looking for some carp fishing, which is both peaceful and productive. The venue in question is Wyreside Lakes Fisheries, a five lake complex tucked away in the beautiful Wyre Valley just south of Lancaster. Here, at least, is a gravel pit fishery where you WON'T have your sport ruined by some manic windsurfer repeatedly falling off in your swim... neither will you ever need fear any other disturbances which can make fishing most other north western gravel pits such an unpleasant experience.

Under the watchful eye of resident bailiff Larry Fitzgerald, Wyreside Lakes has grown into a venue which would be popular even in more fortunate areas, never mind the carp-starved north west.

Initial stocking of the five lake complex took place with 800, 12oz. to 1lb., mirror carp and several thousand roach. These fish were first introduced into the largest water in the complex, the 18 acre Sunnyside Lake. This first stocking took place in March 1984, though the fishery was not opened up to the angling public until some years later. These fish have continued to thrive and, for the last two seasons, Sunnyside has produced carp to over 20lb., with the best fish, so far, being 22lb.

By the time the 12 acre Bantons Lake became available for stocking, the popularity of Sunnyside as a carp venue showed up the need for another water in the complex catering exclusively for the carp angler. For this reason it was decided to move carp from Sunnyside into the new lake. At the time of writing 170 carp, ranging in size from 8lb. to 21lb., have been transferred to their new home.

The fish transferred to Bantons are obviously exploiting their new environment to the full. Fish up to 22 lb. have already been reported, and many of the fish which were weighed in single figures when they were first transferred are already being caught as doubles.

However, despite the removal of some of its residents, it is doubtful whether Sunnyside will ever be totally eclipsed by the new venue. Indeed, some of the regulars feel that there is now more potential than ever for the original water to produce much bigger carp. Especially now that the lake supports fewer actual numbers of fish.

Though the complex, as a whole, is very peaceful there is another smaller water on the site which can provide even more solitude. At only two and a half acres River Lake is by far the smallest water in the complex. It is a very intimate little fishery lined with trees and reeds, and in many respects a classic carp water. The carp have grown and spawned regularly in this sheltered fishery. The best carp caught so far is 19lb. with many upper doubles also in evidence.

Also on the complex is a four acre fly-only trout water. A fifth lake is an 18 acre private carp syndicate. Unfortunately, again due to the dearth of good carp fishing in the area, vacancies in this syndicate very rarely arise.

Overlooking the entire complex are two Scandinavian holiday lodges, sleeping four to six people. These provide very pleasant and comfortable self catering accommodation. This is especially ideal for the carp angler wanting to reconcile a good family holiday (the Lake District is not far away) with some decent carp fishing. A purpose-built jetty for disabled anglers can be found on Sunnyside Lake and in the spacious anglers' room, at the entrance to the complex, there are toilet facilities for the disabled and a tackle shop selling everything you forgot to bring, as well as a range of carp baits. There is ample car parking on site and good pub food can be found a quarter of a mile away.

CARP FISHING IN NORMANDY

Nestling in a peaceful green valley surrounded by the lush and unspoilt dairylands, for which Normandy is famous, lies the Chateau du Lorey; a small chateau with its own, very old, private carp lake. Dating back to the middle 1800's, the spring fed lake was originally stocked for the kitchens but, in recent years, the house has remained empty and the lake has now not been fished for well over ten years.

It is surrounded by gentle grassy banks, overhanging trees and shrubs, including weeping ash and beech, bamboos, laurels, rhododendrons and American Oaks. All provide a fabulous array of leaf and colour as a backdrop to the lake throughout the seasons.

The water has a large, mature head of, predominantly, common carp, with known weights at the time of writing up to 25lb., but, because of the nature and age of the lake, the top weights are as yet to be discovered. Being a private lake, there are no special permits required, which is usually the only way that night fishing is legal in France.

The house itself is welcoming, unstuffy and is neither grand nor gloomy. It has approximately seven acres of gardens, orchards, streams and meadows to the front and side, and behind it is over 140 acres of pasture land and woods. All around is a haven for wildlife.

The chateau offers a complete fishing package to the angler, including day and night fishing, delicious food which includes full breakfast, light lunch, and a three-course dinner, showers and bathrooms, a tackle room with bait freezer, full bar facilities (at English prices!), and a even a 'keep pool' for exhibiting catches!

Attractive and comfortable accommodation is available all year round within the house for the not so dedicated night angler, at a small supplement.

There is no overcrowding because the lake is exclusive to the booked party of anglers, up to a maximum of six, and the lake is not open to the general public at all.

For those perhaps wanting a change of scenery during their stay there are two carp waters totalling 22 acres a short drive away. Created from peat mining works these rich waters are teeming with fish. The carp are virtually unfished for by the French but the waters are known to hold carp in excess of 30lb. The waters also hold 20lb plus pike, perch and zander, tench and specimen bream. All permits are arranged and included in the daily price so there is no extra charge. Regrettably night fishing is strictly forbidden on these two additional waters.

Enquiries are welcomed from single anglers, as well as groups, because it may be possible to share a booking with a small group depending on space availability. Enquiries are also welcomed from anglers accompanied by their wives as private en-suite rooms are available.

The venue is conveniently situated just one hour south of the ports of Cherbourg and Caen, meaning that there are no long and tiring drives and, perhaps more importantly, no lost fishing time. The ports of St. Malo and Le Havre are just over two hours away. The journey, by whichever route, is easy and unhurried.

The taste and life of Normandy is all around. Rolling hills, endless beaches, sparkling water, valleys, country lanes, the Suisse Normande, Camembert, thick Normandy cream, seafood, sand yachting, calvados, cider, cathedrals, chateaux, bustling towns, fishing ports, empty roads, open air markets, patisseries, parfumeries, sidewalk cafes, wines, sunshine, rivers, orchards, apple blossom, dinners by the lake, champagne by the lake or by the bottle(!), tennis, golf windsurfing, picnics, rock-climbing, canoeing, these are just a few of the pleasures to be found in the area.

If you would like to visit the Chateau du Lorey telephone either U.K. 0300-20220, or direct to France on 010 33+ 33 45 68 51. The chateau is English owned so there are no language problems.

The cost of the fishing package is 300 French francs per angler, per day. This includes the fishing, meals and all facilities. There is no extra charge for night fishing. Accommodation, if required, is just 25 francs per night.

FISHABIL

If you haven't seen or heard the name Fishabil yet you are certainly going to in the not too distant future. Fishabil is a specimen coarse fish centre, located in the north-west of France. The lake covers some 86 acres and has been stocked with 36 tons (yes, thirty-six) of specimen fish. Carp, catfish, pike, zander, black bass, tench and... wait for it, sturgeon!

To give you an idea of the calibre of fish that have been released into the lake, there are catfish up to 127 kg (279lb.!), and the carp average over 20lb. The quality of the fish has been matched only by the facilities it offers, making Fishabil an ideal place for the family man with a wife and kids.

In the grounds can be found a luxury hotel with tennis courts and a club house. There are excursions available, an animal park, cinema and horse riding trips all at hand to keep the non-fishing types entertained.

Being a private enterprise night fishing is allowed and all fish must be returned alive. The man behind Fishabil is Raphael Farragi, and he believes that his lake is set to be one, if not the, premier specialist coarse fishery in Europe. The work and thought put into Fishabil is staggering and I would suggest that you book early, as demand for this venue is likely to be considerable. For further details contact Raphael at Fishabil on **France 96 25 27 66.**

CARP FISHERS ABROAD

You have probably read enough articles about carp fishing on the Continent to know taking an unproven trip can be expensive, fruitless, uncomfortable and frustrating – not exactly our idea of a holiday.

Both our fisheries have built their reputation on great catches in perfect carp fishing surroundings. We take the hassle out of arranging your holiday so you can spend more time enjoying yourself catching big fish. Location, directions, night fishing, permits, number of rods, accommodation, native fishermen, etc., etc., are all problems we take care of.

OUR DUTCH FISHERY: Max Cottis and Richard Gardner opened last season with a 3 day haul of 21 grass carp and carp, which included six twenties, five in one night from the Jetty Lake. The season continued well with Jetty Lake alone producing 41 twenties.

CHALET LAKE, FRANCE: Catching carp was consistent, with 95% of parties catching between 20 and 83 ten pound plus carp. Cats of between 20lb. and 45lb. fell regularly to those fishing for them. The giant grass carp did not show until the last week of June when Cottis banked a good fish of 25lb. captured on Andy Nickolson's latest video, 'Carp Experiences'.

Some of the best weeks are still free at both our Dutch and French fisheries so, if you are seriously interested, please contact David or Max to discuss availability and prices.

David Rance, B.Sc., Rose Cottage, Shop Lane, Rodington Heath, Shrewsbury, Shropshire SY4 4RB. Tel: (0952) 770771 and Fax: (0952) 770010

Max Bond, F.M.D., Station Farm, Bentley, Nr. Ipswich, Suffolk IP9 2DB. Tel: (0473) 328147 and Fax: (0473) 328256

GEOFF SHAW'S CARP TRIPS

Well known continental carper, Geoff Shaw, now runs trips (up to seven people) to various fisheries in France, in search of big carp.

The trips are predominantly pioneering sorties and offer carp anglers a great adventure and challenge. Prices for the 9/10 day trips range between £290-£350 depending on the destination. The price includes a meal a day, ferry fares etc. No guaranteed night fishing but lots of fun and a good chance of fishing for some **big** carp.

For an insight into one of Geoff's trips, read Carpworld 12, pages 77-79. Further details from Geoff on 0268 690844.

FURTHER CARP HOLIDAY IDEAS

Free coarse fishing on Trevella Park's own lakes; tench, roach, rudd, carp to 27lb. No close season. Award winning caravan park; holiday caravan hire, caravan/camping pitches. For a free brochure write to **Trevella Park, 6, Crantock, Newquay, Cornwall. TR8 5EW. Telephone 0637 830308** (24 hours).

White Acres Holiday Park, Cornwall. This friendly, family run park can offer you all the amenities which make a terrific family fishing holiday. $4^1/_2$ acres of well stocked lakes, large carp, tench, roach, rudd, bream and ghousties. In addition there is an indoor heated pool complex and top class cabaret each night. Luxury caravans for hire; tents and tourers welcome. For a free colour brochure write to **White Acres Holiday Park, Whitecross, Newquay, Cornwall. Telephone 0726 860220.**

Lakeview Country Club, 'The angling centre at the centre of Cornwall' offers first class facilities, including 4 and 6 person lodges and bungalows. Well stocked lakes containing Cornish carp (20lb+), tench, roach and bream. No close season. Brochures available from **Lakeview Country Club, Old Coach Road,Lantivet, Bodmin, Cornwall, PL30 5HB. Telephone 0208 831808.**

Meadowside Coarse Fishery. No close season. Mirrors and commons to 15lb in the carp lake. Mirrors, commons and crucians to $2^1/_2$lb; tench to $6^1/_2$lb; roach to $1^1/_2$lb in the mixed lake. For more details contact **Meadowside Coarse Fishery, St. Columb, Cornwall. Telephone 0637 880544.**

Avallon Holiday Park on a 180 acre dairy farm has a well stocked, private coarse fishing lake containing carp, bream, tench and roach to $2^1/_2$lb. Self catering, Norwegian Pine lodges on a small, select site; suitable for all the year round holidays. For further details telephone **0502 501501.**

Quality self catering Scandinavian lodges in Bude, Cornwall, overlooking two small lakes containing double figure carp. No close season. Ideal for the family angler, sandy beaches 10 minutes drive. For more details contact **Forda Lodges, Kirkhampton. Telephone 028 882 413.**

Free fishing and no close season at Woodley Farm. Superb fishing in six, well stocked lakes. Choice of nine luxury self-catering cottages - almost one lake per cottage! $1^1/_2$ miles from Shilahill Lakes (carp to 38lb); 10 minutes from Looe (shark fishing) and Polperro; the best of Cornish beaches for the family. Night fishermen welcome. Stamped addressed envelope for full colour brochure to **A. T. Hawkes, Woodley Farm, Herodsfoot, Liskeard. Telephone 0503 20221.**

Pyewell Farm, a delightful 16th century farmhouse in North Devon offers excellent cuisine and personal attention; carp and tench fishing on private lakes. Situated four miles from the North Devon link road and three miles from sandy beaches. Dinner, bed and breakfast £16 per day. For more details write to **Mrs. Steer, Pyewell Farm, Holmacott, Instow, EX39 4LR.Telephone 0271 860357.**

A country bungalow in East Devon, set in its own six acres, sleeps six. Everything provided and pets welcome. Free fishing in a large, unfished pond. Carp estimated at around 15lb; other fishing close by. 12 miles from the sea. For more details telephone **0404891 244.**

Bed and Breakfast or six berth caravan on three private lakes in Devon, containing carp to 20lb+ and other smaller fish. No close season. For more details telephone **0409 27362.**

Shared ownership holiday lodges on the Devon/Somerset border with carp fishing. Specimens to 30lb. Further details telephone **0823 680447.**

Free fishing and no close season at Lowfield Country Holiday Retreat. A beautiful woodland setting, well stocked lakes which have had the recent massive addition of tench, rudd, crucian and small carp. Luxury cottage, lodge or caravans. For more details telephone **Lincoln 052277 717.**

Swan Lake, Wainfleet offers comfortable caravans and cottages on a quiet, country park; all mains. $2^1/_2$ acre lake stocked with carp, tench, etc. Tourers welcome. For brochure, telephone **0754 880469.**

Elmhurst Lakes, Horncastle, Lincs., offer comfortable caravans with bathroom, overlooking a picturesque lake which is well stocked with carp, bream, tench, etc. No close season. For details telephone **0507 527533.**

Nostell Priory Fisheries and Holiday Park offers coarse fishing on some of the finest lakes in Yorkshire. Season, weekly and day permits on three lakes covering 40 acres. Caravan and camp site; holiday and anglers' caravans for hire. Specialist carp tackle and bait shop on site. For full details write to: **Fisheries Manager, Foulby Lodge, Foulby, Wakefield. Telephone 0924 863562. Holiday Park 0924 863938.**

Boroughbridge, North Yorkshire. Self catering or Bed and Breakfast in an 18th century farmhouse on a working family farm. Private carp lake. Ideal centre for a family holiday; close to Yorkshire Moors, Dales and the coast. For details, telephone **Boroughbridge 0423 322045.**

Marlingford, Norfolk. Self catering cottages and lodge beside the River Yare; all mod. cons. Private fishing, river and stocked lakes, carp, roach, chub and pike. Telephone **Norwich 0603 810135** for a brochure.

Excellent carp fishing in Northants. No close season. Camping and caravans. For further details telephone **02805 622.**

Self catering mobile home near Silverstone. No close season. Specimen carp lake. For further details telephone **02805 622**

Self catering apartments on the banks of the river at Ross on Wye. Coarse and game fishing available; carp lakes nearby. Winter, weekends and mid week bookings. For a 1991 brochure, telephone **Riverside Lodge 0989 765558.**

Fishers Pond Fisheries offer a charming cottage on the banks of an ancient carp farm. Densely stocked, doubles only, carp water. Many 20's produced during the summer of 1990. Trout period April-June. For a catalogue and price list, contact **Fishers Pond Fisheries, Pondside Cottage, Fishers Pond, Hants, SO5 7HF. Telephone 0703 694412.**

Excellent barbel, chub and roach fishing on the River Severn. Also seven lakes for trout and carp fishing. Luxury riverside cottages and free fishing. Weekly and short breaks available in 1991. For brochure contact **Severn Valley Properties Ltd., Elm House, Kidderminster Road, Bewdley, Worcs, DY12 1LJ. Telephone 0299 402030.**

Pisces Caravan Park and Fishery, Bedford Bank West, Welney, Cambs. PE14 9TB. In 1988, Carol and Richard Shelton bought the fishery and embarked on an upgrading programme, overhauling the main lake and digging two more. All the lakes were then restocked with roach, perch, crucian carp, adding to the mirror and common carp, bream, tench and pike.

The river is 20 yards from the entrance to the park and is included in the holiday. No day tickets available so with only 14 modern caravans, there is always plenty of room for serious fishing. No keepnets.

The site is $^1/_2$ mile from the village and children under 10 are not allowed.

Carol and Richard Shelton live on the park and run a grocery shop and bait shed. If you would like more information, phone them on **035471 257**, any evening.

Coarse fishing in Dordogne, France. Abundant carp. Full board, magnificent food, river bank boat available. Further details from 12, **Church Park, Mumbles, Swansea, SA3 4DE. Telephone Gaunt 010 33 53800872.**

PETE CURTIS

TAKES A WRY LOOK AT THE CURRENT CARP SCENE – AND A POSSIBLE TACKLE DEVELOPMENT OF THE FUTURE

YEH! JUST SAY CHEESE.
'COS THAT'S ALL YOU'LL BE USING FOR BAIT, FROM NOW ON!
QUICK TIM. IT'S SO HEAVY, I CAN'T HOLD IT MUCH LONGER.
JUST HOLD ON FOR A FEW MORE MINUTES.
THAT'S THE LAST TIME I CAST OUT FOR YOU!!
OOOH, TIM! IT'S SO BIG AND FAT!! IT'S REALLY LUWERLY!!!
AND IF SHE'S SO BLOODY CLEVER, SHE CAN BUY HER OWN RODS!

NAPALM
NEW AUTOMATIC PLAYING AND LANDING MACHINE
JUST CAST OUT, SET THE CLUTCH...
:NAPALM: DOES THE REST!
GO DOWN THE PUB, DO WHAT YOU LIKE!
COME BACK NEXT MORNING, TO, MAYBE, THREE FISH IN THE 'BIG' LANDING NET (£70 XTRA)
'XTRA LOUD 4,000 DECIBEL SPEAKERS.
WORKS OF 4 CAR BATTERIES PER ROD (NOT SUPPLIED)
ONLY WEIGHS 25·7 KILOS!
FREE - CARRYING STRAP, IF YOU BUY NOW!
OR, BUY OUR 'LUXURY TROLLEY', ONLY £99·95P +VAT.
GREAT VALUE AT ONLY ....
:NAPALM: 2 ROD SYSTEM £2,495·00
:NAPALM: 3 ROD SYSTEM £4,469·00
MORTGAGES ARE ALSO AVAILABLE FOR 'THE REDMIRE' 4 ROD SYSTEM.

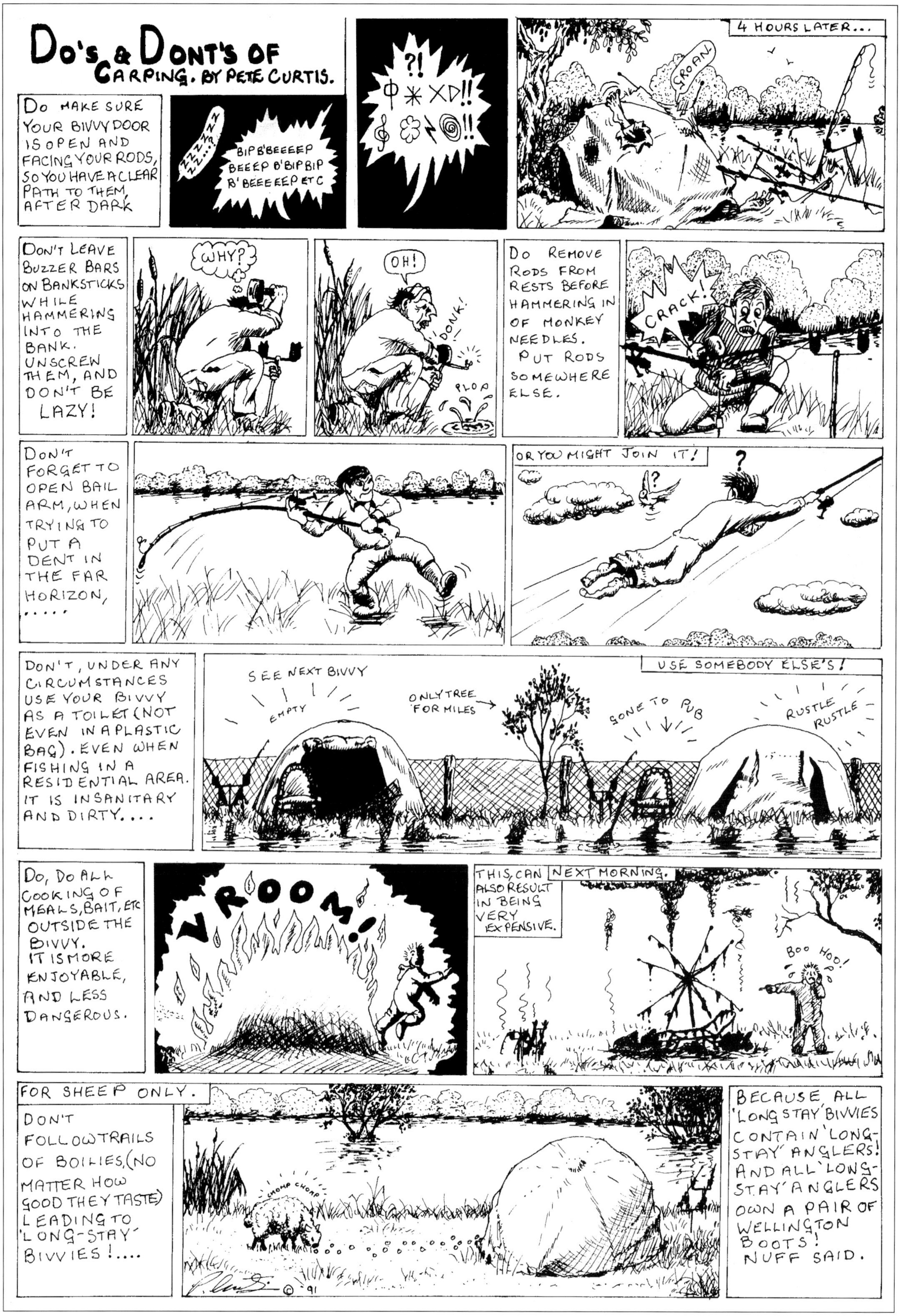
DO'S & DONT'S OF CARPING. BY PETE CURTIS.
DO MAKE SURE YOUR BIVVY DOOR IS OPEN AND FACING YOUR RODS, SO YOU HAVE A CLEAR PATH TO THEM, AFTER DARK
ZZZZZZZ...
BIP B'BEEEEP BEEEP B'BIP BIP B'BEEEEEEP ETC
?! ✱ XD!! !!
4 HOURS LATER...
GROAN
DON'T LEAVE BUZZER BARS ON BANKSTICKS WHILE HAMMERING INTO THE BANK. UNSCREW THEM, AND DON'T BE LAZY!
WHY?
OH!
DONK!
PLOP
DO REMOVE RODS FROM RESTS BEFORE HAMMERING IN OF MONKEY NEEDLES. PUT RODS SOMEWHERE ELSE.
CRACK!
DON'T FORGET TO OPEN BAIL ARM, WHEN TRYING TO PUT A DENT IN THE FAR HORIZON, ...
OR YOU MIGHT JOIN IT!
?
?
DON'T, UNDER ANY CIRCUMSTANCES USE YOUR BIVVY AS A TOILET (NOT EVEN IN A PLASTIC BAG). EVEN WHEN FISHING IN A RESIDENTIAL AREA. IT IS INSANITARY AND DIRTY....
USE SOMEBODY ELSE'S!
SEE NEXT BIVVY
EMPTY
ONLY TREE FOR MILES
GONE TO PUB
RUSTLE RUSTLE
DO, DO ALL COOKING OF MEALS, BAIT, ETC OUTSIDE THE BIVVY. IT IS MORE ENJOYABLE, AND LESS DANGEROUS.
VROOM!
THIS CAN ALSO RESULT IN BEING VERY EXPENSIVE.
NEXT MORNING.
BOO HOO!
FOR SHEEP ONLY.
DON'T FOLLOW TRAILS OF BOILIES, (NO MATTER HOW GOOD THEY TASTE) LEADING TO 'LONG-STAY' BIVVIES!....
CHOMP CHOMP
© '91
BECAUSE ALL 'LONG STAY' BIVVIES CONTAIN 'LONG-STAY' ANGLERS! AND ALL 'LONG-STAY' ANGLERS OWN A PAIR OF WELLINGTON BOOTS! NUFF SAID.

LIPIDS, HNV's &

LIPIDS

Lipids have probably been the most intensively studied of the major biochemical constituents of aquatic organisms. The reason for this being, the high levels of lipids found in many aquatic organisms, and especially due to the lipids containing a wide range of n-3 polyunsaturated fatty acids (PUFA).

There is a wealth of information on the presence of lipids in the fresh water food webs. Freshwater algae contain n-3 PUFA, 18:3n-3 being abundant, but the most common n-3 PUFA is 18:2n-6. The majority of freshwater cyanabacteria (blue-green algae) has 18:2n-6 as the most abundant PUFA.

Another source of n-3 PUFA is to be found in freshwater invertebrates and these can form a large part of a carp's diet. A recent detailed survey established that the majority of aquatic insects, contained a total lipid level of between 10/20% of the animal's dry weight. Larvae of aquatic insects have also been found to contain higher quantities of PUFA's than their adult stages, which leave the aquatic environment.

Because of this wealth of natural occurring lipid, freshwater fish, including carp, have evolved a nutritional requirement that demands a diet rich in n-3 PUFA.

Fish tissue contains predominantly fatty acids of the n-3 series, and so fish diets must provide sufficient essential fatty acids at the n-3 (linolenic) and n-6 (linoleic) series, as well as general lipids, for contribution towards calorie requirements.

The most important problem arising with fish diets and its lipid concentration, is the propensity of polyunsaturated fatty acids to become auto-oxidised by atmospheric oxygen unless **antioxidant protection** is incorporated in the diet. Auto-oxidation reduces the availability of fatty acids to the host. It is also harmful to the fish, because the products of oxidation, such as free radicals, peroxides, aldehydes and ketones, are toxic to fish. They also have the ability to react with other dietary components. It is the control of this oxidative rancidity that is of importance.

ANTIOXIDANTS

Antioxidants are chemicals which are added to feed ingredients, primarily to prevent oxidation of lipids, but other constituents of fish diets can be oxidised, such as carotenoid pigments and tocopherols.

Oxidation can occur in several ways. The mechanism that we should be interested in is auto-oxidation (atmospheric oxidation), which is the method of oxidation of moderately unsaturated fatty acids. This is a process which involves three steps. The first step being initiation. This is where free radicals are formed. This is caused by the presence of light, UV radiation or the presence of divalent cations, such as copper or iron. The second step is known as the propagation step. The free radicals formed in the first step react with oxygen to form more free radicals. The final step is termination; this is where end products are formed. Because the second step forms free radicals, auto-oxidation reactions are autocatalytic.

The formation of free radicals during oxidisation of lipids.

First step. Initiation:

$RH + O_2 \quad \text{catalyst} \quad R\cdot + \cdot OOH$

$RH + \text{Initiator} \quad R\cdot + H\cdot$

Second step: Propagation:

$R\cdot + O_2 \quad RO_2\cdot$

$RO_2\cdot + RH \quad RO_2H + R$

Third step: Termination:

$R\cdot + R\cdot \quad R - R$

$RO_2\cdot + R \quad RO_2 R$

$R\cdot$ = Free Radical
RO_2 = Peroxy Radical

Antioxidants work by chelating pro-oxidant divalent cations, by acting as free radical acceptors, or by donating hydrogen. Antioxidants which are added to lipids and feeds to prevent oxidation, are chemical compounds, such as phenolics and amines. Butylated hydroxytoluene and butylated hydroxyganisole being phenolics, are added at levels of 0.1%. Other antioxidants in use include dilaury thiodipropionate, propyl gallate and ethoxyquin.

The use of lipids (fats/oils) in HNV's is now widespread, and when used correctly, they are extremely beneficial to carp, but when used wrongly, or in an oxidised form, a great deal of harm can be caused. There are disease problems associated with the lipid component of fish feeds. They can be among the most serious, and prevalent of all nutritional problems found in fish.

Too much lipid (oil) in feed causes lipid degeneration. Trout pellets have/should have antioxidants added to them while being constructed, and these are relatively dry. Compare these to some HNV's which are being used.

There is a disease of carp called Sekoke disease. It was at one time a serious problem to the carp culturist in Japan. The disease was caused by oxidised oil, found in silkworm pupae, which was a major feed ingredient. It has been found that a diet containing 10% oxidised oil, caused typical signs of the disease after 60 days, and after a period of 120 days 56% of a carp population had contracted the illness. The disease would have been effectively prevented by the addition of an antioxidant.

What I would like to know is, are the manufacturers of essential oils and HNV's with added oils, also adding antioxidants to their products, especially as some of these products can be sitting on a shelf for a month or two at room temperature.

ABOUT THE AUTHOR

"Who is Charlie Dally?" many of you will be asking. On the other hand, some of you will perhaps recall that he's been writing about bait – very authoritatively – for a great many years. He had a super article about the use of Ion Agar in baits published in the CAA newsletter in the 70's, and periodically sends us high class technical material on the science of bait. This feature is a double barrelled one which will be over the heads of most of us – but welcomed by the real bait buffs among you.

PRESERVATIVES

With reference to the preservation of HNV's and the addition of harmless preservatives.

HNV's containing more than 12% moisture can, and will, support bacteria, moulds and yeast growths, unless they are stored frozen. A fact of life if that microbial growths occur very rapidly in semi-moist feeds. Many of these microbial growths, especially moulds, produce by-products in the process of growing, which are toxic to fish.

In semi-moist HNV's kept at room temperature (21-25°C) mould growth is visible within 3 days. While at refrigerated temperature (4°C) growth is visible within 10-20 days. During frozen storage, microbial growth is completely stopped. Therefore, if you are going to use semi-moist HNV's, use straight after manufacture is advisable, or the use of an antimicrobial additive is required if the HNV material is not to be frozen.

There are many compounds that are used in the feed industry, that will inhibit fungal or microbial growth. Some have general and some have specific applications in food products. The benzoates are wide spectrum antimicrobials, which are effective against bacteria, fungi and yeast. Propionates are used to inhibit the growth of yeasts and moulds.

Choosing an appropriate antimicrobial agent for an HNV mixture is not easy. The study of specific microbial problems, solubility and ease of application of the agent, pH requirements, empirical information and the acceptability of the agent to the carp have to be considered.

A second means of controlling microbial spoilage in HNV's could be the use of special packaging, hermetically sealed bags, but this is impracticable for the individual.

The third method, and the one that I use, is by controlling water activity (Aw). Micro-organisms require an abundant supply of water to grow. Reducing the availability of water in an HNV is, therefore, an

List of Antimicrobial Agents used in feeds

	Limit or restriction		
Benzoic acid	0.1%	Sodium benzoate	0.1%
Calcium sorbate	None	Sodium Nitrite	0.002%
Formic acid	2.5%	Sodium propionate	None
Methylparaben	0.1%	Sodium sorbate	None
Potassium sorbate	None	Ascorbic acid	None
Propionic acid	None		

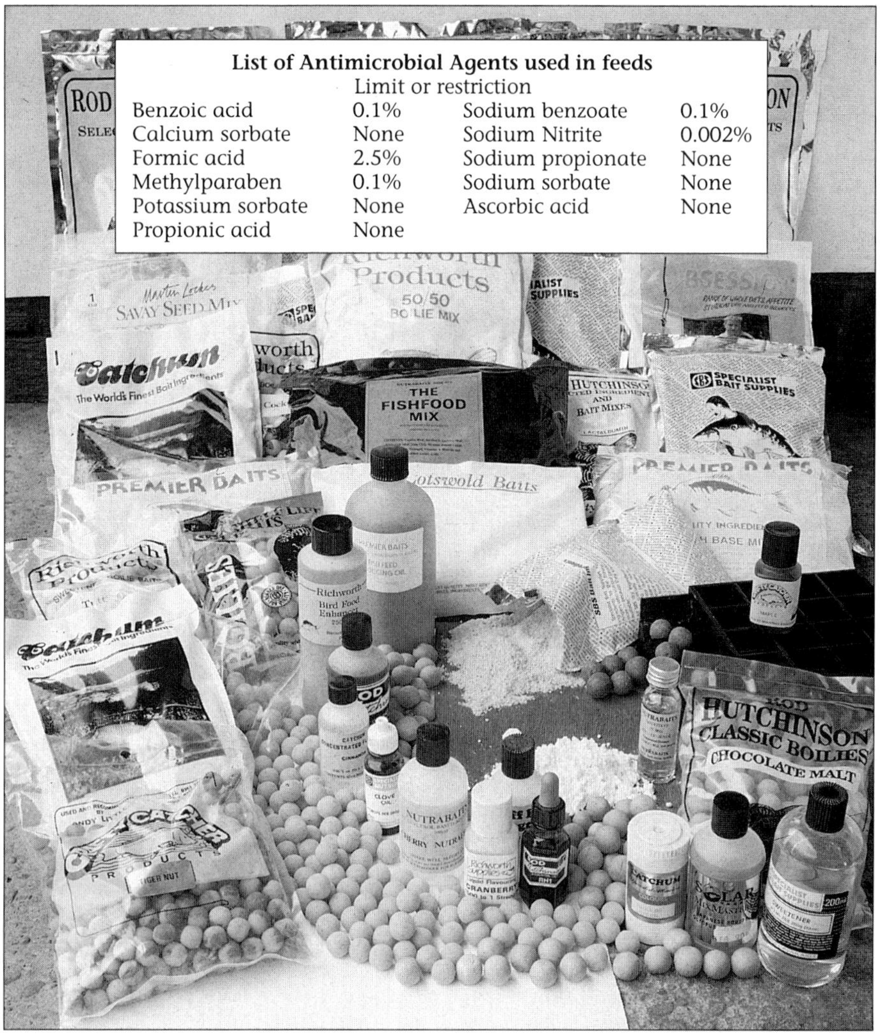
Richworth Products
50/50
BOILIE MIX
Catchum
The World's Finest Bait Ingredients
THE
FISHFOOD
MIX
PREMIER BAITS
Cotswold Baits
SPECIALIST
BAIT SUPPLIES
HUTCHINSON
CLASSIC BOILIES
CHOCOLATE MALT
NUTRABAITS
TIGER NUT

effective way of limiting microbial growth. Water exists in HNV's in three forms: as a liquid, as a vapour and as chemically bound water. Control of water activity involves increasing the proportion of total moisture in the HNV that is chemically bound, this decreases the proportion present as a liquid. Water activity is defined as the ratio of water vapour in HNV's, and the vapour pressure of pure water at the same temperature. The water activity of pure water is 1.0. Small differences in Aw may result in relatively huge differences in the resistance of HNV's to microbial contamination. The approximate lower limits of Aw for the growth of bacteria is about 0.91, for yeast about 0.88 and for moulds 0.80. It is relatively easy to achieve Aw values below these values by adding compounds such as sugar, glycerol, NaCl and propylene.

Air drying ends the process – all the HNV's that I use are air dried. The addition of flavour carrying compounds are added just prior to use.

Charlie Dally

STAINLESS STEEL BANKSTICKS

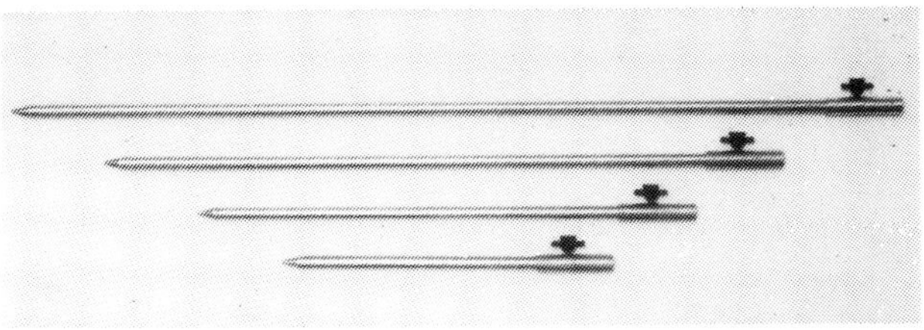

No roll pins or pegs to hold together parts which fit like a banana in a shirt sleeve. All machining is to precise interference tolerances so that assembly requires a press. The Peg Screws allow positive locking with the minimum of pressure. Slim, light and yet stronger than some models of comparable dimensions they look good and function perfectly.
10" Adjustable Ref 242 - £7.45 20" Adjustable Ref 244 - £9.45
15" Adjustable Ref 243 - £8.45 25" Adjustable Ref 234 - £10.45

STAINLESS STEEL SQUARE SECTION BUZZER BARS

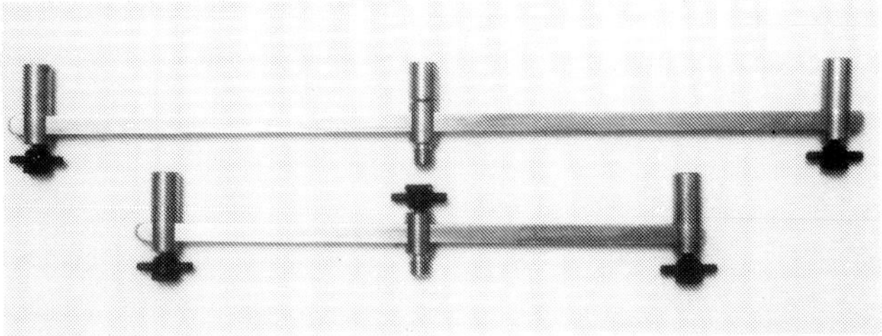

The obvious solution for perfect alignment with no roll pins or pegs so that stability is 100%, these are the ultimate buzzer bar. Single handed adjustment, even with buzzers on, is easy with the peg screws which lock so positively you should never lose one - but if you did the buzzer would still stay perfectly aligned!! The centre adaptor on the two rod bar stops the bar rocking at this point and if you wish you can purchase spare adaptors which enable you to put one at either end of the bar and use two banksticks for greater stability. The converter peg may be removed from the three rod bar and replaced with a 2BA peg screw to avoid looking suspicious when fishing in two rod areas. Altogether the ultimate system.
10" 2 Rod Ref 218 - £12.45
15" 3 Rod Ref 219 - £13.45
Spare Square Bar Bankstick Adaptor Ref 221- £2.85
Spare Square Bar Slider Ref 222 - £2.95

STAINLESS STEEL ROD POD

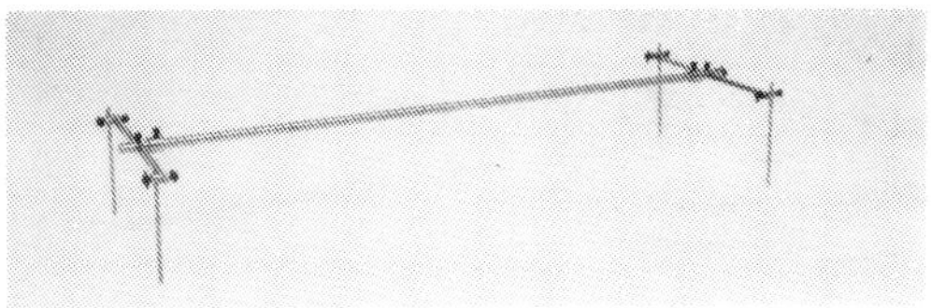

Our Rod Pod is the ultimate in stability, is simple to set up and easy to adjust. It can be taken apart and stored in a matter of seconds. It is designed to take the $^3/_8$" slim Stainless Banksticks which we also manufacture. The pod legs are vertical, giving maximum stability and easy adjustment. Should you require especially long front legs to fish a very steep bank or to fish your rods high, our Stainless Steel Banksticks can be used on the pod for greater versatility. The pod is supplied with or without an ariel holder which takes our square ariel bar. After having used inferior pods you will find it difficult to fault this ultimate rod pod system.
Ref 253 (without ariel holder) - £44.60
Ref 227 (with ariel holder) - £51.05

BUZZ BOMBS

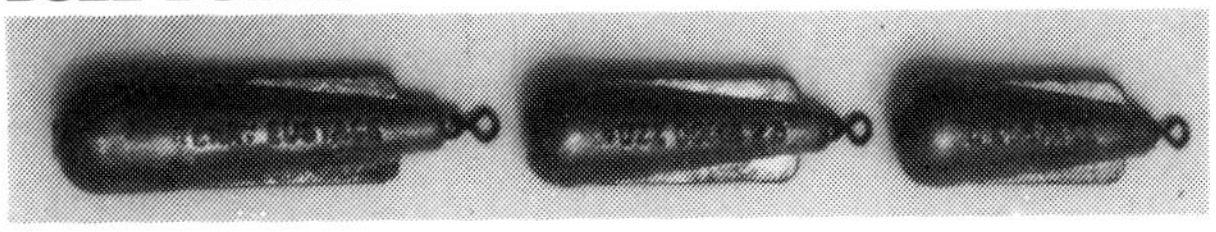

Until the introduction of the Buzz Bomb you couldn't get an aerodynamic lead which lifted clear of weeds, bars and snags on the retrieve. The problem with fluted bombs was that they either spun and twisted on the retrieve and often cast so badly that where they were going to land was pure guesswork. Not only does the Buzz Bomb cast well the positioning of the fins seem to make them even more stable in cross winds than a standard bomb. Swivels used are Berkley 100lb. Three leads per pack.
Ref 204 - 2oz Buzz Bombs - £1.90
Ref 205 - $2^1/_2$oz Buzz Bombs - £2.15
Ref 206 - $3^1/_2$oz Buzz Bombs - £2.35

ROD/LEAD STRAPS

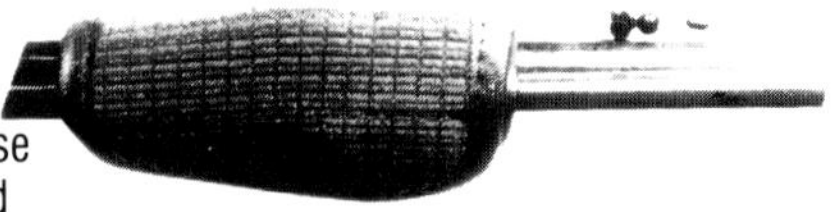

These simple to use items strap the rod anywhere, at top or bottom and can also hold the lead without it rubbing against the rod.
Ref 174 - £3.45 pair

ABEL STOCKISTS GOLD LABEL STOCKISTS GOLD LABEL STOCKISTS GOLD LABEL STOCKISTS GOLD LABEL STOCKISTS GOLD LABEI

MIDDLESEX
Hounslow Angling Centre
265/267 Bath Road, Hounslow
081 570 6156. Also at
Richmond A.C. 081 202 0264

Judd's of Hillington
3 Westbourne Parade
Uxbridge Road, Hillington
Middlesex. 081 573 0196

Middlesex Angling Centre
1288 Greenford Road
Greenford, Middlesex UB6 0HH
081 422 8311

Tackle Up
363 Staines Road
West Ashford, Middlesex
0784 240013

T & S Angling
150 Heath Road
Twickenham, Middlesex
081 892 7660

NORFOLK
Derrick Amies and Son
Gorleston Tackle Centre Ltd.
7/8 Pier Walk, Gorleston, Gt. Yarmouth
0493 662448

NORFOLK
Tom Boulton Fishing Tackle
173 Drayton Road
Norwich, Norfolk
0603 426834

Norwich Angling Centre
476 Sprowston Road
Norwich, Norfolk
0603 400757

NORTHANTS
The Sportsman's Lodge
44 Kingsthorpe Road
Kingsthorpe Hollow, Northampton
0604 713399

NOTTINGHAMSHIRE
Mansfield Angling
20 Byron Street
Mansfield, Notts.
0623 633790

Walkers of Trowell
9-15 Nottingham Road
Trowell, Notts.
0602 301816/307798

OXFORDSHIRE
Catch 1 Tackle
14 The Parade
Kidlington, Oxford
08675 2066

SHROPSHIRE
Kingfisher Angling Centre
8 New Street
Frankwell, Shrewsbury
0743 240602

STAFFORDSHIRE
The Bridge Shop
39 High Street, Measham
Burton-on-Trent, Staffs.
0530 72864

Pickerings of Burslem
4-8 William Clowes Street
Burslem, Stoke on Trent
0782 814941

SURREY
Davies Angling
3a Brook Road
Redhill, Surrey
0737 771888

Guildford Angling Centre
92/94 Haydon Place
Guildford, Surrey
0483 506333

SUSSEX
Fishermans Den
110 London Road
Bognor Regis, West Sussex
0243 866663

SUSSEX
Redfearns Tackle
8 Castle Street
Hastings, East Sussex
0424 422094

WEST MIDLANDS
Terry Eustace Fishing Tackle
372 Chester Road
Sutton Coldfield, West Midlands
021 373 6627

WILTSHIRE
Cotswold Angling Centre
Kennedy's Garden Centre
Hyde Road, Kingsdown, Swindon
0793 721173

The House of Angling
59-60 Commercial Road
Swindon, Wilts.
0793 693460

YORKSHIRE
Eric's Angling Centre
1 Wilfred Avenue, off Selby Road
Leeds, Yorkshire
0532 646883

Westgate Anglers
63 Westgate
Bradford
0274 729570

WHERE IS IT?

1 **A1 Pits**, Notts. – Season permit (available on site)
2 **Angler's Paradise**, Devon – By prior booking (0409-22559)
3 **Arlesey Lake**, Beds. – Syndicate (enquire local tackle shops)
4 **Ashlea Pool**, Gloucs. – Private (very difficult to obtain permission)
5 **Baker's Pond**, N. Humbs. – By prior booking (0430-40350)
6 **Birch Grove**, Shrops. – By prior booking (0742-582728)
7 **Broadlands**, Hants. – By prior booking (0703-733167)
8 **Brooklands**, Kent – Season permit - difficult to obtain (Dartford & Dist. APS)
9 **Broxbourne**, Herts. – Season permit (0932-64872)
10 **Burghfield**, Berks. – Season permit (tel: 0932-562633)
11 **Burton**, Merseyside – Season permit (051-356-0678)
12 **Capesthorne**, Cheshire – Season permit (0625-520061)
13 **College**, Cornwall – Season permit (0392-219666)
14 **Crabmill**, Cheshire – Season permit (Wheelock & Dist.A.C.)
15 **Cutt Mill**, Surrey – Season permit (Farnham A.S. – local tackle shops)
16 **Cuttle Mill**, West Midlands – By prior booking (0827-872253)
17 **Darenth**, Kent – Season permit (0932-64872)
18 **Dorchester Lagoon**, Oxfordshire – Season permit (0865-730851)
19 **Drax Pond**, Yorkshire – Season permit (0757-618641)
20 **Fairlands**, Herts. – Day ticket (available on site)
21 **Harefield**, Greater London – Season permit (difficult to obtain)
22 **Hawkstone Park**, Shrops. – Season permits –difficult to obtain (Wem Anglers)
23 **Heron Pool**, Beds. – Syndicate (tel: 0480-213664)
24 **Heron-Lily**, Gloucs. – Syndicate (0462-816370)
25 **Hollybush Pits**, Hants. – Season permits (0306-883621)
26 **Holmersfield**, Norfolk – Private (difficult to obtain permission)
27 **Horseshoe Lake**, Gloucs. – change of management at time of going to press
28 **Horton Fishery**, Berkshire – Syndicate (0932-64872)
29 **Hyde Lane**, Bucks. – Season permit (enquire local tackle shops)
30 **Johnson's**, Kent – Season permit (available on site)
31 **Layer Pits**, Essex – Season permit (Colchester APS – local tackle shops)
32 **Linear Fisheries**, Bucks. – Syndicate (0908-607577)
33 **Lockwood Reservoir**, Greater London – Private (difficult to obtain permission)
34 **Lymm Dam**, Cheshire – Season permit (Lymm Anglers – local tackle shops)
35 **Mangrove**, Shrops. – Syndicate (0742-582728)
36 **Marlborough Pool**, Oxfordshire – Season permit (Oxford & Dist. A. – local tackle shops)
37 **Motorway Pond**, N. Humbs. – Syndicate (0482-847372)

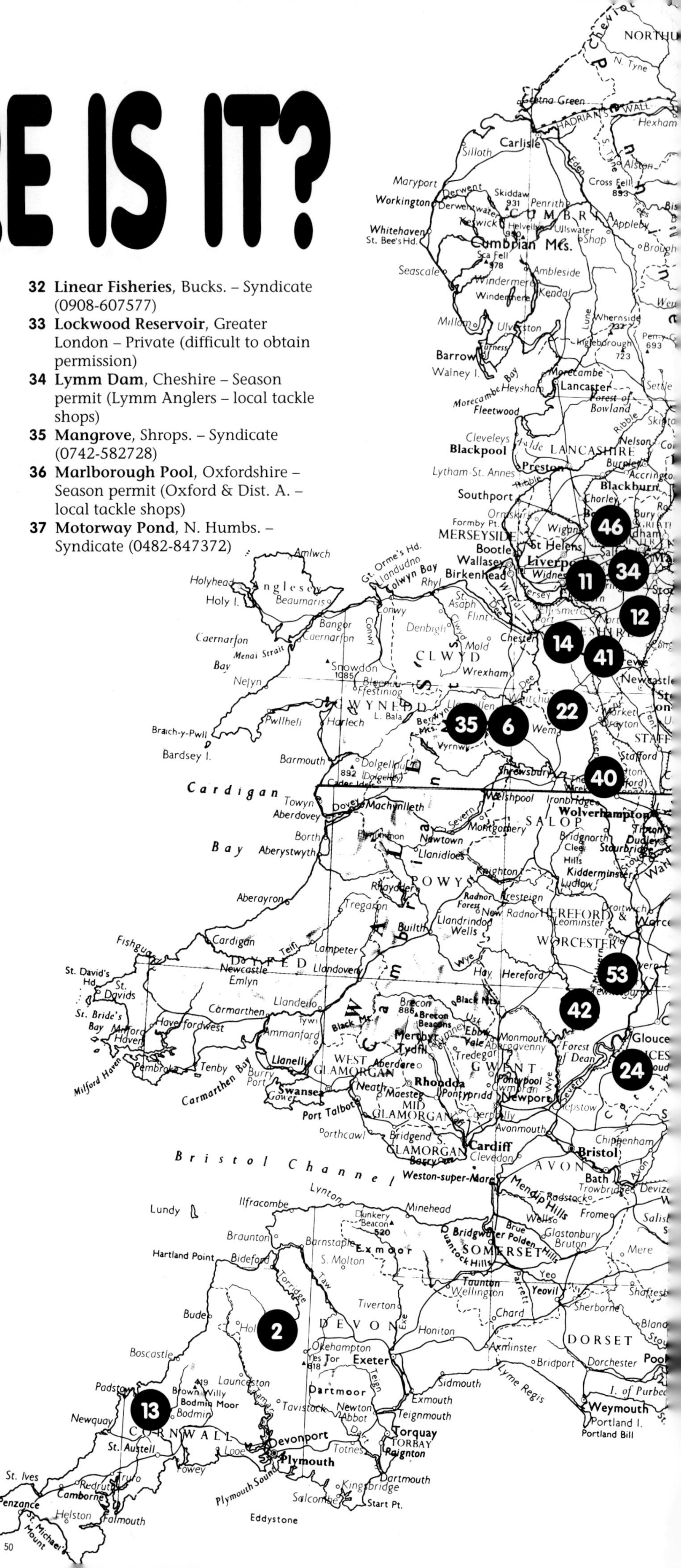

46
34
11
12
14
41
22
35
6
40
53
42
24
2
13
Carlisle
Workington
Whitehaven
Cumbrian Mts.
Barrow
Lancaster
Blackpool
Preston
LANCASHIRE
Southport
Blackburn
MERSEYSIDE
Liverpool
Birkenhead
Wallasey
Holyhead
Anglesey
Caernarfon
Bangor
Snowdon
CLWYD
Chester
Wrexham
Cardigan Bay
Aberystwyth
POWYS
SALOP
Shrewsbury
Wolverhampton
Hereford
WORCESTER
DYFED
Carmarthen
Haverfordwest
Swansea
WEST GLAMORGAN
MID GLAMORGAN
GWENT
Newport
Cardiff
Bristol Channel
Bristol
AVON
Bath
SOMERSET
Exmoor
DEVON
Exeter
Dartmoor
Plymouth
Torquay
CORNWALL
Penzance
DORSET
Weymouth

CARPWORLD'S GUIDE TO SOME FAMOUS CARP WATERS

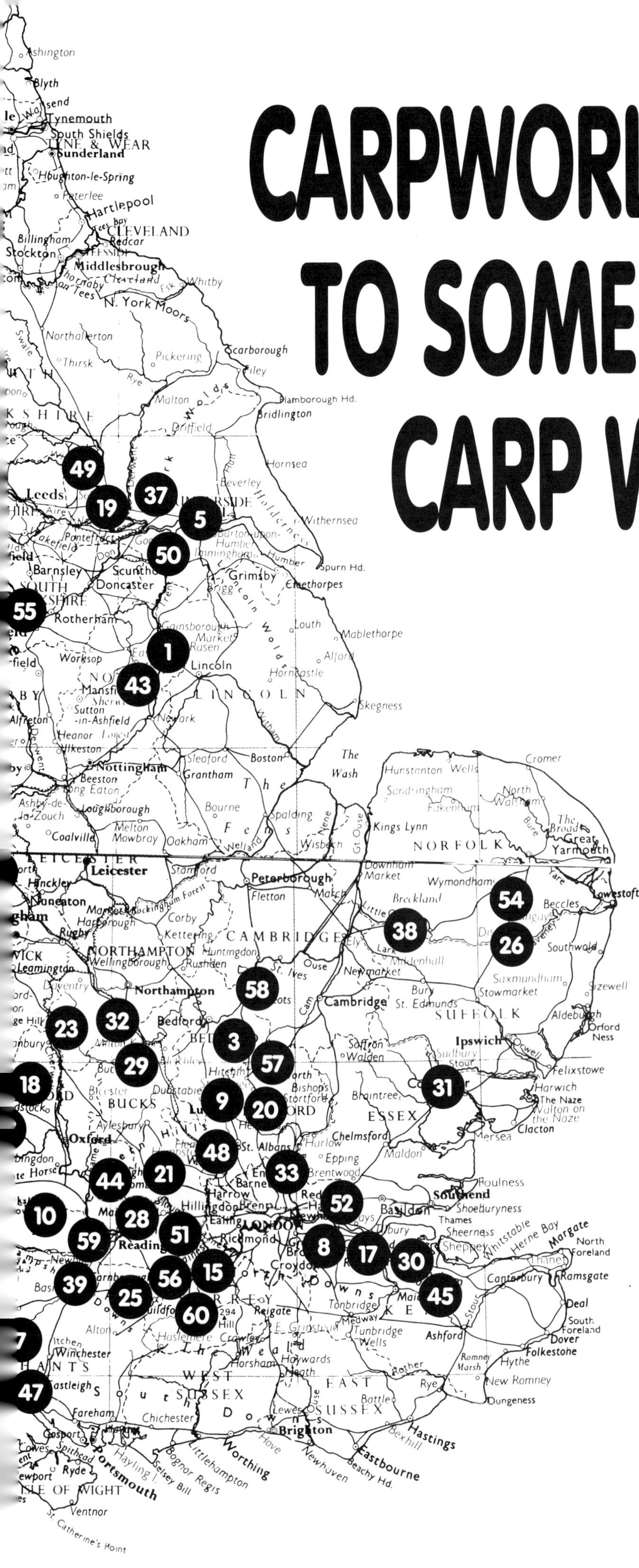

Ashington
Blyth
Tynemouth
South Shields
TYNE & WEAR
Sunderland
Houghton-le-Spring
Peterlee
Hartlepool
CLEVELAND
Billingham
Redcar
Stockton
Middlesbrough
Whitby
N. York Moors
Northallerton
Thirsk
Pickering
Scarborough
Filey
Malton
Flamborough Hd.
Bridlington
Driffield
Hornsea
Beverley
Withernsea
Leeds
Pontefract
Barton-upon-Humber
Spurn Hd.
Barnsley
SOUTH
Doncaster
Grimsby
Cleethorpes
Rotherham
Gainsborough
Market Rasen
Louth
Mablethorpe
Worksop
Lincoln
Alford
Horncastle
Mansfield
Sutton -in-Ashfield
Skegness
Newark
Heanor
Ilkeston
Nottingham
Sleaford
Boston
The Wash
Beeston
Grantham
Hunstanton
Cromer
Long Eaton
Sandringham
Fakenham
North Walsham
Loughborough
Bourne
Spalding
Kings Lynn
Coalville
Melton Mowbray
Oakham
Wisbech
NORFOLK
Great Yarmouth
Leicester
Stamford
Peterborough
Downham Market
Hinckley
Fletton
Wymondham
Lowestoft
Nuneaton
Breckland
Beccles
Rugby
Corby
Kettering
CAMBRIDGE
Southwold
NORTHAMPTON
Huntingdon
Wellingborough
Rushden
Mildenhall
Leamington
St. Ives
Newmarket
Saxmundham
Sizewell
Daventry
Northampton
Cambridge
Bury St. Edmunds
Stowmarket
Aldeburgh
SUFFOLK
Orford Ness
Bedford
Saffron Walden
Ipswich
Sudbury
Stour
Felixstowe
Bishop's Stortford
Braintree
Harwich
The Naze
Walton on the Naze
BUCKS
ESSEX
Clacton
Aylesbury
Oxford
St. Albans
Harlow
Chelmsford
Mersea
Epping
Maldon
Brentwood
Foulness
Southend
Shoeburyness
Harrow
Basildon
Hillingdon
Thames
Ealing
LONDON
Sheerness
Sheppey
Whitstable
Herne Bay
Margate
North Foreland
Reading
Richmond
Thanet
Croydon
Canterbury
Ramsgate
Tonbridge
Deal
Reigate
Medway
Tunbridge Wells
South Foreland
Dover
Ashford
Folkestone
Alton
Haslemere
Crawley
Winchester
Hythe
Horsham
Haywards Heath
Romney Marsh
New Romney
HANTS
WEST SUSSEX
EAST SUSSEX
Rye
Eastleigh
Dungeness
Fareham
Chichester
Lewes
Battle
Gosport
Brighton
Hastings
Bexhill
Cowes
Spithead
Portsmouth
Hayling I.
Littlehampton
Worthing
Hove
Newhaven
Eastbourne
Beachy Hd.
Ryde
Newport
Bognor Regis
Selsey Bill
ISLE OF WIGHT
Ventnor
St. Catherine's Point
49
19
37
5
50
55
1
43
54
26
38
58
23
32
3
57
29
18
31
9
20
48
33
44
21
10
28
52
51
59
8
17
30
39
56
15
45
25
60
7
47

38 **Nunnery**, Norfolk – Season tickets (enquire local university)

39 **Old Bury Hill Lake**, Surrey – By prior booking (0306-883621)

40 **Patshull Pool**, Staffordshire – Season permit (0902-700100)

41 **Redesmere**, Cheshire – Season permit (0625-520061)

42 **Redmire Pool** – By prior booking (081-551-8250)

43 **Sapphire Lakes**, Notts. – By prior bookings (0636-821131)

44 **Savay Lake**, Greater London – Season permit (081-969-6980)

45 **School Pool**, Kent – Season permit (0795-533240)

46 **Smith's**, Lancs. – Season permit (Bolton & Dist. A.C. – enquire local tackle shops)

47 **Somerley Estate**, Hants. – By prior bookings (See Ringwood & Dist. A.A.)

48 **Stanborough**, Herts. – Day permit available on the bank

49 **Three Lakes**, Yorkshire – By prior booking (0757-706605)

50 **Tilery Lake**, N. Humbs. – Syndicate (0482-847372)

51 **Tri-Lakes**, Surrey – By prior booking (0252- 873191)

52 **Walthamstow Reservoir**, Greater London – Season & day permits on site

53 **Watersmeet**, Gloucs. – By prior booking (tel: Watersmeet, Hartpury, Gloucs.)

54 **Waveney Valley Lakes**, Norfolk – (By prior booking (098-686-530)

55 **Wentworth Lakes**, Yorkshire – Syndicate (tel: Wentworth Estate, Rotherham)

56 **Willow Park**, Hants. – By prior booking (0252-543470)

57 **Withy Pool**, Beds. – Syndicate (tel: 0462-816960)

58 **Woolpack**, Cambs. – Syndicate (0954-4593)

59 **Wraysbury**, Berkshire – Season permit (0932-64872)

60 **Yateley**, Surrey – Season permit (0932-64872)

Mike Wilson:

It is generally accepted that carp are not indigenous to this country. The first mention of them, in English literature, is in a pamphlet entitled The Treatyse of Fysshyne with an Angle, published at Westminster by Wynkyn de Worde in 1486 and credited to Dame Juliana Berners (or Barnes). She was the Prioress of Sopwill, St. Albans, Herts. and research has now cast doubt as to her authorship and the date of completion. What is clear, is that the author never actually caught a carp as 'she' states, "the carp is a dainteous fish, but there be but few in England and therefore I write the less of him. He is an evil fish to take for he is so strong enamoured in the mouth that there be no weak harness to hold him. And as touching his baits I have but little knowledge of it and me were loath to write more than I know and have proved."

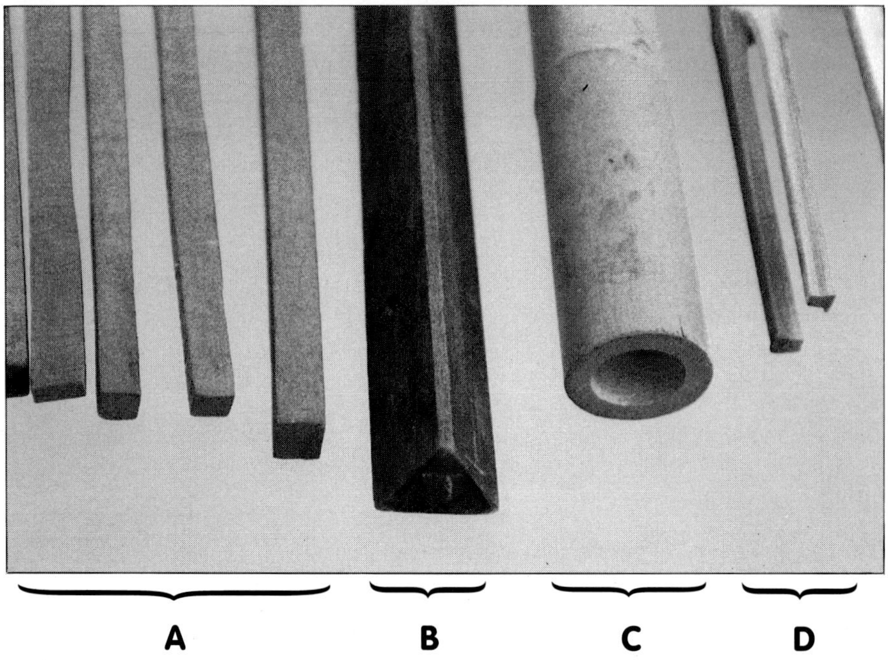
A
B
C
D

A. 50 year old sections of Greenheart. Probably the most important rod making material before cane.

B. Planing Former. Used to ensure all the angles on the split cane are correct. Note the flat on the apex. The cane is glued to this flat whilst planing.

C. The raw cane prior to splitting. Note the wall thickness.

D. Sections of cane after splitting but before planing.

Obviously, carp did exist in the 15th Century and almost certainly were introduced by a religious order, possibly the Premonstratension Order founded by St. Norbert in 1121. The first English Monastery of the Order was founded at Newhouse in Linconshire in 1143 and 33 Houses were established up to 1232. The Order was strict to Custom and they only ate fish and poultry. It is known they maintained some stew ponds. In my view, in their long, slow journey from France to England, the only fish likely to survive the journey in barrels of water would be carp and tench. This is, of course, pure speculation and may only be proved if we could find The Book of Customs, written in France around (after) 1126.

That carp were certainly spreading across the country was not in doubt as Holinshed, in 1571, observed that "Onelie in carps the Thames seemth to be scant." Leonard Mascall, writing on burbot in his Booke of Fishing with Hooke and Line in (1590) says, "If other rivers were stored with them (burbot) it would be good for the common wealth, as the carpe which came of late yeares into England."

Izaak Walton, in the Complete Angler – first published in 1653 when he was 60, also states on carp that, "...that was not at first bred, nor has been long in England, but is now naturalised" and, later, "Sussex being the county that abounds with them." Walton, in my view, caught very few carp (with fixed horsehair lines – he never used a wynch or reel at the time of writing), although he does state he "never saw one above 23 inches."

The lack of nationwide stocks and their famed uncatchability meant that the development of specific carp fishing tackle took a further 300 years.

The earliest known rods date back some 2,000 years B.C. to the ancient Egyptians (William Radcliffe – Fishing from the Earliest Times, 1921). Although the rod material is unknown, Fred Buller and Hugh Falkus, perhaps the most knowledgeable angling historians in Britain today, suggest they were possibly made from papyrus reeds growing along the banks of the Nile. Who am I to suggest otherwise?

Dame Juliana Berners recommended a rod constructed from blackthorn, crabapple, medlar or Juniper as the tip, spliced to hazel and then mounted on a hollowed out 9 foot length of hazel, willow or aspen. When not in use the tip fitting inside the hollow butt section which acted as a staff.

Various other materials have been used over the years, the most important being bamboo cane. The Chinese are believed to have developed the idea of splitting bamboo cane and gluing sections together. A. Courtney-Williams states "that in the book of Tchouang-Tseu (950 BC), an explanation is given as to how to build split cane "Rods", glued and bound. The "Rods" being used as water carriers to transport pails.

Around 1800, only top-joints were made from split cane which was probably square in section. The hexagonal section, well known today, developed over the next 80 years. Although claimed to be developed by American rod builders there is much 'evidence' which suggests that there were a few English rod builders using

CARP ROD BEGINNINGS

this principle years before. To improve the strength of some rods modifications were tried. Such ideas as a solid, spring steel strip, inserted down the centre of built cane, spiral wrapped wire on the outside and 'double-built', (a hexagonal cane length inside an outer hexagonal cane skin. All these ideas failed in as much as the increase in weight far outweighed the benefit of any additional strength.

Over the years, although odd carp were caught it was always a risky business with poor tackle. The general design of rods was very inadequate and, in a roundabout way, was compounded by the publication of Albert Buckley's record 26lb. carp from Mapperley on the 24th July, 1930. His rod was a "common roach rod" with an Allcock's No. 1 Lincoln silk line (8lb. b.s. although Buckley reported it as 3 lb.) and 4X gut (1lb. b.s. – yes 1 lb. b.s.!!) bottom tackle and size 10 hook. A so-called common roach rod in the 1930's was generally a split cane top with whole cane middle and butt, with a length around 11 foot.

When Bob Richards started fishing Redmire (September 1950) he was guided by Buckley's idea of tackle and used an 11 ft. Allcock's Lancer roach rod, 6lb. B.S. Platil, No.10 hook

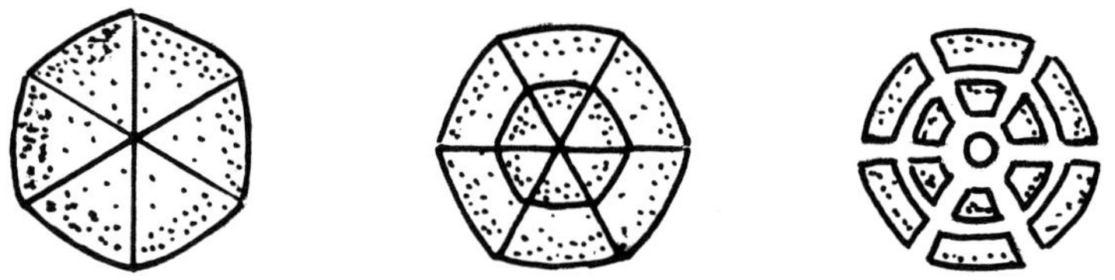

A B C

SECTIONS THROUGH SPLIT CANE

A. Single built

B. Double built

C. Double built/spring steel centre (before glueing)

and an Ambidex No. 1 reel. Richards caught his record fish, a 31lb. mirror on Wednesday, 3rd October 1951. Both he and Buckley had a lot in common; enthusiasm, a slice of luck and an extraordinary amount of angling skill with tackle totally unsuitable for its intended purpose. Even Mr. Sheringham caught his 16lb. fish in the first decade of this century on a 15 ft. roach rod.

The increase in waters holding carp and the published stories of enormous fish fired the imagination. Allcock's Wallis Wizard appeared to many as the most suitable rod available but it lacked backbone for the handling of better fish. The rod was a 3 joint, 11 ft., whole cane butt, built cane joint and top having a total weight of 12 ounces. As a matter of interest it would retail around 128 shillings (£6.40).

It was around 1946, or 47, that Dick Walker and B.B. started work on finding the ideal carp rod. At the suggestion of A. Courtney-Williams (Director of Allcock's), who considered the market too small to develop a carp rod, Dick decided to make his own. The Mark I was little more than 12in. cut from the top of the Wallis Wizard. One of the next two rods was 'double-built'. The fourth attempt proved the ideal weapon, 10ft. 2 piece split cane, 30 in. cork handle with a test curve of 1 lb. The test curve is defined as the weight required to pull the tip through 90 degrees (circle). A rod can cast 1oz. for every 1lb. of test curve with lines of 5lb. per 1lb. test curve, plus or minus 30%. The Mark IV, therefore, was designed to cast 1oz. and is ideal with lines between 6 and 12lb. b.s. A lighter version of the Mark IV, with a test curve of 1lb., was subsequently designed and later christened the Mark IV Avon by Bernard Venables. The Mark IV carp rod was revolutionary. It was tested

ALLCOCKS
SOLID PLAIT
"LINCOLN"
PURE SILK LINE
20 YDS
No E771
2¼ LBS
MANUFACTURED AT REDDITCH ENGLAND
ALLCOCKS
SOLID PLAIT
"LINCOLN"
PURE SILK LINE
20 YDS
No E770
2¾ LBS
MANUFACTURED AT REDDITCH ENGLAND

Line similar to that which was in use in Buckley's days.

by a number of experienced carp anglers and found perfect. At last, a specific rod to do a specific task.

Making rods was time consuming as a fair degree of skill is required. Dick therefore didn't make that many. In a letter to me (20/10/83) he guessed he'd made about twenty MkIV carp, and ten Mark IV Avon, rods.

Demand for the rods increased and, over a few years, J.B. Walker of Hythe supplied Dick with about twenty blanks made by Bob Southwell, Dick finishing them off with cork handle, ferrules etc. for various friends. Subsequently, B. James and Son, of Ealing, supplied Mark IV's, some early blanks also made by Bob Southwell.

New materials followed with glass, carbon fibre and others, until we reach the many and varied carp rods of today.

We all owe Dick a debt of gratitude. If you've never held a built cane Mark IV then ask around until you find one, hold it and appreciate its history. If you own one then treasure it. It's part of our angling heritage.

Dick Walker in 1983.

'B.B.' – Denys Watkins-Pitchford holding the Mk. IV carp rod made for him by Dick Walker. Note also the reel made by Dick. It is an enlarged version of the Hardy Eureka.

The inscription on the rod, which reads: "Built for Denys Watkins-Pitchford by Richard Walker, June 1950."

PROFUMO

The Selby Flier's scored it at last! After a million hours (untrue), and twice as many bait mixes (true) he's finally made it into the magical land of twenty five pound plus carp – and not just once, but twice. The fact that both fish were caught not only out of season, but from an out of bounds stretch of water, too, hasn't dented our man's considerable ego one bit. For the records Jules's two biggies both weighed 27lb+, and he's currently desperately hawking the pictures round trying to make it onto someone's front cover.

Talking about Jules's pictures, our man was a bit taken aback when he glanced through David Hall's coarse magazine for April. A lovely black and white picture of a well composed dawn shot carried the caption "An East Anglian dawn; an unfading memory". It's nice to see that humour is making a comeback in David's mags. The shot was actually one of the Flier's – of Savay Lake looking up from the Sluices. Either someone's memory has faded more than they think, or their geography's a bit bizarre.

Latest from the strange land of carp organisation intrigue is that the famous Kevin Maddocks has resigned his position as chairman of the CAA, and that infamous old soak Nigel Cobham has been voted in in his place. Obviously it isn't our place to comment about the change, so we won't tell you how pleased we are – for the CAA, and Nigel. What a lovely fella; mad as a snake, but then why wouldn't he be?

Strong rumour is that there have been some sweeping rule changes at Rod's syndicate lake. Included in the changes were no invitation to renew for Tim and Mary (thanks a bunch, fella), and a few other major changes aimed at helping Rod catch – and stopping Skid. We don't believe that – although the rule that says that only Rod can fish on Mondays takes some explaining away. It might not stop Skid catching, but it sure as hell will stop him catching on Mondays!

Contributors: Not The Lounge Lizard, Matthew Black, Deeppocket, Deepjoy, Deepthroat, Deepwallet, The Stoke Mafia, Carp Angling Grapevine PLC, Springwell Enterprises, Untrue Rumours Incorporated, The Essex Elite, The Longfield Drinking Team (no problem), The Rotherham Fabrications Factory, Shropshire Morning News, Darenth Fat Boys, The Guildford Bugle, The Yateley Scandal and any other publication we can lift good copy from.

Courageous Rob Maylin has been doing his own selling into tackle shops of his new magazine (modestly described in adverts as the greatest carp magazine ever published). His opening gambit to shopkeepers has been along the lines of "Hello, I'm Rob Maylin the famous carp angler; you must have heard of me." He's now discovered that a surprising number of people haven't. Sounds like a good slogan for a T-shirt, "Rob Who?".

One of the best kept secrets over the last couple of seasons has been the west country reservoir that's been producing some mega catches of big commons to those in the know – mega meaning multiple twenties catches with the odd thirty thrown in. We've had a little whisper that the main man from Mitcham has been travelling west a bit lately. Could our Pete be in on the action there? Sad thing is that all these commons are apparently being moved (officially) to that west country syndicate water which houses the imported thirty pounder.

We know we shouldn't break a confidence, but a carp man's group is going to perform at the May Conference at Dunstable. Isn't it amazing how many carp men have a musical bent? Clive Gibbins on drums – with Mike Kavanagh sitting in on the only number he knows: Chris Ball on guitar; Lee Jackson ditto; and Geoff Shaw; and Kev Clifford coming out of retirement. Andy Bolder will be adding a bit of class, and Happy Haswell will be fronting it all on vocals (seems apt). Missing from the line up will be part time troubadours Fred J Taylor (keen but can't be there); Rod, (probably got the hump about something); Dylan disciple Alan Tomkins; keyboard man Bob James. The Carp Society is trying to keep quiet about the event so it won't discourage too many people from attending!

If Uncle Backstop catches White Spot again he gets to keep it.

Cottis rang us the other day. He'd been on for two hours before he discovered he'd got a wrong number.

We had our lovely mate Chris "Carpbuster" Haswell on just after the season ended. Turns out he's been fishing Darenth towards the end, and although all his mates were emptying the water on his gear (it says here on the back of this cheque) our man couldn't put a fish on the bank, despite having a couple of chances. Ten minutes to go to the end of the session and a big carp leaps invitingly clear of the water a mere thirty yards out. Baits reeled in; recast; stand poised. Chris talks a bit quick, and a bit souvern, so it all started to get a bit confusing at this point. The main, inarguable fact is that Chris and the kid in the swim to his right finished up playing the same fish, which in turn finished up in a bush half way between the two swims. Chris is convinced it's his fish, so he braves the cold (like you do when you're desperate), climbs down the bush, and nets the fish. Three of them eagerly examine the contents of the net, which consist of a twenty nine pound plus carp, with one of the end tackles wrapped round the other one, all of which was immaterial because there was no hook in the fish's mouth. We think there must be a moral to this tale seeing Chris spent so long telling it, but we can't find one – except that a blank's a blank for all that. We've got to tell you that that Carpbuster Special is really special, though. And we still find it hard to believe that they didn't **both** count the fish!

With the rapid growth in carp fishing literature, and the increasing need for carp fishing articles, we felt it might help would-be megastars to achieve the required status – both on the bank and in the weeklies/monthlies/books – if we laid down some guidelines for those lacking the angling and literary talent to be another Chris Yates (i.e. everyone who isn't Chris Yates). Here is the guideline piece. All you have to do is embroider it slightly (but only slightly, otherwise you'll confuse the less imaginative readership). The only other necessary ingredient for megastardom is the catching of some fish that are either big, or rated as difficult. Only Rod fully understands the latter category, and the former will be qualified by how lucky the capture is deemed to be by the unofficial adjudication panel (i.e. the carp fishing grapevine):

First paragraph: Set up on Snake Pit/Harefield/Yateley/a no-publicity Colne Valley water/a midlands pit/a Hampshire Lake/in Kev's back garden. (Kev's back garden has now been re-rated as difficult because of the problems of actually getting to fish the water).

Second paragraph: Had a skinful last night/this morning/this afternoon/on the ferry (be careful; this can be a give away)/on the Air Canada flight (ditto). Constant references to being pissed out of your head are an essential ingredient to acquiring a really macho image, and will even get you through long periods without catching with your reputation intact. If you want to go all the way and you can find an enlightened publication that will allow the reference, you can really impress the boys by owning up to smoking whacky baccy/sniffing coke/shooting whatever it is people shoot/generally being one hell of a guy. Paragraphs of this nature invariably cause great hilarity/fathomless admiration/widespread disgust among real carp anglers.

Third paragraph: Had an Indian (meal) last night/early this morning (your target audience is already in hysterics). Threw some vindaloo at the wall/at another carp angler I hate (preferably named)/all over the table and my shoes (which were at the other side of the room at the time). Called the waiter Sinbad, farted a lot, threw up on the way out, couldn't crap for a week (targeted readership is by now helpless with hysterics).

Fourth paragraph: Got back to the lake in the early hours of the morning/afternoon/evening/the following week. Threw a couple of cankers (carp fishers/wankers) into the lake for the fun of it; fished them out; told them it was a joke; got them to make breakfast; sang to them; gave them a bum rig and a blown bait; cursed the sodding sun for rising and giving me a headache; crawled back to the swim.

Fifth paragraph: Had a thirty/forty hung on the end when I got back/woke up in the morning/woke up in the afternoon/rowed the boat out to the distant snags.

Always finish the piece with the immortal words "That's what carp fishing's all about", an expression invariably used by people who seem to have no idea what carp fishing's all about to people who just carp fish.

(If you fall into the latter hapless majority you will find writing easy and can ignore the above.)

We would like to make the point that the Profumo File is not suitable reading material for anyone of a nervous disposition, with an inflated ego, having no sense of humour, possessing a sense of good taste, who fishes the Colne Valley, or gets upset easily when held to public ridicule.

We were a bit mystified by the great John Bailey's latest article in the marvellous Coarse Fisherman magazine (it says here on the back of this ten pound note). Now we love John, but he does seem to get lost in his own rhetoric a bit at times. This latest article was an attempt to emphasise the need to fish for the right reasons, but we couldn't quite understand how John's described desperation for a big carp because he needed it for a book he was writing quite fitted into the "right reasons" scheme of things.

Naughty Nev's a bit of an authority on model trains. Is it possible to upset people in the land of model railways? If there's a way our Nev will have found it, but as he happens to be one of our favourite people we couldn't care less really. We're just mystified as to how he finds time for model railways when he spends all his life writing, fishing, running NASA, running the Tackle Shop, and upsetting people.

We thought we'd better remind you that Eric Hodson founded NASA. We know you all know that, but if we put it in print often enough Brian Crawford might read it.

Nashy doesn't embarrass easily but word is he was well put out by the description of him in a Daiwa catalogue, and we quote (try and stop us): "No one has caught more big carp than Kevin Nash, an extrovert angler with a king-size reputation for being able to get the best possible results from any big fish water". That's just ridiculous: no one in their right mind could describe Kev as an extrovert.

Sorry to have to report that our old mate and ultimate keenie Baz Griffiths has been made redundant and is zealously pursuing another appointment. In fact he's being so zealous that the last time we rang he was scouring the lakes in France for a fortnight trying to come up with something! Enjoy it while it's there, my son: it might never come your way again.

The Lounge Lizard has become his old unpredictable self again, which is why the last couple of Profumos have lacked a certain *je ne sais quoi.* The latest excuse in a long line of bizarre and increasingly unbelievable reasons for not providing material for his own column is that the roof was leaking and the Lizard had to expend valuable inspiration in roof repairs. (We would have liked a picture of the Lizard wrestling with a leaky roof in the middle of a downpour, which is not to suggest that we believe for one moment that it actually happened.) Perhaps we should have already mentioned that the Lizard has recently moved to a part of Sheffield (Dore) that is so fashionable that people move there just so their address will be Dore. So how's this for inverted snobbery? The Lizard doesn't use Dore in his address, just the postcode!

We should also mention that the Lizard is chairman of the Ritchie McDonald fan club, which means that he is more pleased than almost anyone about Ritchie's recent result. We share the Lizard's and Ritchie's delight, but we weren't too sure about the Angling Times' description of Ritchie as ***delightful*** though. We'll not follow through with that or we'll only finish up with the old finger in the chest routine next time we venture south.